Making Successful Presentations

Related Titles of Interest from Wiley

PRESENTATIONS PLUS: DAVID PEOPLES' PROVEN TECHNIQUES, Peoples

WRITING TECHNICAL ARTICLES, SPEECHES, AND MANUALS, Forbes

A FUNNY THING HAPPENED ON THE WAY TO THE BOARDROOM: USING HUMOR IN BUSINESS SPEAKING, Iapoce

EFFECTIVE MEETINGS: THE COMPLETE GUIDE, Burleson

DINOSAUR BRAINS: DEALING WITH ALL THOSE IMPOSSIBLE PEOPLE AT WORK, Bernstein

COMMIT TO QUALITY, Townsend with Gebhardt

THE POWER OF PEOPLE SKILLS, Stewart

LISTENING: THE FORGOTTEN SKILL, Burley-Allen

WRITE LIKE THE PROS, Bacon

Making Successful Presentations

A Self-Teaching Guide
Second Edition

Terry C. Smith

John Wiley & Sons, Inc.
New York • Chichester • Brisbane • Toronto • Singapore

To all those
who are about to give
their first presentation
and to those who have just given
a less than perfect one.

Recognizing the importance of preserving what has been written, it is a policy of John Wiley & Sons, Inc. to have books of enduring value published in the United States printed on acid-free paper, and we exert our best efforts to that end.

Copyright © 1984, 1991 by Terry C. Smith

Published by John Wiley & Sons, Inc.

This publication is designed to provide accurate and authoritative information in regard to the subject matter covered. It is sold with the understanding that the publisher is not engaged in rendering legal, accounting, or other professional service. If legal advice or other expert assistance is required, the services of a competent professional person should be sought. *From a Declaration of Principles jointly adopted by a Committee of the American Bar Association and a Committee of Publishers.*

Library of Congress Cataloging-in-Publication Data

Smith, Terry C., 1933-
      Making successful presentations: a self-teaching guide / Terry C. Smith. — 2nd ed.
            p.   cm.   — (Wiley self-teaching guides)
      Includes bibliographical references.
      ISBN 0-471-52849-8—ISBN 0-471-52848-X (pbk.)
      1. Business presentations.   2. Public speaking.   I. Title.
      II. Series.
      HF5718.22.S65   1990
      808.5'1—dc20   90-35306
                                                                                        CIP

For information about our audio products, write us at:
Newbridge Book Clubs, 3000 Cindel Drive, Delran, NJ   08370

Printed in the United States of America

91 92 10 9 8 7 6 5 4 3 2 1

Preface

WHAT IS A PRESENTATION? And how does it differ from an oration, after-dinner speech, or other talks? All are forms of public speaking, so there are similarities. For example, a presenter can be entertaining, but the objective is not entertainment. The presenter cultivates thought, modifies opinions, and promotes action. When you give a presentation, you are selling yourself and your ideas.

In every major city there are thousands of presentations on any given day—from the moment the sun rises until long after it has set. These include presentations in large corporations, talks to civic associations, training seminars, club meetings, customer briefings, workplace meetings, "inspirational" talks to salespeople, and countless others. The audiences at these presentations (particularly those in the business world) are becoming ever more critical of what constitutes a good presentation. At the same time, most of the people giving presentations recognize they need help.

Courses in how to give presentations cost hundreds of dollars—some cost thousands. Few give the breadth of coverage this book is intended to provide. It is designed to show you how to eliminate your fears, gain recognition as a good speaker, and have fun doing it!

This is a how-to book on planning, organizing, developing, and delivering presentations. Included are the basic areas singled out by Aristotle in *The Rhetoric* in 350 B.C.: You (the speaker), the Talk, and most important, the Audience. An additional area, Mechanics (artwork, projectors, and other aids), is also covered.

The chapters follow the sequence in which your next presentation will come about, starting with your being asked (or told) to give a talk, and ending with how to handle questions and answers. Thus, you will have a step-by-step guide that can be applied to presentations you will have to give in the near future. The text is supplemented by artwork showing charts, slides, viewgraphs, room setups, and so on. Checklists are also provided at appropriate points.

Perhaps you are wondering if it really takes all of these pages just to cover what to do in a ten- or twenty-minute talk. The answer is Yes, and there could have been many more. You won't use every one in every talk you give. But sooner or later, you'll be able to use most of them.

This revision to the first edition includes substantial amounts of new material that has come to my attention in the past seven years. An entirely new chapter, "PC Graphics: An Aladdin's Lamp for Presenters," has also been added.

The gap between the high and low end of computer graphics has greatly narrowed since the first edition was published. The number of people who use computers to do this work and the tools available have changed dramatically. As a result, visuals that used to be limited to large organizations with professional staffs (or to outside commercial services) are much more readily available.

Feedback from readers of the original version of the book tells me that it has helped thousands of presenters. I'm honored and delighted that the publisher has decided to extend its usefulness in this revision.

This book would not be complete without citing a few of those who have helped point the way.

First, there are those who specialize in teaching the art. Training received from Jim Beveridge, Jack Franchetti, Jack Hilton, Bill Sears, Bill Tacey, Jerry Tarver, and Herb True has proven invaluable. Their earlier work and that of others listed in the Resources and Suggested Reading sections set the stage for my own efforts.

Secondly, there are those experts who, while they do not specialize in teaching the art of presentations in seminars or classrooms, do so day in and day out in the "real world." I'm thankful to have had the opportunity to watch and learn from Skip Boyd, Mark Braga, Frank Brusca, Tom Burgher, Rick Campbell, Tom Hiller, Suzanne Jenniches, Carol LaRotunda, George Mohr, Paul Pan, Geoff Pevner, Robin Raskin, Gordon Rowse, Joe Ryan, Al Spencer, Bill Staben, Gene Strull, John Stuntz, Jack Tymann, and others, many of whom also reviewed portions of this book.

Finally, and most importantly, one learns by doing. So I would like to thank all the organizations who have been kind enough to ask me to talk and all those who sat in the audience.

TERRY C. SMITH

Contents

1. So You've Been Asked (or Told) to Give a Talk   1

2. Planning: "Who, What, Where, When, Why, and How?"   9

3. Getting Your Act Together: Gathering and Organizing   20

4. Developing Your Talk: How to Add Interest   32

5. Adding an Extra Dimension with Visual Aids   57

6. Selling Yourself and Your Ideas   84

7. Practice Makes Perfect   105

8. Check Your Rigging   131

9. It's Showtime   151

10. Questions and Answers: The Speaker's Dessert   168

11. PC Graphics: An Aladdin's Lamp for Presenters   185

Notes   204

Resources   206

Suggested Reading   210

Index   213

CHAPTER ONE

So You've Been Asked (or Told) to Give a Talk

BEING ASKED TO GIVE a presentation affects different people in different ways. I recently asked a group of fifty professionals to jot down one or two words describing how they felt when they learned they had to give a presentation. Some of their answers were: "Anxiety" . . . "Fear" . . . "Concern over quality" . . . "Uncomfortable" . . . "Oh God!" . . . "Anger" . . . "Apprehension" . . . "Uninteresting" . . . "What did I do to deserve this?" . . . "Why me?" . . . "Inarticulate" . . . "I can't do it" . . . "Flattered" . . . "Extra work" . . . "There goes the weekend" . . . "Hot dog! I'll show them" . . . "How will I find time?" . . . and quite a few "Expletives Deleted."

I find it interesting that the overall reaction was a groan, instead of a "GREAT!" Very few viewed the situation as an opportunity to excel, which it is!

Why are presentations considered so tough? Well, first of all you are singled out as an individual. Although you may have a team to help prepare your presentation, you will be up there alone doing the talking. Second, since you will be seeking acceptance both for yourself and your ideas, you will experience some fear of rejection. So, there is some risk involved both for you as an individual and for the organization you represent.

Tough? You betcha! Impossible? Of course not. Success will lie in control of: yourself, your material, and the environment (including the audience). Various chapters in this book deal with each of these in detail as they occur in the presentation process. For the moment, though, you need to overcome that initial discomfort almost everyone feels when asked (or told) to give a presentation. If you are suffering any anxiety, you share it with some pretty famous people: Erma Bombeck, the late Lord Laurence Olivier, and even Sally Forth. As for the less famous, there are thousands of presentations being given every day and virtually all of those speakers are part-timers. So you've got lots of company.

Here's how Lee Iacocca once felt:

> Although I was a member of the debating team in high school, I used to be afraid of public speaking. For the first few years of my working life, I was an introvert, a shrinking violet.[1]

Fear of public speaking can actually be a medical problem. It's called lalophobia. None of the above individuals had it, and neither do you. In years and years of working with thousands of speakers, I've run into only one actual case.

Surprisingly, NBC's Willard Scott's anxiety of public speaking once bothered him so much that he sought medical help. He is now a spokesperson and board member for the Phobia Society of America. According to Scott:

> The first time it happened, I was on the air one morning and there was a commercial break. Before I came back, as they counted the seconds to airtime—ten seconds, nine—my palms suddenly started to sweat, I started to lose my breath; it was like a railroad train was going to absolutely sever me. I had no control over my breathing, and I could barely speak. The only way I got away with it was by acting a little silly, and people thought, well, he's just acting like Willard. They had smelling salts in the studio, and they thought I was having a heart attack. Then it was like waiting for the second shoe to drop. The

SALLY FORTH   **by Greg Howard**

Sally Forth's fear of speaking

Courtesy of Field Newspaper Syndicate

problem caused me to seek medical help because it happened three or four times in a row, right after that. I've worked on the problem for three or four years. I don't think I'll ever get over it, but I believe I've at least been able to combat it; I've learned to live and work with it.[2]

Some of the rumblings going on inside your gut at this early stage may be in anticipation of the anxiety you expect to encounter as you approach the lectern. A point to remember is that those rumblings are natural—to everyone! In later chapters, you will learn how to minimize those butterflies. But most of these initial rumblings probably are not related to actually making the presentation; rather, they may result from one of the most frequently asked questions on earth.

"WHY ME?"

Were you really surprised that you were asked to give a presentation? With the large number of presentations being given each day, *you should be surprised you weren't asked earlier.*

Chances are the person who asked you to speak considers you to be an expert in your field or in the particular aspect to be addressed. That's right. *You* are the expert. You may have never thought of yourself as such, but everyone has expertise in something. And yours is about to be tapped!

By the same token you must believe in what you are saying. (Are you really interested in the topic? You must be interested in what you have to say in order for others to be. If not, perhaps someone else *should* be giving the talk.) The audience wants to believe in you, and you give them that assurance by showing interest in your topic. Put these two ingredients together—your belief (or interest) in the topic, and the audience's belief in you—and a chemical reaction will occur. You will come across as a real person with something important to say.

Why give an oral presentation at all? Why not hand out a photocopy or, if the budget permits, a nice, color brochure? The answer is because these things simply can't match the impact of a live presentation given by a lively individual. The "you" element is crucial. In today's hectic world many people can't be reached by the written word. Their schedules simply won't allow them to peruse written reports chock-full of charts, schematics, and diagrams. Figuratively, you sometimes have to grab them by their lapels in order to get their attention. Couple this with our society's addiction to television and you can see that we really do live in an audio-visual age.

The presentation is a creature of this age.

A presentation is not a lecture. Of course, part of your objective may be to inform, but you usually need to gain information from the audience as well and possibly persuade them to take some action. A presentation is an exercise in interaction, with the speaker presenting new ideas in an attractive, interesting way.

Considering the opportunity the speaker has to adjust to a particular audience, and the ability to engage in dialogue, you can see we are dealing with a very powerful communications tool. Indeed, the word *communication* has a heritage of imparting, participating, and commonality. One of its nearby neighbors in the dictionary is *communion*, which signifies mutual participation or sharing of ideas or feelings. All of these elements are present in a good presentation.

WHAT A GOOD PRESENTATION CAN DO

History is full of disasters that could have been prevented by better communication (Little Big Horn, Pearl Harbor, Kent State, Pan Am Flt. 103). There may be similar disasters—large and small—lurking in the wings at your organization. Whether you are in the business of raising funds, managing an organization, or dealing with government agencies, success depends upon your ability to communicate effectively. How many opportunities have you seen lost because of a poor oral presentation? How many times have you walked away from the lectern unsure of how well you reached your audience? Was the subject a *now* topic, of immediate use? Did it stimulate any dialogue? Was the audience motivated to take action?

A good presentation can be very rewarding:

- The benefits for the audience can involve ways to save time or money, or how to make their lives easier or more successful.
- Your organization can benefit in funding being made available or a contract that is won.
- You benefit from the recognition that comes from making all this happen.

Companies realize that good speakers are a valuable asset. With a few good presentations and some luck, you may find yourself hurried along the road to prominence and promotion.

And yet there are so many examples of people who have failed to live up to their potential simply because they let their fear of public speaking hold them back. Ask yourself, are you so terrified of speaking in public that you would prefer to let others succeed in your place rather than take a chance on yourself? If the answer is yes, go back to your bookstore and buy a book on assertiveness!

WHAT WILL IT TAKE TO IMPROVE?

Unfortunately, there is no magic formula or potion. If there were, this book could have been condensed into an article or perhaps an illustration. Instead of five steps to a good presentation, there are hundreds, and you'll find as many of them as I could think of in this book. Fortunately, none of them are extremely difficult; they do, however, require a commitment to improving your presentation skills.

In giving a presentation your goal is perfection. You want to give a talk where the audience not only shows up, but participates and leaves feeling satisfied, taking some new ideas with them, and inspired to do something. You also want to give one in which all the taken-for-granted mechanics go off without a hitch. This is perfection! *And you and I will probably never see it!*

On the other hand, the very bottom of the scale, the worst talk I ever saw consisted of a script that took one and one-half hours to read and was accompanied by only five visuals which were either unreadable or irrelevant. Certainly, your next talk is going to be better than that one. Indeed, you'll probably be pretty good. And, by the time you've had a chance to combine some of the principles in this book with your own desire to improve, you are going to be terrific.

You've Already Gotten a Big Start

Speaking is a skill you've been practicing all your life. But your experience in daily life has been mostly of one-on-one interactions. Standing before a group is different.

But is speaking to a group really that much different? Place yourself in the audience. Wouldn't you prefer being talked to as an individual? And what's to prevent a speaker from singling out members of the audience, either through eye contact or direct address, and speaking to one person for a while before switching to someone else. This one-on-one approach can have a beneficial effect on both the audience and the speaker, particularly if the speaker begins by selecting individuals he or she already knows and is comfortable with.

Certainly, speaking before a group is a learned skill. If you aspire to become a "golden throat," it will take years of training. But I strongly believe almost anyone can make a good presentation if he or she knows the subject, sets high standards for the talk, and is willing to work hard in preparation. All of us are equipped with the required tools—mind and voice. How we use them can separate us from the crowd.

One Hour for Every Minute

According to *Best Sermons,* a religious magazine, it takes clergymen about seven hours to prepare a twenty-minute talk. That's more than a twenty-to-one ratio. But only twenty people listening to that sermon would represent an equal tradeoff of the time spent listening versus the time spent preparing.

Business presentations require the same or an even higher ratio. Here, the *value* of the presentation establishes the ratio. I subscribe to the theory of making things harder for myself in order to make them easier for my audience. For a brand new presentation, my ratio is one hour of preparation for every minute I plan to speak. This is the preparation level at which I feel comfortable that I'm giving my very best.

Mark Twain once said, "It takes three weeks to prepare a good ad-lib speech." And I'm sure you're familiar with Abraham Lincoln's immortal Gettysburg Address. Only 266 words were delivered from a few notes scribbled on an envelope during his train ride. Originally, some people were offended by the brevity of Lincoln's speech. Later, historians found many drafts in Lincoln's own handwriting which showed that weeks of effort went into that speech, which took but four minutes to deliver but will be remembered for hundreds of years.

It's nice to be able to spread the effort out over a couple of months, but what if you *have* to give your talk tomorrow? If there's absolutely no way out, here's how you might be able to do it and survive. First, isolate yourself so you'll be free from any possible interruptions. Second, adopt a technique the poker players in Las Vegas use. They don't think in terms of thousands of dollars because it might be too frightening. Instead they think in terms of units. Likewise, don't think of your available time in terms of hours. Whatever the available time is, divide it into sixty units as shown in the table on page 7. (Sixty was chosen since it will correlate nicely with any number of minutes or hours you have available. The more conventional percentage values

TIME ALLOCATION FOR PRESENTATION PREPARATION

Units	%	Activity	Comments
1	2	Review the objective	Check with whoever asked (or told) you to speak. Make sure you are both on the same track. Put it in writing.
2	3	Analyze the audience	What do they need (or want) to know? What are their educations, backgrounds, interests? Who are the "friendlies"? "Hostiles"?
2	3	Look for help	Has anyone talked to this group before? Are any existing visuals available? Can you get help with the legwork?
10	17	Research the subject	Collect facts and figures. Look for quotes from authorities. Search out appropriate anecdotes.
1	2	Settle on a theme	What is the main point? How does it match your objective? Can you condense your message to a single point?
3	5	Outline/organize	Begin to put material in logical order. Look for gaps and inconsistencies. Where is it weak? Use as a checklist.
8	13	Prepare storyboards/script	Put narration and visuals together on a single sheet. Do they work together to present the same idea?
7	12	Practice	Go over the material once all by yourself, reading it out loud. Tape-record if possible. How does it sound? Go over it again.
5	8	Revise storyboards	Review storyboards and look for improvements based on results of practice session.
5	8	Dry run	Give presentation to a group of friends or colleagues, using storyboard art for visuals. Ask for pluses and minuses. Check time required.
5	8	Revise storyboards	Incorporate suggestions made during dry run. Strengthen any weak or confusing areas.
8	14	Prepare visuals	Prepare the most effective visuals you can within the constraints of time and money. Check them carefully.
3	5	Rehearse	Using the same group as before, give your narration and visuals one last runthrough. Check time required. Fine-tune if necessary.
60	100%		

are also listed.) Feel free to make adjustments. For example, you might want to increase the amount of time spent on research. Fine, but keep in mind you need to be able to bring personal expertise to the talk. If you have to spend too much time on research, you may not be the right person to be the "expert." If you can obtain help on research or the preparation of final visuals, you can add the units saved to other categories. If absolutely necessary, you can prepare quickie view-graphs directly from your storyboards, again freeing units of time for other activities on the chart. But I would caution against strengthening one area at the expense of eliminating or neglecting another. For example, I would strongly advise against attempting to combine the practice, the dry run, and the rehearsal into a single activity. Doing all three separately is designed to build a degree of confidence you will enjoy having when you speak to your real audience.

You will find each of the activities in this table discussed in detail in this book. But before we close out this introductory chapter, I would like to relate a demonstration that Jack Felton, vice-president for corporate communications of a large multinational firm, uses in his talks on communications. Jack passes out little bags of confetti and asks the audience to take a pinch between their fingers and let it drop to the floor. He then points out that their particular message is just one little flake in the ensuing snowstorm that we refer to as the information explosion—so the message had better be good if they want it to be noticed, received, and understood! Then, after the confetti has reached the floor, he asks everyone to compare the pattern of their confetti with those on both sides. Each, of course, is different— just as each of us is; and so are our messages.

Throughout this book we will be giving you lots of suggestions. But in the end it will be *your* talk. You will have to select what works best for you. And when those things start working for you, there will be one more step in our confetti analogy—*celebration!*

Just like anything else, the more involved you become in presentations, the better you will become. And you can start right now!

CHAPTER TWO

Planning: "Who, What, Where, When, Why, and How?"

PLANNING—THE PROFESSIONAL APPROACH

ALMOST EVERYTHING we come in contact with testifies to the importance of planning. At work, at home, or at play, planning is everywhere—planning, or the lack of it, is easy to spot.

Why is poor planning so easy to spot? The answer is quality; it's the difference between a home gardener and a landscaper. Planning is the professional approach. Every professional—every architect, engineer, purchasing agent, and accountant—knows the importance of planning, and would never think of working without a plan. It's almost impossible to achieve quality without planning.

Why, then, do we often neglect this facet in presentations? Every talk is a unique experience and requires individual planning. Mistakes, misdirection, or lack of attention at this stage will take you farther and farther off course as you proceed.

Planning can be an involved process, and that (plus its importance) is why this entire chapter is devoted to it. However, to simplify things, six aspects of planning are covered. These are the six questions learned by every cub reporter: who, what, where, when, why, and how. (Many feature journalists add an all-important seventh point: WOW!) Your ability to answer these questions now is every bit as important as your ability to answer those asked by your audience at the end of your talk.

THE NO. 1 CAUSE OF POOR PRESENTATIONS

Although your talk obviously isn't very far along at this point, you have a chance right now to eliminate the number one cause of poor presentations. At this stage most speakers concentrate on the *what* in their presentations. They ask themselves, "What in the world am I going to say?" and jumping to that question is often the biggest mistake that can be made. Instead of *what*, the question should be *why*.

WHY AM I GIVING THIS TALK?

"Because I have to," is *not* a good reason for giving a presentation. What you need to begin creating a good presentation is an objective. There can be many objectives in giving a talk. Perhaps you want to:

- Inform or instruct.
- Persuade or sell.
- Make recommendations and gain acceptance.
- Arouse interest.
- Inspire or initiate action.
- Evaluate, interpret, or clarify.
- Set the stage for further action.
- Gather ideas and explore them.
- Entertain.

Perhaps you are aiming for a combination of these. For example, there is nothing wrong with being both informative *and* entertaining—the two are not mutually exclusive. In fact, the two may complement one another. (If you're still having problems with *to entertain* as an objective, think of it this way: What's the opposite of being entertaining? Right, B-O-R-I-N-G!)

Note that these are fairly *general* objectives. This is a good start, but you'll need to be more specific. One way to do this is to put your objective in writing. Many times I've sat in lengthy planning meetings where apparently everybody had finally reached agreement, and someone said, "Well, I guess that about wraps it up," half rising from his chair—only to be stopped by an, "I wonder if we could capture that objective in writing on the board." The result is usually a unanimous moan at the prospect of spending any more time on planning rather than doing. Unfortunately, the result frequently is also the inability to capture in specific terms the objective that had seemed so clear just minutes ago.

Putting objectives in writing can keep you from deluding yourself. Written objectives can also provide a "contract" between you and your superiors. And they can provide the theme for your entire presentation.

> The specific purpose of a speech must be established before any other preparation is started. It should be written in infinitive phrase form something like this example: "To inform the members of Local 306 how observing the rules of parliamentary debate can help assure that all points of view can be expressed by members in union meetings." Once it is written, examine it carefully to determine if it expresses accurately why you want to speak. Revision may be necessary to be certain that the scope of the topic is narrow enough to be covered in the time allotted.[3]

This quote, from William Tacey's *Business and Professional Speaking*, provides a lot of good advice, and I would like to add some more of my own. Starting your written objective with an infinitive phrase is the best way to begin; but while "to inform" is all right, also consider such phrases as "to convince," "to persuade," "to show," "to prove," or "to demonstrate." They make writing your objective a little tougher, but they are usually more realistic. Also, don't be dismayed if your objective is not as succinct as the one cited above. Your first cut may be three times as long as you want it to be, and careful distillation is necessary. If you hit it right off the bat, you had better be suspicious. Writing a *good* objective is harder than you think. Here are some more samples:

- To prove that purchase of a Humdinger-999 will permit the combination of several other data handling systems and supply more complete data usable by all departments at a savings of $350,000 per year in reduced personnel and rentals.
- To demonstrate to the director and staff the need for a new educational program for the disadvantaged in District Three, and to obtain an $80,000 budgetary allocation for Phase I.
- To convince the capital equipment committee that installing robotic paint spraying equipment in Building Twenty-three will increase productivity thirty-eight percent, pay for itself in three years, and eliminate a hazardous working condition.
- To persuade the swim club committee that purchasing a new filter at the end of the season will result in a lower price and guarantee its delivery prior to next year, thus avoiding a possible shutdown.

If you have help in formulating your objective, so much the better. But you may find yourself stuck with a vague assignment. "Bob, work up a talk on the new electronic mail system for our sales reps," or "Could you talk about 'Publishing Today' to our Careers Group?" Converting these command performances on fuzzy, general topics into your own, tailored-to-the-audience's-needs presentation will require a well-thought-out objective.

One way to make writing that objective easier is to visualize the end of your talk. What do you want to happen? Applause would be nice, but it's unlikely in most presentations. Beyond that what do you want your audience to take with them or do?

- Should they be taking something with them that will help them do their jobs better?
- What is going to be different from the way it was before you gave your talk?
- Will they give you their "votes"?
- What decisions will they need to make and when?
- Will morale improve?
- Will productivity increase?

As you develop your written objective, there are two criteria you should apply:

1. Is it attainable?
2. Is it measurable?

Writing an objective that is not attainable, realistic, or feasible will either guarantee failure or provide you with a convenient cop-out: "Oh well, we really didn't expect to achieve a behavioral change with just one meeting anyway."

Here, the problem is often due to multiple objectives. Multiple objectives require multiple talks. Limiting yourself to a single objective (or two at the most) will make your task much easier. Often, attaining goals is like eating a jumbo burger. It's best done one bite at a time.

The second item, measurability, is going to make your life more difficult. In order for the results of your presentation to be verifiable, they must be measurable. Sometimes the results are obvious and immediate. You get a "Yes" or a "Go-ahead." Other times you will need a quantitative method of evaluating results. In a training session, a quiz can measure information transfer. Increased orders from the sales force would be a nice, easily measurable result. So would the percentage of attendees filling out a new form correctly. A before-and-after survey would indicate change. And, there's always getting reelected. Whatever the situation, try to find a way of measuring results, and incorporate the intended amount of change in your objective.

WHO IS GOING TO BE OUT THERE?

Remembering that Aristotle singled out the audience as the most important of the three elements in a talk (*You*, the *Talk* itself, and the *Audience*), you should consider the *who* element next.

You'll want to know your audience's expected size. Your audience might be quite small, say a handful of department heads. Or, it may consist of all the employees in a department. Regardless of its size, it is virtually impossible for you to know too much about your audience. You need to analyze their ages, educations, backgrounds, interests, and—particularly—their needs, so that you can look at your talk from *their* viewpoint.

In his prologue to *The Inconstant*, George Farquhar wrote, "Like hungry guests, a sitting audience looks." Don't send them away hungry. Satisfy their needs.

In the business world, management is primarily interested in four principal factors:

- Reducing costs
- Improving quality
- Shortening schedules
- Increasing performance

All four of these primary interests would obviously need to be considered in planning a presentation to management. Behind them lie a myriad of other interests, needs, problems, and beliefs that would apply to management or any broader audience. These read like alphabet soup. Refer to the table on page 14. Scan the list slowly, and as you do, check off those items that seem to fit both your audience and your objective. Any one of these words can trigger an avalanche of ideas.

Two things are beginning to happen. First, you are beginning to mesh your objective with the audience. Ideally, they fit together like well-turned gears. Second, you are beginning to look at your audience as individuals. Certainly, your objective will have an impact on how you "handle" the audience. In some portions of your

AUDIENCE INTERESTS AND CONCERNS

_____ Absenteeism
_____ Acceptance
_____ Accomplishments
_____ Advancement
_____ Age
_____ Ambition
_____ Announcements
_____ Appearance
_____ Approval
_____ Attitude
_____ Authority
_____ Awards

_____ Beauty
_____ Beliefs
_____ Benefits
_____ Biases
_____ Business

_____ Causes
_____ Caution
_____ Change
_____ Character
_____ Clients
_____ Climate
_____ Cohesiveness
_____ Community
_____ Competition
_____ Conscience
_____ Consolidation
_____ Cost
_____ Courtesy
_____ Criticism
_____ Customers

_____ Data
_____ Delays
_____ Dependability
_____ Design
_____ Devotion
_____ Distinction
_____ Durability
_____ Duty

_____ Economy
_____ Education
_____ Effort
_____ Employees
_____ Employment
_____ Energy
_____ Entertainment
_____ Envy
_____ Equipment
_____ Ethics
_____ Exclusiveness
_____ Expectations
_____ Expense
_____ Experiences

_____ Facilities
_____ Fairness
_____ Family

_____ Fear
_____ Formality
_____ Freedom
_____ Friendliness

_____ Gain
_____ Good Will
_____ Greed
_____ Group Effort

_____ Handling
_____ Happiness
_____ Health
_____ History
_____ Homelife
_____ Hope
_____ Housing
_____ Humor

_____ Image
_____ Income
_____ Individuality
_____ Influence
_____ Inspiration

_____ Jealousy

_____ Knowledge

_____ Labor
_____ Legality
_____ Location
_____ Lost Time
_____ Love
_____ Low Cost
_____ Loyalty

_____ Maintenance
_____ Management
_____ Marital Status
_____ Material
_____ Misconceptions
_____ Money
_____ Mood
_____ Morale
_____ Morality
_____ Motivation

_____ Nationalism
_____ Needs
_____ Newness

_____ Objectives
_____ Opinions
_____ Opportunities
_____ Organization

_____ Parochialism
_____ Participation
_____ Pay
_____ People
_____ Performance
_____ Personality
_____ Planning
_____ Policies

_____ Popularity
_____ Position
_____ Power
_____ Praise
_____ Prejudice
_____ Pride
_____ Problems
_____ Producibility
_____ Productivity
_____ Profit
_____ Promotion
_____ Prosperity
_____ Protection
_____ Public
_____ Purity

_____ Quality

_____ Rank
_____ Recreation
_____ Relaxation
_____ Reliability
_____ Repair
_____ Reputation
_____ Research
_____ Rules

_____ Safety
_____ Salary
_____ Sales
_____ Schedule
_____ Security
_____ Self-Respect
_____ Service
_____ Size
_____ Sociability
_____ Sophistication
_____ Standards
_____ Strategies
_____ Style
_____ Success
_____ Superiority
_____ Support
_____ Sympathy

_____ Technology
_____ Timeliness
_____ Tools

_____ Understanding
_____ Unity
_____ Usefulness

_____ Value
_____ Vanity

_____ Wages
_____ Welfare
_____ Workload
_____ Worship

_____ Youth

talk, you may be forced to generalize for the benefit of the entire audience. During other portions you'll want to home in on specific individuals. Looking at your audience as a homogenous group is invariably a mistake. If you find yourself doing this, more homework is in order.

You want to "give" everyone in your audience something and (if possible) not step on anybody's toes. Doing this requires an individual approach.

If you already know everyone in your audience, you have a pretty good start. Perhaps the audience is a committee that will have to approve your design or request. Chances are that their responsibilities (financial, operational, and so on) will tell you what their individual interests are, allowing you to build portions of your talk around those interests. Also, you may have seen them in other meetings, giving you a chance to analyze their personalities. Which individual requires the thought-out approach? Who is more likely to be captured by a creative idea? Do any of them look on pizzazz as gimmickry? Make these items factors when you consider your approach to the presentation.

What if they are total strangers? Well, your job just got a lot tougher, but not impossible. There are still lots of things you can do:

- Ask for a list of likely attendees and their titles. And, while you're at it, ask for first names—*not* initials. Paste a copy next to your bathroom mirror and another next to your office phone. Look at them every chance you get. Study them in groups of three. Study them forward and backward, matching first name to last name to position, and vice versa. When you finally meet them, they will seem like old friends.
- If possible, get their biographies or personal histories. If your audience is going to be customers at a far-off location, perhaps your field sales representative can help.
- Talk to as many of them as possible in advance. Ask them about their biggest challenges or problems. Talk about what they would like to see at this particular meeting. Ask them what they liked or disliked at previous meetings. Look for ways to incorporate their views in your talk, and ways to meet their objections.

You owe your audience a worthwhile message that is well-presented. In order to deliver, you're going to have to know as much about them as possible. Will they be friendly, but likely to ask probing questions? Will they be hostile? You've got to be prepared!

WHAT AM I GOING TO SAY?

You've probably known the general topic of your talk ever since you were asked (or told) to speak. And, having written out your objective and analyzed your audience, you now have a fair idea of what might be included under your topic.

We will be talking about gathering and organizing information in more detail in the next chapter. For now, you can ask yourself a few more *whats:*

- What do they already know?
- What do they want to know?
- What do they need to know?
- What don't they need to know?
- What shouldn't (or can't) I talk about?

The fourth question refers to too much detail, or (as is the case with many novice speakers) trying to cover the whole world in a single talk. Leave the epics for James Michener and Herman Wouk. Pick one aspect of a subject you are familiar with, that the audience is interested in, and that fits your objective. That's the magic formula.

The "shouldn't" in the final question refers to sensitive information that you would not bring up but would be prepared to handle if it surfaced during the question-and-answer session. The "can't" refers to information outside your area of responsibility that might be inappropriate for you to comment on.

WHERE WILL THE MEETING BE?

You need to know more than just where to show up. We will be talking about room arrangements in Chapter 8, but there are some items you should start thinking about now. First of all, make sure the meeting room is reserved. With the large number of meetings being held these days, suitable rooms are scarce. They need to be reserved as far in advance as possible. If it's not your responsibility and someone else has reserved the room, double-check. If at all possible, visit the room. Will it handle your group comfortably? (If it's in a hotel, don't trust their seating numbers unless you're hosting a brotherhood meeting for leprechauns.) What type of seating and visuals will work best? What kind of audio-visual equipment is available? All of these items are covered elsewhere in this book, but it's not too early to start thinking about them.

There is a special type of talk that takes its name from where it is held. It's called a "workplace meeting." Usually these brief meetings are held right in the workplace. *But they don't have to be.* You can frequently add some importance—even prestige—by getting the meeting away from the workplace. This could be as simple as going outside on the grass or a patio, or using an executive meeting room employees don't usually have access to. You might even want to consider an off-site location.

Perhaps you will be traveling out of town to give your talk. If so, make your travel reservations as far in advance as possible, and don't plan to catch the last possible flight. Reserve a seat on the preceding one and leave yourself a safety cushion in case of weather or equipment problems.

Most of all, make sure you have a good map, right down to the location of the room where the session will be held. More than one speaker, including this one, has faced the panic of not being able to find the right place while the clock merrily raced on. (I know of one highly regarded speaker who even went to the wrong city—where the meetings had always been held—because no one told him otherwise!) As to the room itself, there's nothing worse than arriving early, getting everything set up, and then finding out that you're supposed to be in the room next door and the group scheduled for this room won't switch. Your preshipped materials are already in a given room? That doesn't necessarily mean it's the right one.

One final *where* on out-of-town meetings—know where you can find help locally. Before you leave home, make sure you have the phone numbers of local sales representatives, the meeting coordinator, the hotel, the audio-visual supplier, and others. Keep in mind that you will need phone numbers to reach these people during business hours, plus an emergency number.

WHEN WILL THE MEETING BE?

Here again, you're interested in more than just knowing when to show up. You need to know how much time you have available to speak, and how much time will be available to prepare. In both cases you will have to balance the time you have with the time you need. Furthermore, you will have to factor in *how long you can keep the audience interested.*

Suppose you've been given a single hour to talk about a project you've been working on for the past five years! You say there's no way you can possibly do it? Tough! In fact, an hour might be *too much*. If you have even the slightest doubt that you can keep the audience interested for that full hour, you would be smart to request that your time be cut back. Remember, the effectiveness of a presentation often varies inversely with the time required to give it. George Plimpton has written very effectively about this:

> As anyone who listens to speeches knows, brevity is an asset. Twenty minutes are ideal. An hour is the limit an audience can listen comfortably.
>
> In mentioning brevity, it is worth mentioning that the shortest inaugural address was George Washington's—just 135 words. The longest was William Henry Harrison's, in 1841. He delivered a two-hour, 9,000-word speech into the teeth of a freezing northeast wind. He came down with a cold the following day, and a month later he died of pneumonia.[4]

According to the 1989 *Guinness Book of World Records,* Senator Wayne Morse beat this by a mile back in 1953 when he spoke (fortunately indoors) on the Tidelands Oil Bill for 22 hours and 26 minutes. Zzzzz . . . .

Remember, there is no such thing as a captive audience. Even in an employer/employee or teacher/student relationship where you may be able to hold their bodies "captive," you cannot assume you also have their minds. As Mark Twain said, "No sinner is ever saved after the first twenty minutes of a sermon."

Time management is important for speakers, too. Don't try to do too much in the time available. As mentioned previously, don't try to cover "the whole world." Stick to what's going on in your own "home town." That's probably where your audience is coming from anyway.

When will also tell you the time of day you will be speaking. First thing in the morning? Good, with the possible exception of Mondays. Right before lunch? Bad, because your listeners are likely to be tired, hungry, and checking their watches. Right after lunch? Better, they've had a long break and, hopefully, not too heavy a meal. End of the day? Terrible! They're tired and you may be, too. In this slot, only excellence will do—particularly on Fridays. Planning an after-dinner talk? Okay, if they've been home and have come back to, say, the local school or library. But if it's a business meeting where alcoholic beverages will be served, try for *between* cocktails and dinner. Sometimes the combination of cocktails, hors d'oeuvres, dinner, and wine leaves you with an audience that Arsenio Hall would have trouble keeping awake.

Although this is really the chairperson's job, check every calendar you can get your hands on to make sure that the time and date of your presentation will not conflict with some other, more important event. Don't expect much of a turnout for a talk on high school or college athletics (or any number of other topics) on a Sunday afternoon in January that coincides with the Super Bowl.

You may not get to pick your time. But you *can* make requests and suggestions. For example, if an organization that meets weekly or monthly asks you to speak but hasn't given you enough time to prepare adequately (or to get the necessary reviews and approvals if you represent an organization), tell them you'll be happy to do it, but would like to wait until the following session. They get the "yes" they wanted, and you get the time you need.

HOW AM I GOING TO DO IT?

Fortunately, the answer is that you won't have to do it all by yourself. Commercial artists and professional speechwriters are well worth their fees if you or your organization can afford them. And if you can't, you may be able to find some who will waive their fees because they believe in your cause.

There are many other people available who might help. Enlist the aid of friends, family members, your co-workers, your boss, and (possibly) the organization you will be speaking to. Check with your local community college to see if a speech or English teacher would be willing to help. Or ask your pastor. Or, if your talk has any connection with what your company does, ask the people in its public relations or advertising department. Finally, you could contact your local Toastmasters' organization. There's plenty of inexpensive or even free help out there. All you have to do is ask.

Okay, you've given some thought to the famous five *W*'s, particularly where you want to go and why. The rest of this book will show you how to get there.

CHAPTER THREE

Getting Your Act Together: Gathering and Organizing

SOME BOOKS on presentations combine the previous chapter on planning with this one on gathering and organizing. I have elected to treat them separately in order to make the smaller, individual pieces more digestible. But, more importantly, I have divided them because of their individual significance. In Chapter 2 you laid the concrete foundation for your talk. Now you will begin putting together all those bricks that make up the walls. First, however, you have to find those bricks.

I once heard of a college course in creativity wherein the professor gave each attendee a brick as part of the final exam and told the students to spend the next hour listing every possible use for it they could think of, other than as a building material. Of course, some immediately come to mind: paperweight, weapon, etc. Then there's window prop, measuring device, heat retainer, and so forth. By the end of the hour, the brighter students had each come up with more than 100 uses, proving that even with such a simple subject as a brick, there's no shortage of ideas; all you have to do is capture them.

CAPTURING IDEAS

In *Executive Speaking—An Acquired Skill,* author Joe Powell presents a simple, low-cost method for capturing ideas. "Arm yourself with blank 3 × 5-inch cards. I call them idea cards. Whenever and wherever you get an idea jot it down in the rough, one idea to one card. Forget about spelling or grammar. Just jot down every related raw idea; and capture it immediately because ideas, like snowflakes on a mild day in early spring, disappear on contact."[5] So keep those cards with you at all times. There's no telling where or when an idea will arise.

Some of these ideas will no doubt lead to further research. After all, the audience isn't interested merely in your opinions—they also want facts. Facts that you can gather through:

- Literature searches.
- Personal observations.
- Experimentation.
- Questionnaires.
- Interviews.

All of these are part of doing your homework. In his book *How to Write, Speak, and Think More Effectively*, Rudolf Flesch, one of the pioneers in the field, said, "The only thing that's good enough is to soak yourself in all the facts you can lay your hands on, to become a temporary expert on the subject. You go after the most obvious sources, then after the less obvious sources, and finally you follow up all the stray leads that you can possibly uncover. . . . Legwork is nine-tenths of the job."[6]

Doing a little extra reading saved the day for me once. I was giving one of those "How-Good-Things-Are-Going-To-Be-Tomorrow" talks: you show the good things you've done in the past and explain that while things aren't perfect at the moment, tomorrow will be a brighter day. There were only five people in the room: me, my boss, the president of our particular operation, the chief operating officer of our corporation, and one of his directors. Just when it looked like I was going to get through the presentation alive, the director lit into me for not having done a very good job of detailed step-by-step planning for that "tomorrow" I was talking about. In truth, at that point the "tomorrow" was pretty much a puff of smoke and it looked like my goose was about to be sautéed. Fortunately, my literature search had revealed a quote from a statement by the COO a month before. It said that even the best of leaders sometimes act intuitively and that when you're sailing in uncharted waters there are seldom any maps.

When I first read it, I liked it, and thought it was worth saving. I wasn't sure how I would use it, but I had an overhead transparency made and kept it in reserve as I gave the talk. When the director took me to task for my lack of sufficient planning, I was able to agree with her, saying that I often criticized myself for this shortcoming. However, I added, I had recently run across something that had given me great comfort in this area. I then placed the overhead, with the quote and the COO's name on it, on the projector.

His smile made my day.

Your literature search may yield some quotes from famous people or recognized authorities, anecdotes, analogies, jokes and one-liners, cartoons and other visuals, dramatic statistics, clever twists on words, and interesting "for examples." And don't forget the bait, which is what I call the benefits your audience will obtain if they follow your advice. Your public library is a treasure house of books, magazines, and newspapers that will help. Annual directories such as the *Washington Journalism Review* directory of selected news sources can be a big help. Another is "The Capital Source," published by *The National Journal.*

And don't forget to take note paper with you every time you go to hear someone give a lecture, talk, or presentation so that you can capture any outstanding techniques and ideas.

Collect a lot more material than you will ever need. That way your talk will represent the cream of the crop.

Interviews and questionnaires are another way to get information, and they provide a means of testing the water—particularly if they involve people who will be in your audience. Decision makers are usually glad to help and somewhat flattered to be asked their opinions. Do your homework. Have plenty of questions ready for when the conversation wanes.

As part of the process of interviewing, you may uncover some objections to the position you are presenting (which you will have to work around or overcome). And, when those who objected finally hear the talk, they will recognize the incorporation of their ideas and, hopefully, become members of your team. Speaking of objections, don't neglect alternative approaches or solutions or ignore the "cons" that go along with your "pros." Show that you have considered them and why you set them aside.

Obviously some of the material you gather is going to be too voluminous to put on those little 3 x 5-inch cards that Joe Powell recommended. But be sure to make a list of the main points on a card and file the rest of your source materials. Accordion-style file folders work great for storing your resources, or you might try a three-ring binder or even large envelopes. Think of this as your information warehouse.

As you gather your data, subject it to a value analysis:

- How recent?
- How objective?
- How authoritative?
- How accurate?

Bits of data are like children: once you adopt them, they're yours. So be selective. Sift through your material, picking the most relevant and thought-provoking. But don't clean out the warehouse yet. Just because a piece of material isn't going to make it into the main body of your talk doesn't mean that it's worthless. Some of that material may provide valuable ammunition in preparing for the question-and-answer session that will follow your talk.

ORGANIZING YOUR MATERIAL

Many authorities on public speaking suggest that you organize by beginning at the ending. This will help to keep your main objective in mind, minimize detours en route, and avoid the possibility of an anticlimactic ending.

Another approach is to use the thesis mentioned in Chapter 2 as a "screen" and attempt to "fit" your material through this screen as shown in the illustration below. The bits and pieces represent different facts. Those that can go through the screen will fit your talk. Those that don't, won't. The various holes in the screen represent

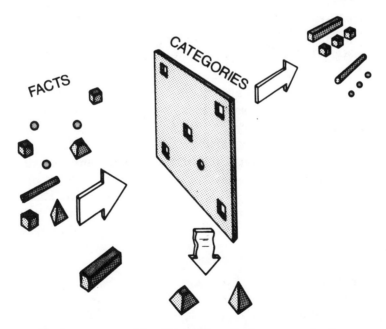

Thesis screen provides filter and preliminary organization.

categories; when the material passes through them, it begins to take on an organizational form.

There are two other approaches you can take in organizing your material:

- Organizing to suit the material and its treatment.
- Organizing to suit the audience.

The best approach is a combination of these two, but let's examine each one in detail.

Organizing to Suit the Material

As you sift through the material, certain expository techniques will begin to suggest themselves. The material will begin to divide itself along certain lines. Some of these include:

- Geographical (sales territories, plant locations)
- Organizational (hierarchy, duties)
- Categorical (types, sizes)
- Appearance (recognition of aircraft, boats, flowers)
- Historical (chronological order of occurrence)
- Operational cycle (engines, pumps)
- Assembly sequence (manufacturing or installation instructions)

I'm sure you can see that some of these categories are closely related. For example, business *organizations* are often based on *geographical* plant locations; *appearance* is often *categorized;* and, *historical, operational,* and *assembly* all bear a *chronological* relationship. In fact, chronological organization is the type most frequently used, but not always because it serves us best.

Organizing to Suit the Audience

There are cases where chronological organization offers a perfect match between audience and objective. Usually these situations involve repeatability—that is, when you want to make sure a step-by-step procedure is followed in assembling or testing some equipment. In other cases, chronological organization is used merely for convenience. It's quite easy to determine what happened first, and then next, and so forth.

In both chronological and historical organization, the facts are presented in the order in which they happened, with no concern for relative importance. And there's the rub. Your listeners are kept waiting to learn the important facts.

There are other ways of organizing material. *Climactic* organization is used by some speakers who are real spellbinders. It derives from novels and other types of entertaining storytelling. With this organization, the plot builds to a high point (or climax) and then drops off quickly. The highlights are kept from the audience until the end, and since they are being entertained (and have some time to spare), they don't mind waiting.

With *deductive* organization, each fact builds on the previous one until an inescapable conclusion is reached. Loved by lawyers (they know the jury can't leave), this organization is fine for presenting a case or offering proof, and it may come in handy for a really tough sell because it starts on familiar ground that the audience already knows or agrees with. But, like the others, it keeps your listeners waiting. Before using this format, you should be certain they will stick around (both in mind and body) for your entire presentation.

The *learning pattern* organization also uses the technique of relating new material to already familiar material. For example, an electrician attempting to learn how an electronic circuit works will first relate it to prior knowledge of common electrical circuits. As a speaker, you can often take advantage of the audience's prior experience to help get new points across.

One final means of organization is the *qualitative* (or *pyramid*) format. It is called qualitative because the emphasis is on quality rather than quantity. Emphasis is placed on the important items and these items are discussed up front, at the very beginning. Like a newspaper article, the pyramid style gives you the point at the very top (the headline), keeps your interest (with the lead), and then gives you the details (in the body). This style is designed for people who may be too busy to read all about it in a report or proposal, and would like someone to merely tell or show them what's important.

Each of these five formats has its own special purpose. The qualitative approach, however, is almost always best for straightforward communication of facts.

Specific Organizational Techniques

Here are some time-tested organizational techniques that embody these principles. At least a few of them should fit your situation:

- The Descriptive Approach (What is it? What does it do? How does it do it?)
- The Events Approach (What happened? Why did it happen? So what?)
- The Progress Report (What was planned? What was accomplished? What's next?)
- The Scientific Approach (Problem, Approach, Results, Conclusions, Recommendations)
- The Shorter Problem-Solution Approach (Start with current status)
- The Best Alternative Approach (Establish need, look at alternatives, choose best approach)
- The Need/Satisfaction Approach (Show or create need, then show means to satisfy)
- The "Tell Them" Approach (Tell them what you're going to tell them. Tell them. Then tell them what you told them.)

The final technique on the list supposedly originated when a young minister asked an old Southern preacher his secret of success for giving such stirring sermons. "Easy," he said. "I simply tell them what I'm going to tell them. Then I tell them. And then I tell them what I told them." Simple? Yes. Simplistic? *No!*

Within the simplicity of this oft-told story lies some of the best advice for presentations and public speaking. *"Tell them what you're going to tell them"* in your opening remarks and explain why it's important to them. Sell them on listening to you. *"Then tell them"* in more detail in the main body of your talk, adding the statistics and proof that will make your approach more logical and believable. Finally, *"tell them what you told them"* in your summary or wrap-up* so they will go away remembering what you said and what you would like them to do.

Repetitive? Yes. *Repetitio est mater studiorum.* Repetition is the mother of all studies. Think back for a moment to the most famous speech Dr. Martin Luther King, Jr. ever delivered. That's right, "I

---

* *Ever stop to wonder why it's called a wrap-up? In any package, the final step is the wrapping. Your summary should wrap everything up into a neat package. Remind them who is going to do what, where, why, when, and how. And, most important, remind them what your idea will do for them.*

Have a Dream." He repeated that phrase nine times in three minutes. Will any of us ever forget it?

BUT WHAT ABOUT OUTLINES?

Most people dislike outlines. I suspect this is a holdover from their grade school days when they were forced to spend hours outlining material. It was often a case of working for the outline instead of the outline working for you. But outlines can provide many benefits. A good outline:

- Supplies a solid framework on which you can build.
- Ensures direction.
- Provides a checklist of important items.
- Helps maintain proper emphasis.
- Keeps your talk from "running away."
- Gives you something your superiors can review.

On the other hand, outlines can be somewhat intimidating. You start by placing the Roman numeral I on the page and then searching for a subject to go with it. *Introduction* is easy enough. But what will be item II? And should this other idea be III, or II.A? If you're an engineer, it becomes more difficult as you sort through the 3.1, 3.1.1, and 3.1.1.1 series.

Also, outlines (at least the *topical* ones that merely list the items to be discussed) don't tell you or your superiors much. True, topical outlines indicate content, order, and subordination, but other than that they don't give a clue as to treatment. Doing so requires expanding the *topical* outline into a *synoptic* outline wherein each topic is followed by a short synopsis. As good as they are, though, synoptic outlines suffer from a fault that also plagues all the others—their inflexibility.

During the process of developing your talk you will be making many changes and improvements. Imagine the erasing, cutting, pasting, or retyping that outline will go through. Instead, think back to those index cards you read about at the beginning of this chapter. Using the cards, ideas can be deleted with a flick of the wrist. New thoughts can be added as quickly as they can be written out. The simplicity, interchangeability, and modularity of the cards make them a dynamic tool for organizing your presentation. In fact, it's almost as easy as dealing a hand of poker or bridge.

Sit down at a desk or large table. Shuffle through the cards once to familiarize yourself with their contents. Now go back and read that first card again, mentally assigning a broad "subject matter" to that card. Then place the card face up on the table and begin reading the next card. If your next card falls into the same broad classification, it goes on top of the first; if not, it starts a new stack of its own. Try to limit the number of stacks to eight or fewer.

As soon as you have "dealt" the last card, you have accomplished your first goal. Your material is divided into a number of groups. Now look over your groups of cards. Some will be quite small. Perhaps these should be combined with other groups. Or perhaps you need more information in these areas. Quite possibly, they are small for some good reason and should remain small (e.g., introductory material). Other groups may be quite large, and you may want to further subdivide these large groups as you did to get your original groups.

Next, look over the groups to decide the order in which they should be presented. Once this is done, shuffle through each group and put each individual card in order.

Now you have arrived at your second goal: your material is loosely organized. Next, go through your stack, rearranging or deleting those cards that do not fit in.

Once you have settled on an arrangement, you can begin writing from the cards, supplying transitional sentences to bridge the gaps between cards. This will give you a first draft which you can polish later.

The index cards enable you to make molehills out of your mountain of an assignment. They give you a quick way of mechanically organizing your material. The result will be a natural, well-thought-out flow of information rather than a script written to fit a preconceived outline.

But even the cards present a disadvantage. They may be small enough to carry around in your pocket or purse but too small to fit visuals and accompanying narration. Sure, you can put your rough sketches on their own separate cards, but eventually a visual and the accompanying narration are supposed to blend together and work as a single unit. It's time to put all your small cards together with the visuals in one place.

Enter the storyboard.

THE MAGIC OF STORYBOARDS

The storyboard combines all the advantages of the aforementioned techniques and eliminates all the disadvantages. The best part of it is its availability. Any 8 1/2 by 11-inch sheet of paper will do, although 1/4-inch cross-ruled grid paper is probably best.

You can make your own storyboards by merely taking some 8 1/2 by 11-inch sheets and dividing them in half with a horizontal line. That's it! The top half of each sheet will be used for your visual and the bottom half for the narration that goes with it, as shown below. Which comes first is somewhat like the question of the chicken and the egg. For convenience, we will start with the top half where the visual goes.

This 8 1/2 by 5 1/2-inch area has roughly the same proportions as a horizontal slide or chart (which is preferable, as you will see in the

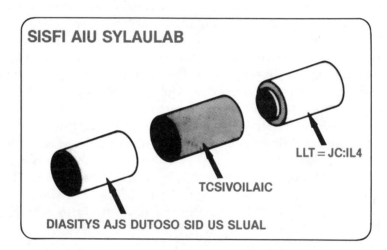

Storyboards supply unity by mating visuals and narration and also supply pace.

chapter on visual aids). So things are already in the proper perspective. And the rather limited area, as compared to a full 8 1/2 by 11-inch (or even larger) sheet, will force you to simplify your visuals. This effect will be further enhanced if you force yourself to use a felt-tip pen or blunt pencil instead of a writing instrument with a fine point.

The bottom half of the storyboard will easily accommodate 120 words of double-spaced typing or roughly the same amount of single-spaced handwritten material. And, since 120 words per minute is well within your top rate of speech, you now have a system that ties visuals together with narration (one visual per idea) and progresses at the rate of approximately one visual per minute. This is an ideal pace for most presentations.

Another advantage to storyboards is that they are team-oriented. Supposedly, the storyboard concept originated in the early days of World War II as part of the production process for animated training films. Producing these films called for the interaction of writers, artists, technical advisers, photographers, musicians, and a host of others, and the storyboard proved to be an ideal link for keeping all their efforts closely coupled. Today the same concept is widely used in the production of television commercials.

For your purposes, storyboards will encourage teamwork between you and your artist (if you are fortunate enough to have one) and you and your superiors. Chances are, your boss will want to review the presentation before you give it. If you work in a large organization, several people—including the legal department—may want to see it. Storyboards come to the rescue. Spiff them up a little with cleaner sketches, and edited and typed narration, and they make an ideal vehicle for review. Just send copies out with an approval sheet and wait for comments.

But if you can get all your reviewers together, there's a better way. Bob Bly described it in an article for *Audio Visual Directions:*

> The quickest way to expedite this process is to schedule a review meeting. Prior to the meeting, arrive at the conference room early and pin or tape your storyboards to the wall in their proper sequence. Be sure to bring pencils, tape, and blank storyboards for the reviewers to work with. At the meeting, the reviewers can resolve any changes they might want to make by pulling storyboards off the wall and pinning up new ones as changes are made. Eventually, you'll end up with a version that has every reviewer's blessing.[7]

Having your storyboards up on the wall provides another benefit. It allows you to view the entire presentation as a unit and measure it against your theme or objective.

Scanning the storyboards will allow you to spot any "mixed messages" where the visual and the narration appear to talk about two different things. Also, watch out for too many "verbal visuals" (word charts or slides) in a row, without any pictorial relief.

NOW LOOK WHAT YOU'VE DONE!

If that reminds you of the scoldings you got as a child, I apologize. I just wanted to point out that giving a presentation is a continuing process of reviewing your material and improving it. This review process starts with checking your outline, editing the narration, and reviewing the storyboards; then continues through the practice, dry run, and dress rehearsal; and often concludes with a critique after you've given the talk.

Certainly, the earlier in this course you make necessary changes, the less drastic the shift and the better the results. So now, before you invest any more time in developing your material, check it out. Ask yourself:

- Does the organization follow the strategy?
- Does all the material fit the objective?
- Are the main points in proper sequence?
- Are the main points properly balanced in terms of coverage?
- Are there any unnecessary duplications?
- Did I gather enough illustrations, analogies, quotations, examples, statistics?
- Will I be able to acknowledge conflicting views and refute them?
- Are there enough benefits to persuade?
- What's new? Does the audience already know all of this?

Having considered all these items and made any course corrections, sail on.

CHAPTER FOUR

Developing Your Talk: How to Add Interest

CAPTIVE AUDIENCE? DON'T KID YOURSELF!

ROBERT BENCHLEY SAID IT BEST: "My attention can be held only by strapping me down to a cot and sitting on my chest. Even then my eyes wander." And so it will be with most audiences. The typical member will resemble the cross-section of a torso frequently shown in television commercials—filled with all sorts of bubbling gases (concerns) trying to get out. Your job as the speaker will be to force a few more ideas in.

Or, consider for a moment the requirements of hypnotism. First, there must be a focal point—in this case, the speaker, who is perhaps even swaying back and forth like the hypnotist's charm. Secondly, the hypnotist needs a fairly comfortable setting—not unlike a meeting room with the lights turned down for showing slides (perhaps shortly after a fairly heavy meal). See, you're starting to drop off already . . . .

Our objective is not to hypnotize, but to enthrall and inspire. And this chapter shows you how to do that by developing your talk's muscles and adding interest. You'll discover how to take those persons in the audience who are dreamily yawning "So what?" and make them mentally shout, "Oh, WOW!"

What Do You Want from the Audience?

Given three wishes concerning an audience, you would like them to:

1. Listen.
2. Understand.
3. Be influenced.

For them to *really* listen, you will have to be interesting and present a message that is worthwhile to the specific group you are addressing. For them to understand, you will have to simplify your presentation, starting on ground they are familiar with or already in agreement on. And, for them to be influenced, you will have to show "what's in it for them"—that the suggested course of action is in their own best interests.

This, then, is the principal purpose of any talk—motivating others to act on your ideas. Tough job? Of course! But, it has always been so. And throughout history, men and women have risen to the occasion. You can, too.

WRITING THE NARRATION

The previous chapter talked about gathering and organizing your information, and the talk began to take shape, much like a patchwork quilt. Now you're going to try to sew all those ideas together into a script.

Getting the Flow Started

Long ago, the movies made "writer's block" a cliché. The typical scene showed the author hurling ball after ball of barely written text into the wastebasket.

Whether they realized it or not, the filmmakers were demonstrating one of the basic laws of physics discovered by Sir Isaac Newton. No, I'm not talking about gravity making the crumpled paper fall into the wastebasket. I'm referring to the law of motion, which states, "A body at rest tends to remain at rest, and a body in motion tends to remain in motion."

Think about it. Don't you have trouble getting started writing? But, once you do get started, don't the words flow fairly easily until an interruption cuts them off? Now take another look at Newton's law and follow these two suggestions:

1. If you have trouble starting at the beginning, start wherever you want. Pick the part that's easiest. Or the part you're most interested in. You can always write that opening later. Save any tough parts for last.
2. Avoid interruptions and distractions that threaten to cut off the flow. Gather everything you'll need beforehand so you won't have to go looking for it. And find a quite place. The library. A vacation cottage. An empty office. Or ask the boss to let you work at home.

Be Conversational. After All, It's a Talk

How do you keep that flow going? Easy. Just imagine yourself talking to someone, and as the words register in your mind, jot them down. You can use your outline as a checklist to keep the ideas flowing and keep you on track. If this doesn't work or proves too slow, try a tape recorder. (Just keep in mind you'll want to do some extra polishing as you put it on paper.) If you used the index cards and storyboard approach suggested in the previous chapter, you have already built a strong bridge between your outline and the narration.

Remember, a presentation is neither a lecture nor a sermon. It is simply talking with people and sharing ideas. It is a skill you practice every day.

Whatever his shortcomings as a public speaker may be, President Bush's strongest point is his conversational style, which gives his talks a good-natured flavor.

PUT EXTRA EFFORT INTO THOSE FIRST FEW MINUTES

You can write your opening first, last, or in between if that suits you, but to keep things in order, it's the first part covered here. But even before your opening remarks, you are going to be introduced.

There are masters of ceremonies who are nonprofessionals and yet give magnificent introductions. Most M.C.'s you will run into, however, will be amateurs at best and your introduction may be, "And now, here's old What's-his-face. Let's see, I had it written down here somewhere."

There are steps you can take to prevent this, of course. Most organizations will ask for some advance information. When they do, resist the temptation to send them your complete history, for surely they will read it word for word. Instead, send them an introduction written the way you would like to be introduced.

Write Your Own Introduction — The TIS Formula

The TIS Formula provides a good model for writing your own introduction. Just remember, "Here 'tis . . . ." Let the T stand for Topic (what you're going to talk about), the I for Importance (why it's important to this particular audience), and the S for Speaker (your credentials on this particular subject).

The entire introduction should take less than a minute to read aloud, and should fit easily on a single sheet of paper (typed double-spaced in a large typeface).

Once it's ready, send a copy to whoever is running the meeting where you will be speaking. And make yourself a copy to take with you when you go to give the talk. When you arrive, find some excuse to go over your introduction with the chairperson or master of ceremonies, who may have lost or forgotten the copy you sent earlier. This may also be the closest your introducer will ever get to a rehearsal.

Writing the Opening

Opening remarks constitute a "warm-up" designed to put you at ease and capture the audience's attention. Here are some examples:

- "I've practiced this presentation all week and I feel pretty good about it. So, if you could just manage to look a little bit more like my bathroom mirror, I'll begin."
- "I have a rather simple idea that I would like you to think about. It could save us $5,000 a year. Now that's not much in a company our size, but it's certainly too much to waste. And, watching the pennies, the dollars will take care of themselves. Here's what I'm talking about . . . ."

Start your presentation by talking about *this particular group* (and not by just mentioning the organization's name). Start by citing some shared relationship if possible:

- "Mr. Jones was correct in introducing me as an engineer from Metro Power and Light. But I'm also a lot of other things. I'm a Catholic, a Jaycee, a father of four. I'm here tonight as all of these . . . ."

Or perhaps you're a high-level executive addressing a group of managers. After the usual "Good morning, it's certainly a pleasure to be here," you reach into your pocket producing a set of 3 by 5 index cards and continue. "Despite these cards, I don't have a well-structured talk. These are just a few problems, questions, or selected topics I thought you might be interested in."

I once saw a general manager do just this. He then proceeded to read the very clever and humorous topics he was going to cover. These twists in management maxims included:

- "A little anarchy can be a good thing."
- "Learn to appreciate your boss. The next one may be worse."

He then went back and covered each item in more detail, showing the practical application of a statement which at first seemed merely humorous. What he was doing was applying the ancient yet effective organizational technique of "Tell 'em what you're gonna tell them. Tell them. And tell them what you told them," which we discussed in the previous chapter. He was giving us a menu of the meal that was to follow, and the appetizer told us it was going to be good!

I've seen a similar card technique used at going-away ceremonies and retirements, where the cards represented questions asked about the guest of honor during the previous week. And, you've probably seen the opening where the speaker approaches the lectern and "accidentally" drops the "well-prepared" talk, scattering the cards and setting the stage for an informal discussion. Or, where the speaker merely sets the cards aside and says, "I'm more used to talking with people one-on-one than I am giving speeches. So, Carol, let me start with you and then I'll move around the room."

Another informal technique involves a flip chart and the comment, "To get us started, I'd like to ask your help in listing concerns." Then you move toward the flip chart easel and uncap the marker to give them time to respond. To make sure they heard you, you might look back at them and repeat, "What are some of the things you're concerned with?" Pause, and if none is forthcoming, continue with, "Well, here's one of the things that worries me." (Or "used to worry me" if your objective is to allay their fears.) Write this concern on the flip chart, again giving the audience time to think. Then ask, "How many of you share this concern?" (Pause) "What other items would you care to list?" Again, pause, and if necessary, add, "Who wants to be first?" And if there's no answer, say, "All right, I admit being 'first' can be tough. Who wants to be 'second'?"—and pause again. (If things haven't picked up by now, call the morgue.)

As the list grows, you are essentially "Telling 'em what you're gonna tell them." Then you check off items on the list as you "tell 'em" in more detail. Then, you perhaps go back and circle each item (or cross it out if you want to show them that the problem has been eliminated) as you summarize and "Tell 'em what you told them."

Lead with Your Ace

Start with your most important item. Be sure to bring out the seriousness of the situation or the anticipated value. Don't neglect the factors of cost, schedule, and performance. And back up your statements with substantiating data.

MAKING IT MEMORABLE

Dale Carnegie training includes a memory aid based on the letters IRA: *I* for Impression, *R* for Repetition, and *A* for Association.[8] In addition to helping you remember things, it can also make your talk more memorable for your audience:

- *Impression*—Make sure they know why your talk is important. What are the benefits? What effect will there be on them personally?
- *Repetition*—If you want your audience to remember, find a way to restate your key ideas in a slightly different manner.
- *Association*—Be sure to start on familiar ground. Tie your talk to something they already know or agree with. Then move on to uncharted territory.

Words that Draw Pictures

Yes, a picture can be worth a thousand words. But some words draw pictures all by themselves. You can make your audience see, hear, feel, or bring all their senses to bear by using picture words. Be *specific*. If you are talking about specific people, mention them by name. Refer to people whom the audience knows or who are in the audience. Use concrete terms. Don't say "electrical equipment" if you mean "conduit." Don't say "crime" if you mean "rape." What do managers, engineers, and accountants think when they hear words like "minimum," "high," "low"? They live in a world of numbers. They deal in specifics. Tell them how you can save twelve months, eighty-six thousand dollars, or fifty-six percent!

Figuratively Speaking—Similes and Metaphors

Use words in an imaginative sense rather than in a literal sense. Figures of speech can stimulate your audience's imagination and add color to your talk. The two major figures of speech are the simile and the metaphor.

A simile is a comparison of two things that do not generally have the same nature. Typically, the simile makes an *explicit* comparison introduced by *like* or *as*. For example, "Her voice was *like* velvet" or, "Their running back was quick *as* a cat." A metaphor, on the other hand, is an *implied* comparison. For example, "That car was a gem" or "Figures of speech are the salt and pepper of presentations."

Be careful not to get carried away into the land of excessive, inappropriate, or (most important) strained metaphors and similes. For instance, "This market is like a river running into the sea, and we are limited only by the size of our bucket."

As they said in the movie, "Metaphors be with you!"

Music to Their Ears

You can develop words and phrases guaranteed to augment the audience's attention. I just used one technique—alliteration—when I repeated the "ah" sound in the previous sentence. Another example would be ". . . power out of proportion . . . ." But again, be careful you don't overdo it and wind up with a "Peter Piper picked a peck of pickled peppers."

You may never originate a line to equal Churchill's "Blood, tears, toil, and sweat" or Kennedy's "Ask not what your country can do for you. Ask what you can do for your country." But I doubt whether General McAuliff knew he was making history during the Battle of the Bulge in World War II when he simply said, "Nuts!" Historic—or at least audience-shaking—rhetoric is not beyond your grasp.

On television, the best example of "music to their ears" rests in the jingle that combines words and music: "Reach out and touch someone" . . . "You, you're the one" . . . "We are driven." For your audiences, you will want to develop short, catchy, mellifluous phrases that keep their attention focused and speak to their specific interests. Consider using, "The beauty of this approach is . . ." or, for transitioning, "But it's not quite enough for us to . . . ." Music to their ears may be product cost ratios or return on investment, among others.

Working in the Facts

Statistics can spice up a variety of talks, especially if you can find an imaginative way to present them. Figuring out how many dollars it will take laid end-to-end to reach from Paducah, Kentucky, to Washington, DC, is a lot easier since the invention of the pocket calculator. Joe Powell, the author of *Executive Speaking—An Acquired Skill* is an enthusiastic speaker who is outstanding when it comes to presenting statistics in terms the average person can understand. For example, after citing a statistic involving millions, he drives the size of a million home by pointing out that a stack of one million dollars would be approximately 100 feet higher than the Washington Monument.[9] His book has excellent chapters on how to create interest with facts and figures, and on how to translate statistics into meaningful illustrations.

Telling Jokes —Dangerous or Delightful?

For some reason, many speakers feel they must begin with a joke. Here's an anecdote from Roger Axtell, author of *Do's and Taboos Around the World.* An executive of a New York insurance firm tells of a colleague who regularly gave speeches to Japanese audiences. It was learned later that at one speech the Japanese translator began: "American gentleman is beginning speech with thing called joke. I don't know why, but all Americans think they must begin speech with joke. You won't understand joke, so I will omit it. But he thinks I am telling you joke now. The polite thing will be to laugh at the end, when I tell you. [Pause] He is getting close. [Pause] Now."

The audience erupted in laughter, even stood for an ovation. Afterward the American lecturer went to the interpreter and said, "You know, I've been giving speeches in this country for several years, and you are the first interpreter who knows how to tell a good joke."[10]

You already have an idea of whether you can tell a joke well. Do you keep your friends in stitches when your bridge or poker group gets together, or at the office, or at cocktail parties, or in the clubhouse? If the answer is no, then don't start to think you will turn into a Whoopi Goldberg or Steve Martin the moment you stand up in front of a group of strangers.

Any jokes you consider should be reasonably short and suited to the audience or situation. Think twice, and then test a joke before using it. Is it appropriate? Is it offensive? Is it really funny?

Although there are reference books on jokes, most of them tend to be disappointing. There are also comedy newsletters you can subscribe to, such as *Orben's Current Comedy*, which is published twice each month.

However, you can also start your own collection with a pair of scissors, some index cards, glue, and a card file. Often, the best jokes to use are those you run across that immediately strike a connection to your field of interest.

Perhaps the best joke to tell is the one you tell on yourself. As Lynne Cheney puts it:

> These days, many public figures put themselves down. Self-deprecating humor is a human, humble touch, and the public responds to it. Abraham Lincoln was an early practitioner. Accused of being two-faced, he replied: "If I had another face, do you think I'd use this one."[11]

During the 1984 Presidential campaign, Ronald Reagan defused the issue of his advanced age nicely when he said, "I will not exploit, for partisan political purposes, my opponent's youth and inexperience." (A political one-liner written for him by Don Penny.)

Tell Them a Real-Life Story

A real-life story can be much more powerful than a joke and audiences love a good story. Here's one from the late Bud Robbins on his early days in advertising:

> Back in the '60s, I was hired by an ad agency to write copy on the Aeolian Piano Co. account. My first assignment was for an ad to be

placed in the *New York Times* for one of their grand pianos. The only background information I received was some previous ads and a few faded close-up shots . . . and of course, the due date.

The account executive was slightly put out by my request for additional information and his response to my suggestion that I sit down with the client was "Jesus Christ, are you one of *those?* Can't you just create something? We're up against a closing date!"

I acknowledged his perception that I was one of those, which got us an immediate audience with the head of our agency.

I volunteered I couldn't even play a piano, let alone write about why anyone would spend $5,000 for this piano when they could purchase a Baldwin or Steinway for the same amount.

Both allowed the fact they would gladly resign the Aeolian business for either of the others, however, while waiting for that call, suppose we make our deadline.

I persisted and reluctantly, a tour of the Aeolian factory in upstate New York was arranged. I was assured that "we don't do this with all our clients" and my knowledge as to the value of company time was greatly reinforced.

The tour of the plant lasted two days and although the care and construction appeared meticulous, $5,000 still seemed to be a lot of money.

Just before leaving, I was escorted into the showroom by the national sales manager. In an elegant setting sat their piano alongside the comparably priced Steinway and Baldwin.

"They sure do look alike," I commented.

"They sure do. About the only real difference is the shipping weight—ours is heavier."

"Heavier?" I asked. "What makes ours heavier?"

"The Capo d'astro bar. Here, I'll show you. Get down on your knees."

Once under the piano, he pointed to a metallic bar fixed across the harp and bearing down on the highest octaves. "It takes 50 years before the harp in the piano warps. That's when the Capo d'astro bar goes to work. It prevents that warping."

I left the national sales manager under his piano and dove under the Baldwin to find a Tinkertoy Capo d'astro bar at best. Same with the Steinway.

"You mean the Capo d'astro bar really doesn't go to work for 50 years?" I asked.

"Well, there's got to be some reason why the Met uses it," he casually added.

I froze. "Are you telling me that the Metropolitan Opera House in New York City uses this piano?"

"Sure. And their Capo d'astro bar should be working by now."

Upstate New York looks nothing like the front of the Metropolitan Opera House where I met the legendary Carmen, Risë Stevens. She was now in charge of moving the Metropolitan Opera House to the Lincoln Center.

Ms. Stevens told me, "About the only thing the Met is taking with them is their piano."

That quote was the headline of our first ad.

The result created a six-year wait between order and delivery.

My point is this. No matter what the account, I promise you, the Capo d'astro bar is there.[12]

TRANSFERRING YOUR ENTHUSIASM TO THE AUDIENCE

So far this chapter has concentrated on how you can build interest with your audience in terms of their mental participation. You are, of course, going to try to capture their minds, but many times you can accomplish this best by capturing their bodies as well. Give them something to do. Get them involved.

There are many ways to build audience participation. If time permits you can try buzz sessions, dividing the audience into smaller groups, appointing a chairperson for each, and asking them to report their findings after a period of time. You might also consider short quizzes.

People love a chance to show how smart they are. Just be careful not to let the situation become threatening. Thank them for their participation. And be flexible when their answers don't match yours. Commend them on their solutions and then express your thoughts as an alternative.

GIMMICKS AND GIZMOS— PIZZAZZ WITH A PURPOSE

For those times when you want to liven things up a little, have fun with your audience, or make a point with a few "indoor fireworks," you should consider gimmicks and gizmos. These little bits of frivolity can make a big contribution to your talk, if you remember two things.

First, the gimmick must be related to your subject, and you must clearly point out that relationship. Nothing could be worse than your audience thinking, "Well, that was interesting, but what's the point?"

Second, one gimmick per talk is enough. Don't overdo this aspect or you may come across as a vaudevillian. Remember, the gimmick is used merely to *underline* your point. It is not the point itself.

With these two rules in mind, the best way to discuss gimmicks and gizmos is to list some examples. Here are some that have worked for me in various situations. I leave their specific application up to you.

Guess the number of beans in the jar has been around so long it even predates this author. No doubt you've seen it in the window of your hardware store, where the proprietor displayed a large jar full of nuts and bolts. Or, perhaps you've seen it at the golf course where the contents were golf tees. Whatever the contents, you were invited to guess the number of items in the jar and the person with the closest guess won a prize.

In giving talks, this technique can be used in a variety of ways. A real container can be exhibited or the jar can be imaginary. For example, you could ask the audience to guess the number of dollars spent by your company on technical reports or pollution control, or the number of miles of road in your county, or any other important statistic you would like them to remember.

At the appropriate point, you or your assistants pass out 3 by 5 cards and ask the members of the audience to jot down their names and their best guesses. Then you quickly check the cards at the end of your talk (or during a coffee break) and while you announce the winner and award a prize, you also drive home the importance of that statistic.

$1,000,000 for your thoughts is a sure-fire way to get a group discussion going. After all, who wouldn't like to have a million dollars? Furthermore, in these times, offering a penny for their thoughts would be an insult. You can actually offer your audience a million dollars for their thoughts—or at least a *chance* at a million dollars. Most states have lotteries, with chances that cost between fifty cents and a dollar and offer potential payoffs up to a million dollars or more.

Buy ten of these tickets and, before the audience arrives, lightly tape them to a flip chart easel. After the appropriate introductory comments, you unveil the tickets and the discussion is on. Give out one ticket for each good idea and use a felt tip marker to summarize the idea on that portion of the chart vacated by the ticket. (Afterward, the ideas can be typed up and sent on to the appropriate person to put them in action.) Rest assured, you'll run out of tickets before they'll run out of ideas.

Just remember, leave at least three to five minutes in your schedule for each idea. Ten tickets are usually enough, even if the audience is much bigger. And if you're using the instant winner type of ticket, ask the recipients to wait until the end of the discussion and rub off the coverings all at once. A really big win could end your presentation prematurely.

You're sitting on a fortune has been overdone, but perhaps you can come up with a new variation. It's frequently used with salespeople to show them what they can do if they get off their posteriors. In this gimmick, money, theater tickets, and the like are stuck to the bottom of one or more chairs. I'm sure you can guess the rest.

One variation is to put three or four pennies in an envelope to show employees how little profit their company actually makes on each dollar of sales. My own variation has been quite helpful in discussing sales techniques with engineers and scientists, who often disdain the selling process. First I lead them into telling me the old adage, "Build a better mousetrap and the world will beat a path to your door," which I then hold up to ridicule, stating that this saying had to have been originated by an engineer. Furthermore, if they want to see why my reaction to this time-honored saying is, "horse feathers," or an even more noxious substance, I invite them to check underneath their chairs. There, taped to the bottom in an envelope, is a small wedge of Gruyère cheese, which in our mousetrap analogy suggests bait. "Bait" leads to "benefits," and the discussion is on.

A wedge under each chair is nice, but let me suggest an improvement. Once, quite by accident, I didn't have enough cheese to go around. The individual sitting on the "empty" chair actually stood up, turned the chair upside down, and was slightly miffed at not getting any cheese. Voila! A great example of what happens in real life when there's no benefit for someone.

Making it bubbly involves something most people have seen on TV, the plop-plop of two Alka-Seltzers hitting a glass of water. The recognition is instantaneous, particularly if you use the big blue box as a prop.

You can use this as an opener, saying what a tough time you are having generating your own enthusiasm and then giving the bubbling glass to someone in the audience who looks less than alert. Or, you can use the effervescence of the concoction to lead into a discussion of enthusiasm itself.

A few pointers. Have the tablets out of their protective foil wrappers and ready to go. (Tablets, box, and glass can all be hidden behind the lectern.) Warm water will increase the effervescence. And, if you really want to be colorful, add a drop of food coloring to the tablets ahead of time and let them dry.

How barriers prevent results can be used in many discussions on negativism, prejudices, and similar attitudes. A volunteer from the audience is asked to pour water from a pitcher into a glass. The volunteer holds the pitcher; you hold the glass. In the other hand you hold a piece of paper or cardboard. As the volunteer attempts to pour, you position the paper above the glass. The results can be hilarious; some prodding may be necessary, but eventually the volunteer will attempt it. Then ask why the water isn't going into the glass. You're sure to get words like "blocking" or "barrier" in the response, which is just what you want.

If the floor is carpeted, the little bit of spillage will dry quickly with no harm done (although I wouldn't recommend this bit for the corporate boardroom). If the floor is tile, beware. The wet spot could be hazardous. One wipe with a paper towel, though, and you're back in business.

I use this gimmick to demonstrate the disadvantages of reading a speech and how the written page can be a barrier between you and your audience, disrupting eye contact. I'm sure you will find your own uses.

Beat the clock is another audience participation gimmick where the premium is on quick response. Let's say you are instructing a group of foremen on the importance of short but satisfying answers to questions. Get a volunteer to field questions. The volunteer is timed from the start of his or her answer; sixty seconds is usually an adequate limit. If a satisfactory answer is provided, a small prize is awarded, along with any suggestions for improvement.

A final exam that's fun can help you maintain attention and interest throughout a day-long session. Early on, tell the group there's going to be an exam. They'll feel challenged—perhaps threatened—and will take notes and hope they will pass!

At the end of the day, ask them to put away their notes, print their names on the top of a piece of paper, and then (to save time) have them fold up the papers and pass them up to the front.

At this point you unveil a flip chart with a one-, two-, five-, ten-, and twenty-dollar bill lightly taped thereon. (Include a fifty-dollar bill if your sponsoring organization has sufficient resources.) Then, announce the rules of the "test."

For each correct answer to a question, there is a prize, starting with one dollar. Of course, the one-dollar question is pretty simple and the subsequent questions get progressively harder, leading to the grand prize. Select the test participants at random; you can make a point of this by tossing their folded sheets high in the air. Pick up those that land closest to you, stand on edge, or whatever.

The questions should deal with those points that you particularly want the audience to remember. Although the questions will get progressively tougher, your goal is to make a point, not to save money. Be generous. You might even want to offer a second individual a chance at any missed questions. If you gave a good presentation, you should have no money left over at the end of the test.

Up, up, and away is another grand finale you can use to dramatize the fact that you're trying to get a fundraiser or some other event off the ground. Have an artist letter the event's name on a piece of *lightweight* cardboard. Then attach helium-filled balloons to the sign. Mix the colors—the more the merrier. Use a lot of balloons, and fill them as full as possible. The whole contraption can be stored under a draped table until the right moment. But, be sure you do a test flight beforehand. Otherwise, the results may be just the opposite of what you're trying to convey.

The goldfish gimmick involves both an opening and a closing. I'm not sure where you'll be able to use it, but it worked so well for me once, I thought I would pass it on.

I was giving a talk to higher management and I wanted to point out that people in the communications industry are sometimes treated like second-class citizens. Of course, the audience wasn't aware that this would be part of my message.

My title slide was very straightforward, but included an illustration of a goldfish in a bowl. My narration went on to point out that "working in communications is sometimes the equivalent of living in a goldfish bowl," which immediately started them thinking in terms of high visibility, etc. While I agreed this was occasionally the case, I then proceeded to show them a series of slides showing what the goldfish bowl analogy really meant. The first showed a boss berating a worker. The next showed the worker arguing with the spouse. Then the spouse punishing a child. Followed by the child kicking a dog. Another of the dog chasing a cat. And finally, a slide showing the cat relieving himself in the goldfish bowl. Along with the last slide, I announced, "And that is why I say working in communications is sometimes the equivalent of living in a goldfish bowl."

When the laughter subsided I went on to say, "Now listen up, you *cats*," and cited a few points, trying to keep things on as positive a plane as possible. At the conclusion, I mentioned that it was not unusual at this type of meeting to present the audience with some sort of reminder such as a pen set, calendar, or lucite paperweight, but since they already had many of these, I was going to present each of them with something the likes of which they had never gotten at a meeting before. Then, with some help, I gave each a small bowl with a live goldfish in it!

It literally brought the house down. Being managers, they started tapping on the sides of the bowls to "keep things moving." Some combined their resources to see if they could increase productivity. (Unfortunately, with all the pandemonium going on, the next speaker didn't stand a chance. A coffee break had to be called.) After the meeting was over, some of those fish traveled coast-to-coast. And, most importantly, all of those *cats* got the message.

Something everybody's interested in—*sin* can help you with a ho-hum audience that already knows *as much* as you do, but doesn't know *what* you're going to say. Standing before a blank screen you announce that your topic for today is going to be something everybody is interested in—*sin.* And as you hit that key word you also flash it on the screen—preferably in large, Old English letters. Then you go on to say you'd like to expand on the topic somewhat. And in your next slide or viewgraph, the word *sin* grows to *sinergism* (again in Old English lettering).

You quickly point out that you know it's misspelled, but the important thing is not how to spell it but what it can do and how to achieve it. The slide changes and *synergism* appears while you go on talking about how, if they all work together, the whole can be greater than the sum of the parts.

Then give some examples, followed by your summary. "And, in conclusion," you tell them, "let's all go out there and *syn!*" (Again with the visual in Old English, but with another reverse twist on the spelling.)

Look what the competition's doing (to us) is useful in getting bigger budgets for advertising, public relations, and the like. First you gather a number of pieces of cardboard the size of magazine or newspaper pages and tape them together into one continuous piece that will fold up accordion-style. Then you select a recent issue of a magazine or newspaper in which your company ran an advertisement (the bigger the issue, the better). Then cut out *all* the ads in that issue and paste them on your pieces of cardboard.

What you now have is a visual that arrives at the meeting room folded into a compact shape, but which, when you use it, unfolds, and unfolds, and unfolds, and . . . . (You'll need as many as six or more volunteers from the audience to hold it up at various points along its length.) It may even surround most of the group. The result is a visual that shows how easily a single ad can get lost, and the importance of a consistent campaign.

In public relations the same technique can show how much competition there is for space and the need for increased efforts.

If you're still worried about being too entertaining, keep in mind that people will pay significantly more for entertainment than for education. Ask any university faculty member. The average college professor would have to work for a thousand years to match the annual salary of a national-network talk show host.

These are just a few ideas to start you thinking. There are many more. Just keep your eyes open and use your imagination.

TYPING A TALK

Even though you don't plan to read your talk to the audience, you'll want to write out the talk completely as part of the preparation process. And if there's the slightest possibility you might be reading it or want to have it up there as a crutch, it should be in a useful format.

Chances are that whoever types your talk will do so under lighting conditions only slightly dimmer than those in a modern operating room, and that the material will be at normal distance for reading. What a surprise you'll get when you get up to give your talk and discover the lectern is equipped with a seven-and-one-half-watt light-bulb, while your script is at a distance only a person badly in need of bifocals would appreciate.

To help overcome these and other pitfalls, here are a few things you or your typist should consider:

- Use a large typeface. The IBM Selectric typewriter can use an Orator ball (element) that is excellent. Other brands of interchangeable-element typewriters have similar balls. Modern word processing equipment also works well. Laser printers, such as the Hewlett-Packard HP LaserJet II (a sample printout is shown on page 49), can give you large, bold type that even Mr. Magoo could read.
- Set your typewriter for double or triple space and double that between paragraphs or thought groups.
- Type on legal-size paper ($8^1/_2 \times 14$ inches) but use only the top 11 inches so that the script will sit up higher on the lectern. This will make it easier to read and give you better eye contact because of the shorter angle between the audience and the script. You can also tape a pencil about six inches long—not the one you got with your golf scorecard—to the lectern at a spot that will make your $8^1/_2 \times 11$-inch scripts rest comfortably at a more readable height.

THIS IS A SAMPLE OF A SCRIPT PREPARED ON A LASER JET SERIES II PRINTER. THE FONT STYLE IS CALLED PRESENTATIONS I. THE CHARACTER SET IS 58.

Typing the script with a large typeface is a must if the script is to be read.

- Never split a sentence by carrying part of it over to a new page. Try to avoid splitting paragraphs.
- Put six periods at the end of each sentence to make sure you won't miss any pauses and inadvertently run two sentences together.
- Make sure the narration is typed the way you will *read* it and that there aren't any built-in booby traps. For example, I once saw a speaker misread WW II as "World War Eleven." Numbers are generally a lot easier to read if they are written out (e.g., "Two and three-quarter million dollars" versus "$2,750,000").
- Of course you'll want your script typed or printed on one side. And you won't want to bind it since you'll be sliding finished sheets to the side rather than turning them. (Sometimes the lectern light will reflect off sheets being turned and have the audience thinking they're watching an hourglass demonstration, with the sand—or pages—running out bit by bit.)
- If you're using visuals, you may want to indicate when they occur by using a few key words, a rough sketch, or a copier machine reduction in an expanded left-hand margin. And you should mark *exactly* where they should come on.

Remember, the script is a working document. Chapter 7 talks about marking a script for emphasis, pauses, and other narrative devices. But there's a lot to do before you get there—starting with editing.

REVIEWING THE ROUGH NARRATION

You are probably at least vaguely familiar with the editing process that occurs in creating movies, television news, newspaper articles, and the like. Exactly the same process applies in speeches, which must be edited for both time and value. And unless you perform this function for the audience, the audience will perform it for you—figuratively tripping the trapdoor that will drop you out of their minds.

By the time you edit it you should have your material typed. If you were fortunate enough to have someone else do your typing, this will have gotten you away from the script for a while. Typing will also cut down on some of the "personal involvement" in the handwritten version, and the phrases that seemed so brilliant when you wrote them may have lost a little of their luster. All this can be restored with polishing.

Now lean back and read the script *with your ears.* How does it *sound* to you? Read it all the way through, lightly underlining or circling any words or passages that are stumbling blocks for your *ear.* Then go back and read it again. Mark any additional items that need attention and start effecting the needed repairs. Remember, you're talking to a group of people. This is not a doctoral dissertation.

Do any sentences seem too long to your mind's ear? What will they sound like when they're actually spoken? Great strides are being made in applying conversational styles to writing. Certainly the same should apply to any talk. Instead, it's sometimes tempting to conjure up images of some "great orator" out of the past and let your sentences run on and on. It's easy to forget to strive for brevity or to fail to pause often enough for paragraphs and sentences.

How is the flow or continuity? If a musician were to score this talk, would it move sluggishly like a funeral dirge or bounce along like an up-tempo swing tune? One talk might resemble a caterpillar crossing a set of railroad tracks—two great peaks with a long flat spot in between. Another talk might sound like the staccato burst of a machine gun—with nearly the same deadly results.

Your talk's continuity or flow can be improved in a number of ways. Certainly, having your material in the best possible order is a good start. As you review the typed narration you will probably see some improvements that can be made in the arrangement.

Variety is needed. For example, the short sentences that we recommended earlier can have all the rhythm of a ride down railroad tracks on a minibike, if you use too many of them in a row. It's bump, bump, bump as you bounce across each tie. You can sometimes avoid this by combining some short sentences. Another good idea is to repeat certain words and phrases. For example, if one sentence said, "One of the important features of this model is its instrumentation package," your next sentence could begin, "This instrumentation provides . . . ."

Connecting words and phrases also help—"thereby," "therefore," "accordingly," and "however"; as well as phrases like "so that," "as a result, you get," "at the same time," and "this means that." Be sure to alert your audience when you shift gears by using such transitions as, "So much for the legal situation. Now let's take a look at . . . ."

Enumerating your points can help your audience keep track of where you are and represents a "contract" wherein you promise to deliver a certain number of key points and they promise (you hope) to stick around. Each new number you cite will at least provide an opportunity to recapture any of those present who may have momentarily drifted away. You can minimize the latter by limiting yourself to three main points.

While we're on the subject of talking about things in *threes,* consider the three-sided triangle. It's often used in construction because of its strength, and to some it even has a religious significance. In speeches and presentations it can be used to add strength and rhythm, as in John F. Kennedy's ". . . the energy, the strength, and the devotion which we bring to this endeavor will light our country and all who serve it."

Does your talk suffer from "I" trouble? As you read through it, do you keep hearing the word "I"? Just as too much focus on oneself makes for dull conversation, the same is true for speakers. The audience wants to know what's in it for *them.* So you'll want to be frequently using words like "you" and "your." Count the number of times you use "you" and "your" versus the "I's" in your talk. The ratio should be at least 10 to 1.

Will anything in this talk cause an unpleasant jolt? Will it be offensive? Is it subject to misinterpretation? Sometimes there are attitudes hidden in words and you can't afford to ignore them. Such word choices that are not to be taken lightly include cheap vs. economical; profit vs. earnings; incompetent vs. unsuited; and gift vs. contribution. Frequently you will hear speakers talk about "you people." I would avoid this because it implies the speaker belongs to another group or class. Furthermore, some might even consider it an ethnic or racial slur. You can upset a young adult by unthinkingly referring to him as a "boy." But if that young adult also happens to be black, your thoughtlessness could really generate some fireworks. The same danger exists when speakers refer to women as "girls." People who are so insensitive that they make these errors deserve whatever happens to them. But other, less obvious mistakes are easy to make if you aren't careful in reviewing your phraseology.

Quit While You're Ahead

Things do not get better every time they are revised. (Sometimes they get worse.) There comes a time when enough is enough. Free-lance writer, producer, and media consultant Peter Schleger asks:

> When should one stop revising? There is no true answer. Perhaps one must simply take a step back and ask, "Does it look right, does it sound right, will it be effective?" It may not be perfect, but let's go with it. Everything can always be made better.[13]

Getting Management Approval

If you work in an organization, you'll want to keep your bosses informed about what you're doing. You don't want to show them something that's too rough, but you also don't want to go too far and be asked to make a major change of direction at the eleventh hour. My advice is to send them periodic steps in the process—thesis statement, outlines, storyboards, narration—and make them members of the team. This should result in relatively easy changes along the way rather than a last-minute major redo. It's an iterative process that differs in every organization.

Again, Peter Schleger:

> The review process is different in every organization and is dictated by corporate culture and managerial styles of individuals within the organization. One of my clients had a reputation for being reserved and shunning publicity. Today, the organization encourages its managers to get out into the community. Its former review policy would have taken a defensive stance, making certain to say nothing controversial. Today,

it aims to be exciting, a philosophy reflected in reduced anxiety about saying the wrong thing.

Some small companies have no review process, where the only one responsible is the client. Perhaps this is too lax, but it reflects the way they run their businesses. One division of a recently broken-up communications company would not allow a project, any project, to start without the approval of a vice president.[14]

The 4-S Formula

Here's an easy-to-remember formula you can use to improve your speeches:

Shortness + Simplicity + Strength + Sincerity = A Good Talk

Shortness —In addition to shortening your sentences, narrow the focus. Don't try to talk about the whole world, or even about all aspects of the small part you are involved with. Beware of information overload. If you include too many details, your talk will not only be too long, but your audience will most likely be faced with a mixed bag of ideas. Unless the audience finds an item useful or interesting or (preferably) both, scratch it out. Remember, in terms of emphasis, less is more. Limit your points. You want to be sure to finish before your audience does.

Simplicity —Avoid gobbledygook, bafflegab, bureaucratese, and other long-winded styles that use more words than are required. Why say "before the actual time that" when a simple "before" will do the job just as well? Other examples include "at the present time" (now), "due to the fact that" (because), "in the event that" (if), "by means of" (by), and a host of others. Learn to trim off the fat and leave the meat. Talks that are sensationally simple can be simply sensational.

Strength —You want an active audience, so use hard-hitting, active verbs. Minimize your use of the passive voice and you'll help minimize the possibility of a passive audience.

So you say it's been a while since your last course in English grammar, and you'd like to hear more about active and passive voice. Briefly, in an active sentence the subject performs the action (John threw the ball). In a passive sentence the subject is acted upon (The ball was thrown by John). Even in these simple examples you can see the passive voice is inherently longer and requires extra mental effort. Worse yet, in some passive sentences the "actor" is unknown (It has been decided that . . . , It has been reported that . . . , etc.). It's a great technique for obscuring blame, but a bad technique for getting credit—and it is *always* confusing.

Sincerity —Show the audience that you really care. Let them know you understand their problems and you are doing what you can to help solve them. Look for places to use "I know" and "I care." Jack Kemp, Secretary of Housing and Urban Development, uses a nice phrase, "People don't care how much you know, until they know you care."

And, trim those hedges. Get rid of those qualifying phrases (It is felt that . . . , It is believed . . . , and It is quite possible that . . .). Sometimes hedging is absolutely necessary, but don't let it become a habit where you start hedging ninety percent of the time. Leave the weasel words for the lawyers. And, while we are debasing those denizens of the docket let me digress with a derogatory ditty from a Speechwriter's Letter compiled by Dr. Jerry Tarver, at the University of Richmond:

> There was a Speech Writer in Hell
> Who wrote for the Devil so well
> He got a raise in his pay
> To an ice cube a day
> And the Lawyer was removed from his cell.[15]

THE BIG FINISH

There's one part of your talk I wanted to save for the end of this chapter—and that's the ending of your talk. People in show business talk about a big finish, about ending on a high note. If you were to plot audience interest level during an ideal talk, the curve would shoot almost straight up as a result of a good opening that captures the audience's attention and interest. Then the curve would tend to flatten out and maintain that level if the talk is very good. For most talks, however, the curve would drop down a little as the speaker moves through the main body.

Now here's an important point! Picture the speaker as having to carry a heavy lead weight throughout the talk. And the longer the talk, the heavier it becomes. That weight, of course, is time. And it drags the audience interest level down with every sweep of the second hand. Given too long a talk, that weight will make the interest curve look like the first big dip on a roller coaster.

To combat this you should do two things. First, shorten the talk to try to keep it from entering the twilight zone. Second, top it off with a big finish. That's big, not long.

Your talks may not rival a Broadway production, but think of the opposite extreme. How many talks have you seen where the speaker suddenly said "Thank you" and sat down? Your first reaction was probably, "Gee, is it finished?" followed by, "Maybe I dozed off."

The ending of your talk should never be a surprise to the audience. Change your voice tone. Step forward to meet them for questions and answers. Use phrases such as, "Now that I have finished presenting my case, let me stress one indisputable fact," or "And in conclusion," or "Let me sum up." After a movie or slide presentation, some people will take the lights getting brighter as a sign that it's time to wake up. You might take advantage of this to summarize and capture those few who would sleep through Judgment Day.

Best of all, give them a well-thought-out summary. "Tell 'em what you told them."

Ask for the Order

Any book on sales skills has a chapter entitled, "Ask for the Order" that points out the importance of never letting a discussion with a customer end without attempting to get that all-important signature on the dotted line—at least figuratively. Speakers don't often want their audiences to sign a sales contract, but they usually want something unless their purpose is strictly to inform or entertain. As a speaker, you want permission to give the presentation again at some higher level. Or you want approval to move on to the next phase. Or you want the audience to send their senator a letter. But, you have to make sure you "ask for the order" or you'll be throwing a plop! (That is, tossing out ideas and watching them go "plop" because either nobody knows what to do with them, or they weren't asked to do anything.)

And you not only want to ask for the order, you want to make it easy for them to say "yes." For example, if you want them to write their senator, plan to supply a stamped, preaddressed envelope.

Ask yourself right now, "Will this audience do what I want them to?" Hopefully, the answer is yes.

Never End with Just "Thank You"

Remember the speaker whose ending was so abrupt the audience was surprised by his "thank you" as he sat down? I suppose a simple "thank you" can be sincere, particularly if it's preceded by a good summary and separated from the end of that summary by a sufficient pause. But "thank you" is so short it doesn't often satisfy the needs of the audience, and all too often it comes across as "thank God that's over."

"You've been a good audience," is almost as bad as "thank you." They're not kindergarten kids. How about closing with, "I enjoyed joining you, thanks for your attention, good luck to each and every one of you" or, "Walt Whitman, the famous poet, once wrote 'To have great poets, there must be great audiences.' To paraphrase, I'm certainly no poet, but I thank you for being such a great audience. Good night and God bless every one of you."

Start working on that ending now. You'll get a chance to test how good it is during the dry run and dress rehearsal. The next step in preparing your presentation, though, is to take a look at what's going to go with your narration—the visual aids.

CHAPTER FIVE

Adding an Extra Dimension with Visual Aids

AROUND 10,000 B.C., during the last period of Paleolithic culture, humans drew leaping bison on the walls of a cave near Altamira, Spain. Today, historians wonder why. Possibly there was some early religious significance. Or maybe prehistoric persons painted merely for their own enjoyment. Well, as long as opinions are being ventured, I'll advance one of my own. Perhaps it was a training session, and the prehistoric presenter had found that the use of visuals added an entirely new dimension to explanatory grunts.

Farfetched? It seems as good an explanation as the others. Why not? Almost 12,000 years later, training experts would be laboring over drawings of their own—curves and bar charts that can increase comprehension and retention by as much as 500 percent.

Research conducted by the Wharton School of Business at the University of Pennsylvania dramatically proved the effectiveness of visuals in business presentations. In the study, 123 MBA candidates tested the influence of overhead transparencies in meetings. When visuals were used:

- Average meeting length was 28 percent shorter.
- Group consensus was faster and there were fewer cases where consensus was not reached.
- Decisions were more often made on the spot, either during the presentation or after some discussion, rather than being deferred.
- And, most interestingly, presenters using visuals were judged as more professional, persuasive, and credible.

USE VISUALS—IT MAKES SENSE

We learn through our senses, using each one to a varying degree. Taste accounts for only one percent, and touch only one-and-one half percent. Smell is three-and-one-half percent, and hearing is a surprisingly low eleven percent. The remaining eighty-three percent of the data we gather is from sight! Learning is largely a visual phenomenon.

In addition, some interesting statistics have been generated on retention, as shown in the table below.

	Retention After	
	3 hours	3 days
Tell Only	70%	10%
Show Only	72%	20%
Show and Tell	85%	65%

Visuals can communicate ideas faster, more effectively, and more memorably. Wouldn't you like to have your talks be memorable?

I'm sure you are familiar with the old Chinese proverb, "One picture is worth a thousand words." Let me offer an example. One of the simplest equations in mathematics is:

$$(a + b)^2 = a^2 + 2ab + b^2$$

But if you've never been exposed to math, it may be a little difficult to understand why the quantity $a + b$, when multiplied by itself, will yield a squared, plus two times ab, plus b squared.

How easy an illustration makes it! First we take two lines, one the length of a, and one the length of b.

Then we "square" these two lines (or multiply them by themselves).

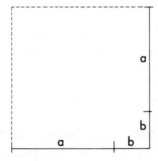

And as we complete the diagram, we can see that we will obtain an area that measures a, squared; another that measures b, squared; and two that measure ab.

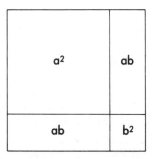

Now, I dare say that visual could save at least the thousand words cited in the proverb if you're dealing with a mathematical klutz like me. If only my math instructor had mixed a little geometry in with his algebra. If only he had said, "Look, dummy, what do you want me to do—draw you a picture?"

One more thing about this example. Sometimes visuals can so vividly depict a fairly complex idea that the presenter doesn't have to explain it—he can simply pause for a moment and give the audience the pleasure and satisfaction of discovering *for themselves!*—and that's magic. When the members of your audience figure it out themselves, retention rates can soar to ninety percent or more.

Visuals can aid your talks in so many ways. They can:

- Arouse interest
- Encourage participation
- Prevent misunderstandings
- Persuade
- Focus attention
- Save time
- Reinforce ideas
- Add humor
- Enhance credibility
- Explain the inaccessible

Visual aids can do all these things, and one more. By promoting better understanding, they lead to more agreement, *increasing the level of consensus.*

WHY SOME SPEAKERS AVOID VISUALS

With all of the benefits visual aids provide, it's hard to imagine why anyone would work without them. Four reasons that come to mind are:

- Cost
- Time
- Effort
- The "Show Business" Syndrome

Visuals for a presentation can cost a lot of money. The artwork for a single professionally prepared slide might cost between forty and fifty dollars, or even more. But there are many techniques you can do all by yourself. With only twenty dollars' worth of supplies you can prepare an entire presentation. So, financial costs shouldn't stop you.

As to time, the only instance where you don't have enough of it to produce some sort of visuals is the purely impromptu talk where you are called on to speak right then. Even in that case, you have the opportunity to grab a piece of chalk or a marker.

Certainly, good visuals take effort. But isn't that what a talk is all about? It's been said that good visuals can "make you look more professional and better prepared." More than that, they are proof of how much you care about your audience.

The show business syndrome takes two forms—both losers! The first is, "I'm the star up here, and I don't want to share the spotlight." Indeed, some people can do this, but they are rare indeed, and usually work as actors or entertainers. The other aspect of the show business syndrome is just the opposite. "Visuals? Who needs all that pizzazz? This isn't a dog and pony show!"

Today's audiences are becoming more and more attuned to visuals. We live in a visual world. Without the visual, there's a missing ingredient. Some of us grew up in a world of radio, where we sat on the floor and listened to Jack Armstrong, Lux Radio Theater, and the like, with visual images racing through our minds. Perhaps you remember. Now explain it to today's generation. They're likely to say, "Yeah, but where was the picture?"

VISUAL AIDS—NOT CRUTCHES

Visual aids should be a supplement to your talk, not a substitute. They are supposed to complement your speech, not carry it.

Slides are not a substitute for a script. How many times have you seen speakers read the visuals to their audience—as if they couldn't do it themselves? Having a speaker use a pointer while doing this is even more insulting.

The purpose of visuals is not to serve as cue cards, but as a checklist of key ideas that you will expand on, adding a handful of words to explain or emphasize.

Some speakers go so far as to collect visuals and then build a speech around them, creating a trap. Instead, you must build the visuals around the talk.

SELECTING THE RIGHT TYPE OF VISUAL AIDS

There are a multitude of visual aids at your disposal. The factors influencing your selection include: your objective; the size and importance of the audience; the location (room); your budget; time available to prepare; the number of times the visuals will be used (amortization); and the complexity of the message. Each of the types has its advantages and disadvantages, as shown in the table on pages 62–63.

VISUAL STYLES

Having looked at the various types of visual aids at your disposal, you must now consider different "styles." These include:

- Lists and Tables
- Pie Charts and Maps
- Block Diagrams, Schematics
- Bar Charts and Alpine Charts
- Color vs. Black-and-White
- Cartoons
- Three-Dimensional Art and Photography

Lists and Tables

Called word charts, these are quickly and cheaply prepared by using either mechanical or hand-lettering. Six lines of type (plus title) with six words per line should be the limit.

ADVANTAGES AND DISADVANTAGES
OF VARIOUS VISUALS

	For	Against
Chalkboards, Markerboards	Usually available. Casual. Produced as you talk. Adaptable. Mistakes easily corrected. Little or no cost.	Dull. (Use colored markers.) Slow moving. (Write in advance and cover with screen or chart paper.) Low visibility. "Body blockage." Audience size limited.
Chartboards	Can be formal or informal. No projection equipment or processing required.	Won't suit large audiences. Large size adds to preparation time when done by hand. Photos require large, expensive blowups. Hard to transport. Awkward to handle during presentation. Low impact value.
Flip Charts	Can roll up for transport. Easy to make and use. Chart pads, markers, and easels readily available. Good interaction between speaker and visuals. Inexpensive.	Wear and tear with repeated use. Large size can add to preparation time. Audience size limited to 40 or less. Low visual impact.
Overheads	Rapidly becoming *the* visual of choice in business presentations. Quick and economical to prepare either by hand or on standard office copiers. Projectors readily available. Usable in normal room lighting. Easy to carry and store. Changes: additions, deletions, order possible during presentation. Detailed pictorials possible. Suitable for any size audience.	Projectors tend to be big, heavy, and can block the view. Keystone images are likely unless top or bottom of screen is adjusted perpendicular to projected beam. Mechanics of switching and positioning visuals can be distracting. Full-color transparencies are expensive and take time.
Slides	Generally considered "higher quality" than overheads. Compactness for storing and carrying. Projectors readily available. Fast and smooth operation. Suits any size audience. High impact. Color photos economical to produce. Long life.	Darkened room decreases eye contact and inhibits note-taking and discussion. Once loaded, slides are "locked-in," making changes during the presentation virtually impossible. Artwork can be expensive. Extra time required for photographic processing.

	For	Against
Movies	Shows motion. Suits any size audience. High interest level.	Projectors harder to come by and transport. Audience focuses on visual (rather than presenter). Darkened room eliminates note-taking and interaction during the presentation. High costs and long production time. Hard to revise. Rapidly becoming the "wave of the past" in business presentations. Being replaced by video in most situations.
Video Tapes	Shows motion, high interest level. No photographic processing required. Easier and faster to produce than movies. Large-screen, video-beam projectors can enlarge the speaker's image (for large audiences) or show audience reaction shots by way of a camera when speaker's visuals are not on the screen.	Audience focuses on visual (rather than presenter). Larger audiences require multiple monitors. Very large audiences will require video-beam projectors. Different recording formats require different playback equipment, especially in foreign countries. (Tapes are not interchangeable.) Professional production costs are high.
Models, Mock-ups, and Props	Added "reality." High-impact value. Versatility. Props and products are readily available.	Models take time to prepare and can be costly. Use limited to smaller audience, depending on size of prop.
Video Teleconferencing	Connects two or more widely separate locations. Saves travel time and expense. Provides timely resolution of problems. High-tech, state-of-the-art aura.	Cost. Requires full-time staff of professional operators in dedicated facility. Older slo-scan variety is barely tolerable. Full motion VTC is better. But nothing matches being there face-to-face when possible.
Electronic Presentations	The wave of the future. Charts prepared on a computer are shown directly on a monitor screen (small groups) or projected, bypassing the need for slides or overheads. No costs for visuals. Changes are easy. Smooth transitions (or special effects) between visuals.	Initial cost of equipment. Equipment for larger audiences not readily available. Requires familiarity with computer graphics techniques.

Lists and tables are useful as a checklist of key items you will expand on verbally, for side-by-side comparisons, short quotations, and so on. Be careful not to overdo the use of this technique. Three word charts in a row should be plenty.

In general, tables are less attractive and harder to decipher than graphic presentations. However, they do allow for presentation of numerical values accurate to whatever decimal level you choose.

Pie Charts

A pie chart is simply a circle divided into sectors. Each degree around the circumference equals 0.277 percent or, to make it easier, every 3.6 degrees equal one percent. Some protractors come with a percentage scale. If not, a little work with a scratchpad or pocket calculator will do the trick.

As shown on page 65, pie charts tell at a glance the relative value of any component to the whole. They are simple and nontechnical, and will work with any audience. When using pie charts, try to keep the number of slices down to six or fewer.

I once needed to show a particular pie chart to an audience that had seen it many, many times before. Problem: How to keep them from getting the ho-hums. Solution: I got a real pie from our cafeteria, cut it into correct portions, had our art department label the pieces and our photographic department shoot it. Results: It worked great on the audience. Unfortunately the artist and photographer required three pies to get just the right shot. Next time I'll wait until after they've had lunch.

Maps

Maps show locations (offices, plants, and markets) and how quantities are distributed geographically. They can also be used for size comparisons (How many times will Rhode Island fit into Alaska?), and as artistic backdrops, such as on title visuals. Next time you're tempted to merely list locations, try a map instead. Imagine what the information on the facing page would look like if a map were used showing the Middle Atlantic states at normal size and enlarging or reducing the other regions proportionately.

Sales Leadership

Southwest Region	41%
Northeast	23%
Middle Atlantic	17%
Central	12%
Pacific	7%

Sales Leadership

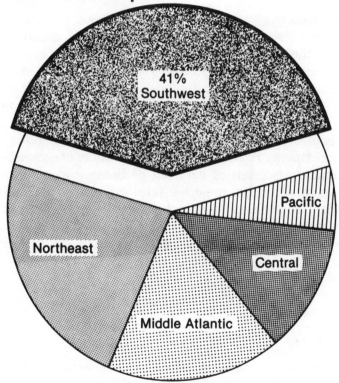

Pie charts (and other illustrations)
make relationships clearer and more interesting.

Block Diagrams, Schematics

These show how things flow, fit together, or relate to one another. The organization chart is a prime example. Using more than a dozen blocks on these charts is courting disaster. Fewer would be better. Consider showing just the major portions on an overall chart and then expanding on each portion with a piece of follow-up art.

If you're preparing a schematic of an operating system, consider using outline drawings of the various components instead of merely blocks with titles. In other words, have a pump look like a pump or a disk drive like a disk. These "icons" will add interest and aid understanding.

Bar Charts/Column Charts

Bar charts come in a variety of styles. All are good for comparisons. In the simplest version, the bars extend horizontally and there is only one scale—the lengths of the bars. Sometimes there are two scales. Here the bars are usually arranged vertically with the height of the bars measuring quantity and the horizontal scale usually representing time. (Vertical bar charts are more properly referred to as column charts.)

More sophisticated bar charts can be prepared by dividing the bars into their component parts, increasing the number of comparisons that can be made. Also, sets of bars can be brought together for direct comparison of different categories (sales and assets, men and women, e.g.). Other basic arrangements include the *sliding bar, deviation, range,* and *overlap* arrangements shown on page 67. Additional symbols can be added to any of these to show milestones, goals, current values, and the like.

Alpine Charts

In alpine charts the various values are connected to one another rather than to the base, forming a curve. Curves are much better than bar charts for showing trends—particularly where more than two items are involved. Curves are the most useful form of graphic presentation and far more are drawn than any other type. Most frequently the vertical scale represents dollars (or some other dependent

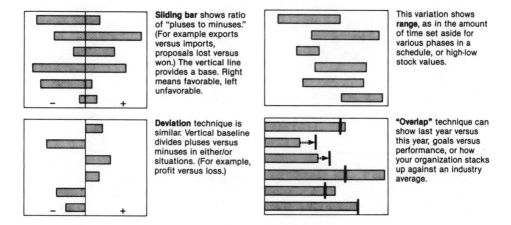

Sliding bar shows ratio of "pluses to minuses." (For example exports versus imports, proposals lost versus won.) The vertical line provides a base. Right means favorable, left unfavorable.

This variation shows **range**, as in the amount of time set aside for various phases in a schedule, or high-low stock values.

Deviation technique is similar. Vertical baseline divides pluses versus minuses in either/or situations. (For example, profit versus loss.)

"Overlap" technique can show last year versus this year, goals versus performance, or how your organization stacks up against an industry average.

Types of bar charts

variable) and the horizontal represents time. Many other combinations appear in engineering and other technical fields. Keep in mind that the length of the vertical axis in relation to the horizontal axis will have a marked effect on the impression given, as shown in the diagrams below.

Since you should be using all your visuals in a horizontal format (more about that later), you needn't worry about the left curve. But suppose the format shown on the right produces a chart that is as

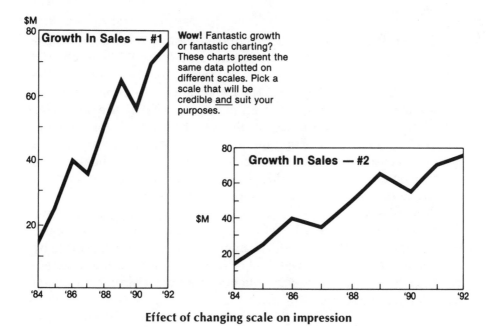

Wow! Fantastic growth or fantastic charting? These charts present the same data plotted on different scales. Pick a scale that will be credible <u>and</u> suit your purposes.

Effect of changing scale on impression

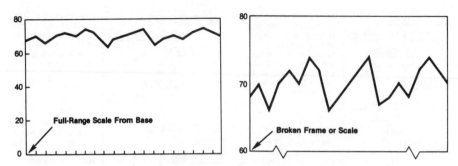

The broken frame or depressed zero curve will accentuate peaks and valleys, but you must indicate the break. Beware of the risk of misinterpretation.

Full-range scale vs. broken frame curve

flat as the plains of Kansas, and the minute variations are important. In this case, consider the "broken frame" or "depressed zero" curve. The illustration above shows what can be done. This technique accentuates the *differences* between totals. At the same time it can be deceiving in terms of the totals themselves. Make sure the scale is clearly marked and the break is shown.

Log Charts

The broken frame makes some technical people nervous, but there is another scale they love—the logarithmic (or log) scale. On the logarithmic scale, equal distances represent equal ratios. (See the illustrations on page 69.) Thus, the log scale can do things an arithmetic scale cannot. Often referred to as ratio charts, the log scales show the relative importance of change at various levels and the relative rate of change. For example, a one-dollar increase in the price of a one-dollar product is one hundred percent, while the same increase on a five-dollar product would be only twenty percent. Yet an arithmetic scale would show both the same way.

A log scale would reflect the smaller percentage of growth. Thus these charts have a special usefulness for showing relative changes. For example, an arithmetic scale might show production rising by increasing amounts, whereas the log scale would present a more accurate picture, showing that production has been rising—but by *decreasing* percentages.

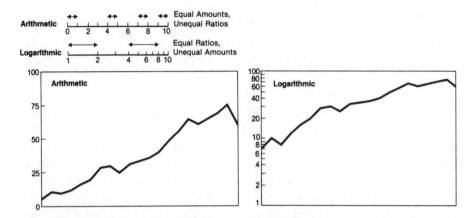

The arithmetic version shows steady growth with a calamitous dip at the end. The logarithmic shows a decreasing <u>rate</u> of growth and puts the final dip in perspective. The first dip of only two units represents a twenty percent drop, whereas the final dip of fifteen units is also twenty percent.

Arithmetic and logarithmic plots

Color Versus Black-and-White

As proof of the desirability of color visuals over black-and-white, one need only consider the sales figures for television sets in this country. All those people aren't spending all that extra money purely as a status symbol. Color makes watching TV more interesting, more enjoyable. And, in a presentation, color can do even more. Color can be used to trace the flow or to code various parts, thus clarifying the message. It can even reinforce your message by using a simple underline or by using red for a "no," "stop," or "problem" message, and by using green for "go," "money," or "solution."

Informal presentations need not be limited to black-and-white. Color pens can be used to add color to overhead transparencies, and the sensitized sheets used to make the transparencies come in a variety of colors. Even black-and-white photos can have a light blue, yellow, or sepia tint added to give them some semblance of color, and some added interest to your audience.

Do watch out for the rainbow or Joseph's cloak appearance—limit yourself to a few colors and then use them consistently. Also keep contrast in mind. You'll want dark colors on a light background or vice versa. Using colors in the same range next to each other spells trouble.

Cartoons

Although they take a fair amount of skill to prepare, cartoons can add a little levity to a presentation, and are welcome in the proper circumstances. By definition, a cartoon shows things in an exaggerated way—the more exaggerated, the better.

Photographs can often be used as "cartoons" by adding a funny caption. For example, you might take a picture of a fortune teller and label it, "long-range planning." Or, gather up all the old brushes in your house, set them afire, shoot the scene, and label it, "Reduce brush fires." Many times a "bad" photo that would be thrown away has just the right facial expressions. Photos of children are particularly easy. Gather up all the pictures you can find and have a go at it. You should come up with a few *good* ones.

Sometimes a word chart alone can do the trick. I once had to give a presentation to some financial managers to justify my new departmental budget. Knowing that controllers are always on the lookout for extravagance, my first chart was a childish scrawl stating, "This presentation didn't cost much." They loved it.

Three-Dimensional Art

Unless one suffers from a vision problem, one sees things in three dimensions, giving one depth perception. Three-dimensional artwork can add another type of perception (understanding). For example, a three-dimensional cutaway is vastly superior to a two-dimensional cross-section in terms of realism and interest value. The extra preparation time is usually well worth the effort.

Photography

Photography automatically provides a three-dimensional atmosphere, a view of reality. Many times I have seen slide presentations in which the speaker had a professional artist draw some common object such as a mousetrap. Why pay an artist dollars to draw a mousetrap when you can buy one at the hardware store for a few pennies and then photograph it for a few pennies more? Even if an object costs more than a few pennies, it certainly costs far less than hiring a professional artist who would charge for a good drawing.

Furthermore, the photographic treatment will be far more realistic—particularly with some shadows obtained by adding side lighting and standing the object on its end or elevating it from the surface with a hidden support.

Slides do require photographic processing, and you may elect not to use photography where artwork would be quicker and cheaper—especially if you are using charts where large photographic blowups would be required.

Standard Formats

Many organizations strive for a consistent look in their presentations by using standard formats for their visuals. In some cases this consists of a standard background, perhaps black, blue, or a top-to-bottom gradation. The format may also call for a horizontal bar that the title will fit into, or a horizontal line below the title, separating it from the rest of the visual, and a similar line as a bottom border. Both of these are good techniques, but they often get carried too far. Watch out for standard mastheads that contain the organization's logo and its name (sometimes in type larger than the title of the visual). Having this same information at the top of every visual takes up valuable space without conveying any new information. At its best it is distracting; at its worst, boring. Company loyalty is an admirable trait, but save the logo for the lower right-hand corner of your illustrations. Keep the logos relatively small (about the same size as a capital letter in your text). And avoid spelling them out at all costs.

VISUAL TECHNIQUES

Now that the various types and styles are familiar to you, take a look at some visual techniques that will make your presentations more dynamic.

Dynamic Visuals

The term "dynamic" applied to a visual may mean that it is forceful, or that it actually moves, or both.

A touch of imagination can make a visual more forceful. Suppose you wanted to cite one of the basic truths your service function is based on, but you didn't want to look like you thought you had just discovered it. You could prepare a visual that looked like the old-fashioned stitchery on the Whitman Sampler candy box. The letters spelling out your point would appear as cross-stitching. Actual thread or yarn would be nice (if you have the time and the skill), but X's drawn in a cross-pattern with felt-tip color pens will also do the trick.

Certainly parts of a chart can be made to slide, "grow," or rotate, as can parts of overhead transparencies. There is even a polarizing technique that can be used to simulate motion on overheads and 35mm slides. Multiple-projector slide shows can also add a degree of animation. Keep in mind, however, that the motion should be used to make a point—not just for its gimmick value.

Progressive Disclosure

In themselves, "verbal visuals" (word charts, lists, and tables) are perhaps the least dynamic type of aid. And yet, there is a technique that will greatly enhance their effectiveness. It's called progressive disclosure.

One of the problems with showing an audience a list of five or six items is that they may have reached item six while you are still talking about item three or four. Since your audience can think much faster than you can talk, this is only natural. But it doesn't make for a good presentation.

Of course, you can read all six items and then go back to explain them one by one. But this still supplies your listeners with an excuse to take a mental excursion. The cure is progressive disclosure—showing your audience each item at the rate you want them to consider it.

In the write-as-you-go presentation on a chalkboard, viewgraph, or chart, progressive disclosure simply "happens" as you move along. But this can be time-consuming, and there are other techniques.

Using an overhead projector you can place a sheet of paper over the transparency, blocking out the light. Then slide the sheet down a step at a time, revealing as much as you choose. On charts, the same effect can be achieved by lightly taping a strip of blank paper over each line of text and pulling the strips off as you progress. Slides offer similar possibilities requiring only one piece of artwork. A six-step list would be shot in its entirety and six negative slides (white letters on black background) produced. Only the sixth slide would be used as is.

Working "backward," the sixth (final) line on the fifth slide would be opaqued or blanked out, then the fifth *and* sixth lines on the fourth slide, and so on. When shown in the reverse order, a normal progression or build-up will occur. A variation, called build-and-subdue, calls for toning down previous lines with a shade of gray, further highlighting the one currently under discussion.

Progressive disclosure is applicable to more than lists and tables. A complex series of overlying curves could be developed one curve at a time; areas of a plant can be shown with pieces of equipment to be moved or modified; side-by-side comparisons of new versus old can be made; or what's inside a piece of equipment can be displayed by removing the cover. The possibilities are endless.

Overhead transparencies can be used very effectively for this purpose. The material to be added is simply placed on another transparency that will be placed over the first at the proper moment. To ensure proper alignment, one side of the addition is usually taped to the base visual using pieces of transparent tape as hinges. Used in reverse, this same procedure can be used to take apart the composite image.

Similar effects can be obtained with flip charts, particularly in showing "old versus new," "ours versus theirs," or other side-by-side comparisons. In this case a piece of blank chart paper is cut vertically and placed over the right half of the table, drawing, or whatever, so it obscures the new, improved version. At the proper time it is flipped back and—*bingo!*

The pulloffs mentioned earlier have other uses. For example, picture a big dollar bill that peels away in various sized pieces to reveal a caption stating where that particular portion of income went. (This is an interesting variation of the pie chart approach.)

In addition to pulloffs for your charts, consider stick-ons. Suppose you had a list of alternatives and wanted to dismiss each one as you finished discussing it by sticking a "NO" on top, leading to a final "YES." (To avoid looking too authoritarian, you could ask the group's opinion on each item after you've finished making your point. Just in case, you might have a few "MAYBE'S" standing by and, possibly, an extra "YES.") The same possibilities occur with arrows, stars, checkmarks, x-outs, O.K.'s, and so on.

There are commercially available stick-ons in pads. 3M produces the Post-It™ pad in high visibility yellow in three sizes ranging from 1 1/2 by 2 inches to 3 by 5 inches. These stick-ons can be moved about (reused) to show transfer of information in a computer, rearrangement of seating, or almost unlimited other changes. On a viewgraph, the same effect can be achieved with a small scrap of colored transparency, pushing it about as needed.

MULTI-IMAGE PRESENTATIONS

Most presentations involve a single projector with a single screen. However, the situation occasionally calls for something a little more sophisticated. Enter the multiple-projector show. These shows can get as complicated and costly as you like (and can afford) with any number of projectors programmed by a computer. This section covers the simplest form, the sort of thing you can do for yourself.

Sometimes these are referred to as dual-screen presentations, but this is a misnomer, since an attempt should be made to use a single, large-width screen so there is no line (or screen edge) between images. Therefore, "dual-projector" would be more appropriate; however, the term generally used in the trade is "multi-image." Regardless of the name, the important thing is how to improve your presentations using these techniques.

Although you can certainly get more information on a wide screen by using two projectors and still have it be readable, that is not the purpose of a multi-image presentation. Rather than adding more *detail*, the purpose is to add more *interest*. This is usually done by having a photo slide next to one with text or a curve. A movie can also be run next to a slide. (Don't forget to insert a black blank to make sure that side of the screen goes dark while the movie is being shown.)

The first time I ever saw a two-projector presentation, the technique was used very effectively for describing a number of components that made up a piece of equipment. As a photo of each component was shown on the left side, a series of slides on the right presented first its nomenclature and location, then its electrical characteristics, then its mechanical characteristics, then its performance curve, and so on. Then a photo of the next component accompanied by its nomenclature and location was presented and the process was repeated. Thus, the audience was never in doubt as to which particular component was under discussion at any given time, and the illustration slide added interest and a point of reference.

Note that the illustration slide was "held" on the left without being repeated as the series on the right progressed. There is no need to insert duplicate slides so that both sides change simultaneously with each sequence. In fact, repeating slides for this purpose will only tend to distract the audience.

Normally, in presentations of this type, the speaker works with a projectionist to avoid having to worry about whether to push the right or left button. The speaker cues the projectionist, who pushes the correct button by referring to a cue sheet. (See the sample cue sheet on page 75.)

Talk Title **Manufacturing Improvements**

Adv		Right Title/Description	Tray Pos	Left Title/Description	Tray Pos
L	R	Title	1	Speaker's Photo	1
L	R	Aerial View	2	Acreage statistics	2
L	R	List of Departments	3	Blank	3
	R	↓ ↓	–	Employee #'s	4
	R	↓ ↓	–	Hourly Rates	5
	R	↓ ↓	–	Defects Ratios	6
L	R	~~~	~~~	~~~	~~~
	R	New Equipment	13	Capital Investments	16
L	R	Robotic Welder	14	↓ Movie ☀ (Blank)	17
L		Cost Figures	15	↓	–
	R	↓ ↓	–	5-Year Saving Curve	18
L	R	Automated Wire-Wrap	16	Photo	19

Projectionist's cue sheet for multi-image presentation

Another valuable advantage of a dual projector setup is its usefulness in making "before and after" comparisons. This is usually done as a side-by-side progression: that is, showing "before" on the left next to a black blank slide, then adding "after" on the right.

One of the problems that can arise in a dual-projector presentation is a hideous color combination between the left and right slides. I've seen some that would drive an audience to nausea, given enough time. This is usually the result of the speaker pulling slides at random from his or her desk drawers and then attempting to put together a dual-image presentation. Certainly some existing slides will be used, but the presentation should be planned for side-by-side viewing using storyboards similar to the one shown on page 76. Once the order is established, every effort should be made to stick with it to avoid mismatched colors.

Another good technique is to use a black background for text slides with white or yellow words—or both in combination, yellow for the title and white for the body. The black background avoids any color mismatch with the slide on the other side. It will also prevent a bright word slide from overpowering a color illustration slide. Finally, since

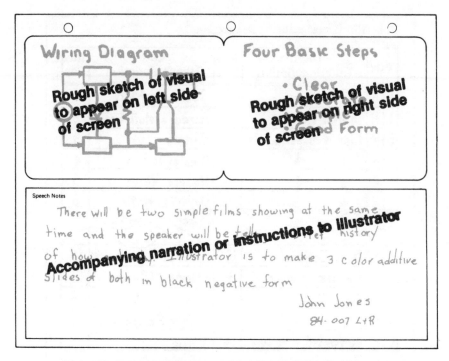

Storyboard form for dual projector presentation

the black background will result in a slide that has no projected "edge," it eliminates overlapping images or gaps at the center of the screen, or having one slide misaligned in height.

Although alignment can be a problem, you shouldn't rule out using both projectors to project a "single" image from one side of the screen to the other. This can be very effective if you want to show something really big, such as a mountain range, sea surface, city, long lists, rows of products, and so on, where the subject matter lends itself to this technique.

Try to put titles on one side. If they must run across both sides, *never* make the split in the middle of a word. Whatever the subject, care should be taken in shooting and mounting the slides and aligning the projectors. Then the audience will be able to adjust to any minor misalignments.

Another good use of dual images can be found in humorous warm-up presentations for sales meetings, retirements, banquets, and the like. Here a photo is usually presented on the left, next to a black blank. After a short period to let the image sink in, a funny caption (in small but readable type) is flashed next to the photo. When the laughter reaches its peak, both sides go blank for a moment and then the process repeats itself. If the photo is so hilarious that it becomes the punch line, a "straight" caption can be used first.

This technique can be accompanied by a live narration. However, my own preference is to use some fast-moving music to avoid having the words on the screen compete with the narration. The technique requires a special knack for this sort of thing, inside knowledge of the subject, and the ability to come up with a hundred ideas and then use only ten. And you usually need a fairly large audience to get the necessary reaction.

Multiple-projector shows require more planning, plus larger screens and more projectors to carry (or rent), but they are really not that difficult and they certainly increase the interest level. Consider multi-image presentations where you need impact and where the presentation is important enough or will be given frequently enough to justify the extra effort.

REVIEWING THE ROUGH VISUALS

The time to edit your visuals is now, when they are in the rough sketch or storyboard form, not after all the time and money has been spent finishing them. Here are some things to look for:

Are your visuals in the horizontal format? Audiences prefer the horizontal to the vertical. (And so do projectionists, since the horizontal image makes more effective use of the screen.) Our vision is peripheral, and our eyes can cover a horizontal area faster and more easily. The vertical format tempts us to make seven points whereas we would be more likely to use only five in the horizontal. Also, the lower the bottom of the chart or screen, the greater the probability people in the back rows won't be able to see it.

Do you have a title visual? You didn't plan on starting with a log-log curve, did you? Your audience needs something to help them stop "excursioning," and you need something to get you through the introductory, "Good afternoon, ladies and gentlemen, my topic for today is . . . ." Your title visual should include the topic, identified in six words or *less*; your name (particularly if the pronunciation or spelling is unusual); your organization's name, seal, or logo; the specific date; and some "interest" art, if possible.

How about the rest of the titles? Do they summarize or make the point? "Schedule" doesn't make a point. "Delivery in 3 Weeks" does!

Think in terms of "headlines" that will tell the audience what they are supposed to get out of the visual. Try to get a sales message in your titles. "Next Year's Preakness Winner" is going to get a lot more attention than "Horse, Side View." Rhetorical questions are another interest grabber—for example, "What has been learned?" And, of course, there's always "Benefits."

Too many verbal visuals? Word charts should be limited in terms of the number used and the number of words on any given chart. Remember, pictures lighten visuals, words make them heavier. Use bullets or sock dots (●), "interest" art, color, and progressive disclosure to help break the monotony. More than three word charts in a row without any visual break is dangerous. After the third such chart they all look the same.

As to the number of words on a single visual, try for a title plus a *maximum* of six lines with a *maximum* of six words in each line. For tables, try to stay within five lines deep and four columns across.

Will it be readable? There is a group of speakers who tell their audiences, "I know you can't read this in the back row, but . . . ." I hope their reward for irritating audiences in this manner is to spend eternity engraving the Lord's Prayer on the head of a pin.

Often the cause of unreadable visuals, particularly slides and view-graphs, traces to their being shot directly from printed material. After all, if you can read it on an 8½ by 11-inch page, you ought to be able to read the same material on a six-foot-wide screen. The truth is that viewers in the last row may be as much as seventy feet away, and to them that screen will be only two inches wide. So while the projector may magnify, the end result for some of the audience may be reduction. The art for visuals and that for printed matter require distinctly different approaches. Visuals require less detail, fewer words, larger letters, simpler grids, and heavier lines. Recycling or at least reprocessing will be required. The KISS formula (Keep It Short and Simple) was never more important.

Does each visual achieve unity? That is, does it develop one, and only one main point? Or, is it full of points competing for the audience's attention? Even in technical presentations an audience should be able to comprehend your visual in less than fifteen seconds, and your accompanying narration should keep it up there *no longer than one minute.* (Ideally, the narration will add detail and emphasis, not explain the visual.) Two of the major causes of poor presentations are:

- Too few visuals
- Too much detail on a single visual

Each of these shortcomings feeds on the other. Now let's move on to our next to last topic.

MAKING YOUR VISUALS

If you have access to a PC, a laser printer, and the know-how to use them, making your visuals will be a snap. (See Chapter 11.) Or, perhaps you are part of a large organization that includes an art department, then getting your visuals produced is quite simple. All the artists will want is a reasonable amount of time and a charge number. Similar professional services, which are available to the public, have phototypesetters and other equipment that can make lettering a snap. Depending on how much value you put on your own time, their charges are often a bargain. But you don't always have the time or a budget, and in some cases, you don't want to look too "fancy." In that case you can easily do your own low-cost visuals.

Low cost does not mean poor quality or unprofessional results. These shortcomings are usually the result of lack of time and effort *and* not knowing a few tricks of the trade.

Use the right supplies. You can find some of the things you will need in your company storeroom, or in an office supplies or art supplies store. Such things as transfer lettering, pressure-sensitive tapes and patterns, transparency pens, chart markers, clip art, and stock or made-to-order slides are available. One way to find out what's available is to ask. Another is to browse through the stores or catalogs. Organizations you might want to contact are listed in the resources section at the back of this book.

Use the KILL formula. Much like its partner, KISS (Keep It Short and Simple), the KILL formula means Keep It Large and Legible. In order for your charts to be readable from fifty feet away, the letter size will have to be *at least* two inches high, with the same amount of space between the lines.

If you're using color, you need contrast—dark letters on light backgrounds. (Vice versa is nice on slides.)

If you're using slides, it may be a little hard to determine adequate letter size. There are two ways to go about it. The first is to use the 6W test, wherein you move away to a distance six times the width of the visual and then take a look. (This also applies to viewgraphs.) The other is to hold the finished slide up to the light and attempt to read it with your naked eye. If the visual fails either test, you should try again.

Cut, cut, cut. Eliminate any unnecessary lines, symbols, or words. Don't use "in the event that," use "if." Imagine that you're doing a roadside billboard. Simplify as much as possible. Deletion automatically places more emphasis on what's left. On the other hand, spell out any abbreviations or acronyms that *might* be confusing.

Be creative. Add interest art. If you're talking about time, add a clock. Words like heat, cold, misalignment, vibration, growth, and drift all suggest an imaginative lettering style. If you're talking about going from dollars to cents, you might start with a chart showing a large dollar sign. Then, as you talk, you progressively peel away parts of it until what you have remaining is a cents sign. The only limit in this area is your own imagination.

Show the customer's system. Let's suppose you make disc brakes and that's what your presentation is about, keeping in mind that your customer makes buses or airplanes in which your brakes are eventually installed. Wherever possible, you will want to show or relate to the total system. Your title visual provides a good opportunity for this and gets your presentation off to a good start. Later it may be appropriate to show where your equipment is located in the total system or how it attaches. You'll also want to show their system at the end of your talk by mentioning benefits, conclusions, and recommendations.

The nuts 'n' bolts of flip charts. Leave at least two inches of free space all the way around. This is particularly important at the top (so that the gripper bar won't cover part of your title) and at the bottom (where there may be some curling from having been rolled up). If the chart paper is thin, use double sheets (taped or stapled together) to prevent showthrough or premature disclosure of the next chart, and to prevent bleedthrough of the markers. Make corrections by mortising—that is, put a clean sheet directly beneath the area to be changed and cut through both with a razor blade. You will now have a clean piece of paper that will *exactly* fit the hole in the original. A little tape on the back and no one will ever know.

Flip chart pads measuring 27 by 34 inches are available for around ten dollars. In a pinch, manila file folders can be opened out to make suitable charts for small audiences. (Needless to say, they are easily filed when you're finished.)

If you find working on the large pads to be tedious, you can work on 8 1/2 by 11-inch paper and then enlarge the image. One of the easiest ways to do this is on a PosterPrinter by Varitronics (Varitronic Systems, Inc., 300 Interchange Tower, 600 South Highway 169, Minneapolis, MN 55426; 1-800-637-5461). This copier will give you a 23 by 33-inch enlargement in only seventy seconds. It's lightweight, simple to use, and affordable. It produces a black image on various color papers or various color images on white paper. The samples provided by my local blueprint company took the enlargement with very little loss in sharpness.

Doing your own overheads. The most glaring mistake you see in this area is the use of office typewriters to prepare the visuals. Even the large typefaces for the interchangeable-element typewriters are marginal at best. If you don't have transfer or photo-composed lettering at your disposal, try hand-lettering. Pens are available that are specifically designed for working on transparencies. A one-quarter-inch ruled sheet below the acetate will ensure alignment and neatness. (Word processing equipment or personal computers coupled with modern printers offer big advantages in this area. Refer to Chapter 11 for more information.)

By all means, use frames on your viewgraphs. They will:

- Keep the transparencies from sticking together.
- Give you a place to write "stage whispers."
- Block spillover light from the projector.
- Provide a firm base on which to tape overlays for progressive disclosures.

A service for turning 35mm color slides into overhead transparencies is available through 3M's service centers. Most office copy shops can also make a transparency from your black-and-white original.

Producing 35mm slides. Here are a few things to keep in mind if you are shooting your own slides. First, clean up the area. Next, add people for interest and scale. Now get in closer. If you are showing a person doing something, the hands and what is being worked on are probably more important than the rest. (If you are working from an existing photo, crop it and reshoot.) Sometimes slides can be shot directly from printed matter without the halftone dot pattern becoming too obvious.

Artwork for slides should be prepared in the 2:3 ratio of the finished slide. (For example, six inches high by nine inches wide.) Simple word slides can be prepared using a carbon ribbon typewriter and a three-inch-high by four-and-one-half-inch-wide typing area. (Shoot it as a negative and consider using pastel dyes or overlays to add color.) Of course, transfer or photo-composed lettering will usually work best. Three-dimensional letters can also be used.

Personal computers can be used with any of several hard-copy devices to make good do-it-yourself visuals. Recently, some major companies have been offering professional-level computer-produced slides. Xerox, 3M, and Genigraphics® have systems on the market that really bring the computer age to slide production. Various techniques and equipment are discussed in Chapter 11. There are companies that will make a slide for you for $10 each, and on up. (See the Resources section, *A-V Suppliers.*) Among the advantages are:

- Speed (overnight, or in an hour with your own system)
- Retrieval (stored on floppy disk)
- Easy revisions
- Up to 4,096 colors
- Various type fonts and sizes
- Automatic conversion from spread sheet (tabular) form to pie charts, bar charts, graphs, etc.

Props and three-dimensional models. In the theatrical world, "prop" is short for "property." But the word "prop" also means "to support." In presentations, both meanings apply. Consider a credit card held up as a prop during a discussion of deficit spending. Or, as Admiral Grace Hopper (U.S. Navy Ret.) does in discussing computers, hold up a piece of wire cut to 11.78 inches long to illustrate how long a nanosecond is. (11.78 inches is how far light will travel in a nanosecond.) Look around you. Good props are everywhere.

With a little skill and some work you can turn out credible models using styrofoam and other materials at hand. If the "equipment" is in existence and almost square or rectangular, you can make a 3-D model by carefully photographing all four sides, mounting the enlarged photos on cardboard or foamcore, cutting along the outline, and gluing the pieces together. Engineering or architectural drawings will yield similar results.

In their book, *In Search of Excellence—Lessons From America's Best-Run Companies,* Thomas Peters and Robert Waterman tell of a balsa wood model (constructed out of materials purchased for fifteen dollars at a local hobby shop and assembled over a weekend in a hotel room) that helped a team of engineers from Boeing win the contract for the U.S. Air Force B-52 bomber.[16]

MY FAVORITE VISUAL PRESENTATION

I've worked on a lot of multi-media presentations. Some with up to fourteen projectors, controlled by a computer. But my all-time favorite was relatively simple—at least to the audience. The audience numbered close to a thousand, and the speaker was the president of a well-known electronics company. Feeling that slides would be pretty ho-hum and lacked motion, I asked our audiovisual people if they could show video—with one very important factor. Our executive would not follow a script and (even if he did) we would not know precisely how long he would talk on a particular subject. He might take thirty seconds, a minute, or a minute and a half. It would not do for him to finish a particular topic and then have to wait for the next scene to come on. Nor would it do for the scene to end and a new one to start while he was still talking about the previous one. Of course, he probably could have paced himself to the scenes, but that would have given him a lot to think about. "Just leave it to us," we said. And he did.

My AV experts put together a system that had two playback units and two tapes. Scenes 1, 3, 5, etc., were on one tape, and scenes 2, 4, 6, etc. on the other. Thus, we could have scene 1 playing for as long as required, with scene 2 on standby. A control box allowed us to do a smooth dissolve between the two. (Those of you familiar with motion picture production will see the similarity to A and B rolls.) As a backup we had a standard slide projector hooked up to a video camera. Fortunately we never had to use it. With another camera we were able to show an enlarged view of the speaker or shots of the audience, with switching controlled by a director.

Sounds pretty complicated? Well, it was for me too. But it was a piece of cake for our audiovisual specialists. It you work in a large organization and are preparing a program for an executive-level speaker, you might want to discuss this approach with your audiovisual department.

THAT'S ALL, FOLKS

Of course, that isn't all. When I was planning and organizing this book, I stored all my notes for each chapter in the largest envelopes I could find. This chapter overflowed its envelope, and I still haven't covered everything. One could easily write an entire book on visuals, and some people have. Three such books are *How to Put on Dynamic Meetings* by Chester K. Guth and Stanley S. Shaw, and *Planning and Producing Audiovisual Materials* by Jerrold E. Kemp, and *The Visual Display of Quantitative Information* by Edward R. Tufte. But perhaps the best way to learn about how to use visuals is the "hard" way—by doing it. You'll find a few more tips in Chapter 7, Practice Makes Perfect.

CHAPTER SIX

Selling Yourself and Your Ideas

ALL OF US ARE PART-TIME SALESPEOPLE

WHILE I PLANNED this chapter I thought, "What are you doing writing this? You're no salesman."

But that's not true. While we may not be selling a product, all of us are selling ourselves and our ideas every day. This is particularly true in presentations.

Throughout this chapter, the terms "sell" and "customer" are used. These broad terms can denote anyone (our managers, spouses, co-workers, or others) we are trying to persuade to buy either our products or ideas.

In giving presentations, many speakers approach their task as merely to inform their audience, and the results are usually lackluster. The better speakers present ideas *and* also persuade and promote— they sell.

To some, selling is a dirty word. Those who would demean selling think in terms of the door-to-door huckster, ignoring the fact that *Vice-President, Sales* adorns some of the finest desks and doors in the United States. Or, they feel that successful salespeople are born—just like speakers, no doubt—when both selling and speaking are learnable skills.

There are other reasons for avoiding selling, but perhaps the biggest is fear of rejection—indeed, most of the other reasons may be subliminal cop-outs for this particular one. Fear of rejection traces back to the earliest moments of our childhood and stays with us all our days. Successful salespeople overcome this barrier by learning not to take personally the rejection of a product or idea. Better still, they figure out what to do differently after they experience a loss, and press on to the next opportunity. They have a commitment that takes them beyond the fear of risk. And, above all, they employ strategies they know will maximize their chances of winning. We will be taking a look at some of these sales strategies later in this chapter. But first, let's establish their tie to presentations.

THE WAY YOU PRESENT INDICATES HOW WELL YOU WILL PRODUCE

Audiences form an immediate impression of your ability to perform from how well you come across in your presentations. Thus, your presentations are a reflection of your total professional capability. Being right just isn't enough; you must also be persuasive. To do this, you must first be sure of yourself and then radiate positive emotional stimuli throughout your presentation.

In fact, your presentation begins before you have even opened your mouth. It begins the moment you walk through the door or toward the lectern. Make sure you are well-groomed. Smile. If any hands are offered, grasp them firmly. Let the audience know you are in control—both of yourself and the situation.

Be Positive—Sell Weddings, Not Funerals

Dr. Norman Vincent Peale and his book *The Power of Positive Thinking* have provided inspiration to a host of sales personnel and others. One of my favorite stories in this area comes from Russ Johnston, a salesman, who says:

> You've got to have the right perspective to succeed in selling. When Goliath came against the Israelites, the soldiers all thought, "Wow! He's so big we can never kill him!" David looked at him and said, "He's so big I can't miss."[17]

Recently I sat in on a presentation where a general manager was discussing a possible shortfall in billings. But he never referred to it as a "shortfall." Instead, he called it a "challenge." And do you know what? Six months later he met the challenge by making his bogey.

Elsewhere in this book the evils of canned presentations are discussed. But good presentations do, indeed, come in cans: "I can," "You can," "We can."

Given the right circumstances, you can transfer your own positive outlook to the audience and get them to give you a positive reaction.

Make sure your audience knows where you are coming from and what your recommendations are. If you appear unconvinced, wishy-washy, or uncommitted, they will be very unlikely to give you a go-ahead. Avoid hedging. Instead of saying, "I think," use "I'm sure" wherever possible. Don't talk about how hard it was to develop your new technique, talk about how well it works. And, don't read your talk!

Abraham Lincoln once said, "If you would win a man to your cause, first convince him that you are his sincere friend." So, you want to be friendly, credible, somewhat informal, sincere, and authoritative (and—perhaps—thrifty, brave, clean, and reverent, too). Reading your talk puts a mask over any or all of these traits.

Improving Your Personal Sales Ability

Often, a competition can be so close that the customer picks the presenter as much as the product. In his book *The New Oratory*, Anthony Jay says:

> I keep hearing about decisions made after totally unemotional logical discussion based exclusively on objective facts, but only in management books. Most narrow decisions, I am convinced, come down more often than anyone yet accepts to primitive tribal acclamation, to a man or a small group of men winning the confidence and respect of another group. I do not even think it wrong that it should be so—very often this is in fact the most important remaining consideration. But we are taking a great risk if we are not aware of it when we are casting our presentations. I doubt if an unsuitable group can effectively persuade their audience that they are suitable, but I have no doubt at all that a suitable one can in the course of a presentation convince them that they are unsuitable.[18]

Part of what Jay is saying is that to be most effective, one should try to match the presenter(s) to the audience, picking individuals who already know the customers and are compatible. Failing this, one would seek out presenters who are at least credible, likeable, capable, and self-assured. But what if you are it, for better or worse?

Well, there are ways to shade things toward the better. One way is to develop that elusive quality known as charisma, and one way to build charisma is to do something new:

- Find a new hobby.
- Join a new group.
- Read a new type of book.

- Visit a new town.
- Try a new food or drink.

Any of these can help ease burn-out or the blahs and make you a more interesting, more persuasive personality. One word of caution, however: it's not just how interesting you are, but how interested you are in the *other person* that will help you sell.

Now the stage is set for persuasion.

THE PROCESS OF PERSUASION

Look up the word *persuade* in a thesaurus and you will find many synonyms: influence, win over, coax, convince, make willing, induce, convert, sell. Behind these words lies a process that is rooted as much in emotion as in logic. Anthony Jay talks of an "intellectual judo . . . using the force of the other man's opinions and prejudices to win your argument," and he cautions against wrestling when you should use that judo. "You have to get inside his mind at the planning stage and build your presentation on the foundation of his knowledge, prejudices, attitudes, experience, and needs."[19] These needs can be for a product, for economic benefits, or even for psychic gratification (for example, the customer's desired self-image can create a psychic need). The customer's experience will include not only past successes and failures, but habits and even moral upbringing. Prejudices include all the obvious ones plus smoking, eating, and drinking habits. Find out what "bugs" your customer/manager. Modern television commercials to the contrary, there is absolutely no way you can antagonize and persuade at the same time in a presentation.

Good salespeople not only know their subjects well, they also know their customers. They do this not in an attempt to be manipulative, but out of honest concern for their customers' needs.

ASSESSING CUSTOMER NEEDS

If you've ever taken a course called Marketing 101, you may remember that selling consists of identifying customers' needs and then influencing the customers to work with you to satisfy those needs.

The process starts with gathering all the information you can on the customers' business: Volume. Market Share. Their Competition.

Profit. Problems. Requirements. Expectations. This advance work will allow you to talk to the customers in their own language, not so you can tell them their business (they already know it and will resent such attempts as being arrogance on your part), but so you will be able to ask educated questions that will give them a chance to tell you more that you need to know. Other items you will want to consider include: your competition, availability of funds, who the real decisionmakers are, and past track records.

Now focus on their specific needs. To be a seller, you must have a product or an idea that will do more for your customers than the money or other resources in their possession. Unsatisfied needs are prime motivators. Determine the need. Ask yourself whether the customers will relate personally to your solution. Will it appeal to their special interests to be stylish, avoid trouble, and save time or money? Next, design your presentation to these interests and you will significantly improve your chances for acceptance.

In their book *In Search of Excellence—Lessons from America's Best-Run Companies*, Thomas Peters and Robert Waterman cite an outstanding example of how knowing your customer can lead to a successful sale:

> Another friend described for us why, in a recent major computer system purchase for a hospital, he chose International Business Machines. "Many of the others were ahead of IBM in technological wizardry," he noted. "And heaven knows their software is easier to use. But IBM alone took the trouble to get to know us. They interviewed extensively up and down the line. They talked our language, no mumbo jumbo on computer innards. Their price was fully twenty-five percent higher. But they provided unparalleled guarantees of reliability and service. They even went so far as to arrange a back-up connection with a local steel company in case our system crashed. Their presentations were to the point. Everything about them smacked of assurance and success. Our decision, even with severe budget pressure, was really easy."[20]

LOVE THY CUSTOMERS

A couple is talking. Suddenly one asks, "Do you love me?" And the answer is, "Of course!" To which the first replies, "You never show it!" Obviously, you "love" your customers. And you had better show it! One way is to acknowledge their importance.

Napoleon once said, "Ask me for anything—except time." Today he might say, "Time is money." Time (and attention spans) become more and more critical as you go up the management/customer ladder. An executive's time is extremely valuable and could easily be filled with things other than listening to your presentation. In seeking an audience, prepare a one-page interest grabber and then present this proposition in person or over the phone. If possible, ask for only ten minutes. (You can say a lot in ten minutes. Just look at the thirty- and sixty-second TV spots.) Be sure to state that's all you need. Then suggest the listeners leave some time open in case they would be interested in further discussion.

Once you have your appointment, be punctual. Build in extra time to guarantee on-time arrival. You may run into construction, heavy traffic, transportation breakdowns, an accident, or other delays. Don't rush; plan on killing some time in the parking lot or in the reception area. Remember that in some big industrial complexes, it may take fifteen minutes to get someone to meet you and escort you to the individual's office.

If you are running late, be sure to call and explain the difficulty and *ask permission* to come ahead anyway.

If you control the meeting room setup, you can make the audience feel important by providing attractive place settings (name tags, note pads, water, and agendas). Note pads can even be "personalized" to a specific meeting. Agendas can be prepared as small booklets containing a schedule, a list of key personnel and their telephone numbers, and a local map.

By all means you will want to remember those all-important words "please" and "thank you," but even more so, you will want to remember the customers' names. Dale Carnegie says the two most important words in the English language are YOUR NAME. And, if it's true with you, it's certainly true with your customers.

With a little advance preparation, you can make your customers feel like old friends (see page 15). Even without it, you can still do a credible job. When introduced, make sure you get the name. If you don't, ask that it be repeated. Find a way to use it in the conversation as soon as possible, and associate the name with the individual by matching the two in some way if at all possible. Take on large groups one at a time and don't be embarrassed to check back on names you think you've "gotten."

SALES STRATEGIES

Where do you go from, "Nice weather we've been having," or, "Did you have a good trip?" This is the critical juncture where you must capture the customers' interest. You must shift their attitudes from a skeptical "So what have you got?" to "Oh boy! How can I get one?" as you present your ideas. Ideas, fortunately, are like eggs—they can be served in many ways. You might elect to open with:

- A startling statement or question. ("Do you know that one of your departments is literally throwing away $70,000 each year?")
- Major benefits. ("Rearranging our outpatient center would save time and money, and improve the quality of service.")
- Product demonstrations, models, or mockups. (Here you actually show that something is smaller, works better, or is easier to handle—perhaps in a side-by-side, old-versus-new demonstration.)
- A statement of customer needs (e.g., setting up a "problem/solution" approach).

Notice that in each of these approaches you put your advantages up front by telling the customers why they should listen and, thus, winning their interest.

Sledgehammer or Velvet Hammer?

You can knock something down with a sledgehammer or stroke it with a velvet hammer. If you are demolishing a building you would use the former. Trying to get a cat to purr would call for the latter. The approach for people lies somewhere in between.

There's an excellent example of salesmanship in Meredith Willson's musical *The Music Man.* A supersalesman, Professor Harold Hill, comes to River City, Iowa, selling band instruments. None of the other salesmen can understand why Hill does so well. "Why, he doesn't even know the territory." He soon shows them why in the song "Ya Got Trouble," pointing out that it's "Trouble with a capital T, and that rhymes with P and P stands for Pool," informing anyone who will listen that the new pool table installed at the billiard parlor will soon be the downfall of the town. From there it's a short jump to the solution—a boys' band—and the upbeat, foot-stomping march, "Seventy-six Trombones."

There's a great marketing lesson there, and it's worth heeding. What if Professor Harold Hill had started with "Seventy-six Trombones" and either dropped "Ya Got Trouble," or saved it for last? Would he have been as effective? Of course not. "No Sir-ree!"

The technique Harold Hill used is sometimes called "setting up a straw man" (need or problem) which you can then knock away with your solution. This might even involve the fear of the competition's doing something faster or more cheaply, or the fear of falling behind technologically.

Both of these techniques can be used effectively if used with caution. Be sure you know when enough is enough. Don't overwhelm your customers. Sometimes they will want to push the answer around until it becomes *their* answer. Let them! When this happens they "own" the solution.

"Reading" your audience by using good eye contact can tell you if you are in danger of overwhelming them. And encouraging their participation through questions and answers can lead the way toward "ownership."

The Soft-Sell Approach

With few exceptions, most of us are more comfortable with the soft-sell approach—particularly if we are on the receiving end. Let me quickly point out that "soft-sell" does not in any way indicate less effort or enthusiasm on your part. It's more of a perception on the part of the receiver.

None of us would grab a customer by the lapels and shout, "Now, look!" But there are other ways to overwhelm a customer. For example, are you taking a "committee" with you to make the presentation? When you and your group outnumber the customers, it puts them on the defensive or encourages them to call in their staffs, changing the nature of the meeting. You might want to take along one of your brass or one expert, but any more will decrease the intimacy and/or make you seem less capable.

Instead of beating customers over the head with how great your product is, you might invite them to join you in constructing a "key factors chart" showing how your product compares with the competition's. Let them identify whether each factor gets a plus or minus in each column, and then discuss the logical choice.

Another aspect of the soft sell is to use phrases such as, "I'm here merely to point out something. Any decisions will be in your hands." And then make sure your tone of voice matches this statement throughout your presentation.

The poker player who holds a full house or better can, of course, afford to be soft-spoken. Let's suppose you have a multi-functional piece of equipment that does the work of three separate pieces currently in use, at a reduction in overall cost. Obviously, the user is not going to throw away the equipment now in service. But you have a very strong case for replacements or new installations. Make sure they fully understand the one-for-three benefit. Then, you can make them an offer they can't refuse (or at least can't ignore).

One more way to avoid overwhelming your audience is to start on familiar ground. Start with principles they already know or agree with. Then move on to the more complicated or opposite view. As the information becomes more complicated, cut down on the shake, rattle, and roll data. Give the audience only as much as they need to understand and to agree. In presenting opposing views, start "slowly." Remember Mark Antony's speech in Shakespeare's *Julius Caesar?* Because of the sensitive situation following Caesar's assassination, Mark Antony started, "Friends, Romans, countrymen . . . I come to bury Caesar, not to praise him." Indeed, by the time he finished he had praised Caesar quite a bit.

Certainly you won't start by telling your audience what it's going to cost them. (Unless the cost is so low you want to startle them.) Instead, start by telling them what your product or service will do for them. Thus, when cost does come up, you have set the stage for answering the question with, "Not as much as you might think."

Sometimes you can make the cost seem like less by showing how it might be shared by two or more parties, or how the equipment might perform more than one function. In the case of replacement, it's possible that the new approach will pay for itself over a period of time. For example, you can find the costs of repairing older, less reliable equipment, or the cost of the increased energy it uses, and deduct those costs from the new. Or, you can cite the basic investment in the existing equipment and the advantages of updating it with a relatively inexpensive modification (compared to replacement). In either case the customer is saving money in the long run.

Be Flexible, Give the Customer a Chance to Talk

Have you ever wondered why God gave us two ears and only one mouth? So we could enjoy stereo? Perhaps. But I wonder if He just might have been trying to tell us that we ought to do twice as much listening as talking.

In giving a presentation it's hard to spend *twice* as much time listening as talking. But, don't neglect this important sales strategy before, during, and after your presentation.

Don't launch into your presentation too quickly. Try to find out more about the customers. They may want to talk about their backgrounds, desires, interests, ambitions, or motives. This is particularly valuable at the onset of a less formal, one-on-one presentation or at the coffee session that may precede a meeting with a larger group. Try to set up a process where they talk and you listen. Give them feedback, reinforcement, agreement. Focus on *them.*

During your talk, don't insist on plowing through your script, dismissing any customer comments as quickly as possible so that you can get on with it. If someone in the audience says, "That's an interesting idea, have you thought about trying it on . . . ?", don't say, "Yes, we've already thought of that; now, as I was saying . . . ." Given a chance, the customer may tell your story for you. The presentation *really* begins when the customer starts talking. Welcome the two-way flow and control it. If you ignore it, you will miss valuable clues, antagonize the customer, and probably lose the sale.

Instead, use effective questions to keep the dialogue going. A general rule in selling is that the person who asks the questions has control. You can ask questions to determine needs, discover likes and dislikes, check agreement or listening, feel out objections, determine whether the customer is ready to "buy" or whether you should keep selling, and other information. Questions such as, "Can you tell me more about that?" or, "What do you think?" will often flush out your quarry. After you ask, be patient. Let the customer answer fully.

If you've really "heard" your customers' needs, you may be able to make the sale by explaining a single aspect of your product or idea. Anyone can tell a customer one thing. The good listeners make it the *right* thing.

"You Can Rest Assured"

Naturally, the customer is looking for a definite commitment—assurances—on your part. These take the form of promises, which in order to have teeth are sometimes backed with penalties in terms of reduced price or increased quantities for nonperformance.

But there is another type of assurance that we touched on a few moments ago when we were discussing letting the customer do the talking for you, and that is the testimonial. Having a third party do your talking can make your listeners less skeptical, particularly if the third party is an independent authority on the subject.

Testimonials can be delivered in person (or even by satellite link), via movies or video tape, on audio tape accompanied by slides of the authority, *short* quotes on charts, or even copies of a letter. Be sure to ask permission to quote, and if the individual is present, introduce him or her properly.

IBM uses this technique quite effectively in selling computers to small businesses, giving potential customers a chance to see how businesses similar to theirs have profited by installing a computer. Westinghouse and other companies have also used the same technique to allow customers to share their thoughts on quality with employees.

I once saw a testimonial save the job of a representative for a leading manufacturer of projection equipment. Problems arose in demonstrating a sound/slide system and the rep, who found himself unable to operate the equipment, began making excuses in front of forty potential buyers *and* his district sales manager. As the noose grew tighter, the rep was saved by a projectionist in the audience who came to his rescue with an unsolicited testimonial about how he had used the same type of equipment countless times and had never had the slightest problem.

The projectionist was somewhat unkempt in a flannel shirt with his T-shirt showing, and his beard, long hair, and mode of dress set him apart from the others in the room. But *everybody* listened! Unfortunately, the rep in his three-piece suit didn't. If he had, he probably would have been smart enough to ask the projectionist if he could fix the problem during a short coffee break.

Product Demos and Samples

Back in Chapter 5 we talked about models, mockups, and props (e.g., holding up a credit card while talking about deficit spending). All of these are valuable, but they can't equal a product demonstration. It allows you to show the actual product and why it is better than its fourteen competitors.

If your product is small enough to hold, hold it at chest level as you talk about its benefits. Then tell the audience what to look for as you put it to action. Let the way you handle the product show your esteem.

You may even have a chance to give the customers some hands-on experience using it, or possibly even leave behind a sample. Everyone

**When demonstrating models or equipment, be sure to
hold the item high enough for the audience to see.**

likes something for nothing. If you're lucky, they will test it. Even if it
just sits on their desk a while, it will serve as a reminder. Be sure your
telephone number is attached.

Selling by Semantics

Using the wrong words in a sales presentation can block the sale.
And, while using the right ones may not clinch it, they certainly don't
hurt.

As a comparison, consider:

- Cheap and flimsy *vs.* inexpensive and lightweight.
- Council for Responsible Nutrition *vs.* Vitamin Lobby.

Some words can be loaded in two directions, depending on which
side of the fence you are on:

consumer advocates	pro-choice
environmentalists	pro-life
fair trade	productivity
free enterprise	right-to-work laws

You also need increased sensitivity to words that might be considered sexist or even racist.

Try these words for positive impact:

assured	first	proven
bargain	free	quality
best	guarantee	reliable
biggest	heavy-duty	results
compact	improved	rugged
demonstrated	long-life	safety
discovery	money	save
easy	new	smallest
efficient	only	you

And be sure you back up any opinions with facts.

Startling statements or attention-getters ought to be prefaced as such:

- "I know you will find it hard to believe. We had to double-check our figures when we first ran across this, but . . . ."
- "Now pay attention to these sales numbers, because they get pretty big. There are eleven districts with two systems per district—that's twenty-two systems—and each system has eighteen terminals, for a grand total of three hundred and ninety-six terminals!"

Look for hard-hitting slogans or themes that tie your major benefits into a neat, compact package:

- "An aerodynamic solution to an aerodynamic problem."
- "Separation means stability."
- "Easy to operate. Drives like a car."

SOMETIMES YOU HAVE TO BE A DIPLOMAT, AS WELL AS A SALESPERSON

Sometimes it will seem as though you've been handed a gallon bucket and told to go milk a cobra. As mentioned earlier, when you have to persuade an audience that might be hostile, move slowly. Don't establish your position too early. If the audience is well-educated, you would be wise to present both sides. Sometimes a minus can even be turned into a plus. For example:

Transporting the unit in the horizontal position will require that it be thoroughly sealed so that the hydraulic fluid won't leak out.

However, sealing the unit in this manner will actually prove to be an advantage since it will ensure both cleanliness and lubrication during transit.

One must always stay alert to the possibility of changing negatives into positives. Once I was in a meeting where an engineer was explaining a trailer that was full of test equipment which was available to the electrical utility industry for use at various power plants. As he explained the pieces of test equipment and their functions, someone asked, "But haven't you been having a lot of problems with this equipment?" Indeed they had been, and the engineer quickly told them so, ticking off three examples on his fingers. But then he quickly shifted gears to point out that that was precisely the beauty of installing all the test equipment in the new trailer. It had eliminated the problems by providing a permanent yet mobile installation within a controlled environment.

On another occasion I was called in to do some consulting on a coal-fired electrical generating plant. The manufacturer was worried because the plant wasn't producing quite as much power as had been specified, resulting in reduced income for the utility and raising the possibility of litigation.

I had studied all the various documents and became more and more confused. During a meeting to discuss the problem, I found myself put on the spot for an opinion on how to approach the customer. Somewhat at a loss for words—and certainly at a loss for ideas—I decided to try the "ask *them* a question" technique. "So, what's the *good* news?" I asked. Silence. And then someone in the far reaches of the room slowly answered, "Well, for the amount of electricity it produces, it burns a lot less coal than we ever thought." Sensing an opening I quickly asked, "How much less coal, and how much would that coal be worth?" A few pocket calculators came out and a number was forthcoming. "And how much revenue is the customer losing because of the diminished output?"

By now I'm sure you've guessed what I was hoping. The savings were a near trade-off for the loss, providing an avenue of approach in discussing the problem with the utility.

I will always remember the joy of turning this negative into a positive (or at least defusing it to a stand-off), so much so that I refer to it as the "coal versus kilowatts" caper.

In this case the negative involved the situation. What can you do if the audience itself is negative? Sometimes you can turn objections around by using the "feel . . . felt . . . found" formula. In other words, "I can see why you might *feel* that way. . . . I've often *felt* that way myself. . . . But after studying all the possibilities, here's what I *found*. . . ."

I'm sure you've heard of "win–lose" situations where in selling a product or idea there's no gain if you give up and the customer wins, nor is there any long-term gain if you beat the customer into the ground and he signs just to get rid of you. The real sale is a "win–win" situation in which customers feel you understand them and their situations and can help them solve their problems.

You can't arrive at the win–win point by telling customers they are wrong. You might get there by the Socratic approach, wherein you ask a series of questions that have to be answered in the affirmative, leading to the final, big "Yes" that you are seeking. You might also make a series of suggestions and let the customer arrive at a conclusion. Perhaps you can provide two alternatives, each of which accomplishes your objective. If the customers have complaints, hold back on your reply until you are certain that you have all the information you can get, and they've gotten the complaints off their chests. And, be ready to concede minor points, while hoping to win the big one. Be careful not to rob your customers of their sense of control.

Psychiatrists and counselors use similar techniques where they let you arrive at solutions to problems with their guidance. Would-be sellers would do well to study their patience.

Above all else, when a program has problems (cost, schedule, performance), play it straight and be honest. As Mark Twain said, "You've got a lot less to remember when you tell the truth." Honesty, trust, and sincerity are head-and-shoulders above style, pizzazz, and slickness in sales techniques.

SELLING COMPLEX PRODUCTS, PROJECTS, OR PROGRAMS

The world we live in becomes more sophisticated every day. So much so that the scientists, technicians, or other experts are the only credible salespeople in some situations and must therefore do their own selling. The technical presentation actually becomes the point of sale as they try to convince an audience (of one or many) to buy their products or services, or to entertain further proposals or demonstrations. In this situation, a number of problems arise:

1. Usually, the audience will have seen many such presentations. Indeed, they may have already seen a similar one on that same day.

2. The "expert" giving the presentation has spent most of his or her career learning the technical expertise and may lack the interpersonal polish referred to earlier.
3. Because they are the experts, they occasionally engage in displays of technical arrogance in front of customers who have the same, or almost the same, level of expertise.
4. They feel that good technical work will sell itself. They deal in functions and features, and neglect to sell the benefits.

Marketing strategist Peter Johnson cites a number of ingredients in the making of an awesome speaker—ingredients that will capture CEO-level interest:[21]

- Topic or title that will immediately spark interest
- Appearance, image, class
- Dynamic/Interactive format
- Vocal animation
- Movement
- Content
- Intelligence
- Notable visuals
- Tangible "take home" value.

Let's take a closer look at that last item.

The Functions, Features, and Benefits Approach

The *function* of an item is what it does, and knowing what it does helps the customer to understand what it is. *Features* are the technical gee-whizzes that allow the item to perform its task. Features help customers to understand how it works, and that can be fairly interesting. But *benefits* are what it does for *them,* and that's the real payoff. Customers are interested in:

- Cost. (Will it save them money?)
- Schedule/Time. (Can they get it more quickly? Is it faster?)
- Performance. (Is it better? More reliable?)

Expressing features as benefits gives them the wallop they need to become vivid and forceful. Don't talk in vague, general theories; talk specifics. Don't sell radial tires; sell improved mileage, durability, and all-weather road handling. Don't sell aluminum siding; sell maintenance-free exteriors. Don't sell a ten percent cost reduction; sell a million dollars saved. To get customers to turn loose with their cash, show how the benefits of your approach outweigh the cost. This can be in terms of dollars or time saved, or perhaps the customers' own reputations. Do you have better service? Better financing? What do you have to offer that's better? Before customers stick their necks out, they have to know what's in it for them. Otherwise, their tendency will be to say no, to play it safe. Find a way for them to minimize any risks involved.

The Really Tough Sell

Selling can be tough, there's no doubt about it. I once found myself wondering what the toughest sales jobs have been in recent years, and what role presentations played in the selling process. The audience I picked was the bankers who would have to put up the money, or the board of directors who would decide on the go-ahead. The three ventures I selected were Federal Express, *USA Today*, and Autotrain.

Sure, they all went on to become major successes. But think about the situation at the time. Picture the banker saying, "Let's see, you want to start an airline that will carry only packages? And every package will have to go to Memphis? And you can do a better job than the major airlines who already carry packages?" The first time Frederick W. Smith presented this idea was in a paper for an economics class at Yale. He got a C. Fortunately he came from a wealthy family, so he was able to "put his money where his mouth was" to the tune of $8.5 million, but he still had to raise $70 million more from venture capitalists.

Back to our banker. The next person to come see him is Gene Garfield, who wants to start his own railroad called Autotrain to haul passengers and their automobiles between Washington and Florida. Hasn't this guy heard what's happening to railroads? The federal government can't even find the forms for starting a new railroad. (This didn't stop Garfield. He wrote a new one for the ICC.) Whoa! Send the guy who wants to go into the buggy whip business back in!

Finally there's Allen H. Neuharth, who wants his board of directors to let him start another newspaper. Never mind the fact that Gannett already owns eighty-eight dailies. Never mind the fact that newspapers are being folded all over the country. (I can't believe I said that.) Al's will be different. For one thing, airlines and motels will give them away free. "Free." There's a word sure to catch every board member's attention.

Researching the literature on these three outstanding but seemingly improbable ventures, and following-up with correspondence and phone calls, led to some very interesting observations on presentations.

It's a good thing Fred Smith didn't give up on his idea when the professor gave it a C. I wonder where that professor is now? We know where the idea is—everywhere. From its start in 1973 to its going public in 1978, passing the $1 billion mark in 1983, and climbing above $5 billion in its fiscal year 1989, Federal Express has been an outstanding success due to the gung-ho entrepreneurial spirit of its founder and his followers. Their approach to presentations (and everything else) is that image is all-important and is fostered by an obsession with quality. You'll find it in all their presentations.

Gene Garfield, the founder of Autotrain, is a lawyer/natural scientist—not (according to him) a marketing type. But that didn't stop him from selling Autotrain, which was a labor of love. Garfield started from zero, raised $7 million initially, and then went to $40 million. First-year revenues were $34 million. The stock was originally 50 cents a share, went public at $10, and eventually reached $63.

In a telephone conversation, Garfield told me his presentations approach consisted of a barnstorming tour to railroad VPs. He called chairmen directly, fearing others would turn him down. The presentations lasted from five minutes to four hours. Garfield hired an industrial designer/artist to do a *large* rendering of the rail cars as the cornerstone of the presentation. He thought graphs were too stilted and ordinary, but he also developed a business plan as a backup for the MBAs to read.

Of the three entrepreneurs I researched, Al Neuharth is certainly the best showman. Some of his critics even saw him as a hustler or huckster. As chairman and president of Gannett he had little to prove in taking the risk of starting *USA Today*; but he is a driven person, an entrepreneur.

During the development and subsequent selling of the idea, there were any number of presentations made by and to Al Neuharth. Some of the more interesting ones are chronicled in *The Making of McPaper*[22] by Peter Prichard. Here's a synopsis:

- In listening to a presentation concerning timely deliveries, Neuharth shouted, "That's B____ S____!" to the presenter. The presenter respectfully disagreed, pointing out that he had been out with the trucks, timing them. He then bet Neuharth $5 they could do it. The corporate limo followed the trucks, and the presenter won his $5 and a top position.

- Conversely, another presenter on vending machines found himself laboriously explaining to Neuharth how gravity works, and was told by Neuharth that he "knows damn well" how gravity works.
- A series of presentations was made to the board of directors over a period of time, before asking for "go." At the first presentation, someone bumped into a flip chart and knocked it into the lap of a director. The presentations covered production, distribution, readership, and advertising. Neuharth moved gradually, knowing it would take time to sell. In the summer of 1981, a lot would have voted "no go." Later, closer to the vote, Neuharth had an informal meeting with four outside directors. At one point, the presenter of a business plan hedged when asked what his confidence level was. Neuharth saved the day by presenting an escape route: they could pull the plug while losses were modest and salvage parts. At the final meeting the vote was unanimous (12 to 0) to go.
- At an annual meeting of 300 Gannett executives, Neuharth got ten minutes into his presentation before making the announcement about *USA Today* and got a standing ovation (delay served as teaser and allowed him to dispense with routine matters).

The lessons taught by these three big leaguers can be of value to us all:

- "If at first you don't succeed . . . ."
- Quality/image can be unbeatable persuaders.
- Seek out the *real* decision makers and contact them directly.
- Good artist's concepts or models will bring an idea closer to reality.
- Planning and attention to detail have no shortcuts.
- The biggest problems will often come from financially oriented members of the audience.
- On big projects you can get a "yes" (go-ahead) one bite at a time.
- "Faint heart [lack of confidence] never won fair lady [the prize]."

"AND, IN CONCLUSION . . ."

No book on selling would be complete without covering the *close*, and so it is with this chapter. You might be inclined to think of the last sentence or two of your talk in terms of something that might produce applause. That would be nice, *if applause is the result you are after.* But in the business world, you are more likely to have other types of approval in mind.

You are more likely to be seeking money or other resources, permission to present your ideas at the next level, a signature, a request for a proposal, or some other form of commitment from your customer or management.

So, you will want to do two things:

- First, summarize your benefits, conclusions, or recommendations. (Many briefers assume these are obvious after the logical buildup. *They are not.*)
- Then, "ASK FOR THE ORDER!"

Be Sure You "Ask for the Order"

Picture the timid door-to-door seller who presents the product, says, "Thank you," turns, and walks back down the path hoping the prospect will call out, "Wait!" What do you think the chances of making a sale under those circumstances would be?

Some of us are so afraid of rejection that we never ask for the order, reducing the probability for either a yes or a no answer to zero. Asking would at least raise the odds to fifty-fifty. And, by meeting objections, stressing benefits, and providing favorable alternatives, we can tip the balance further and further in our direction.

The worst thing about not asking for the order is that the audience may think you are seeking advice or hand-holding as opposed to endorsement or resources. (Even worse, they may subconsciously hope you won't ask for action on their part. The response may call for fortitude, which might be in short supply.) Be sure they know what you want.

Don't Demand Immediate Results

An immediate O.K. is nice, but if you don't get it, don't push too hard. To do so may class you as the door-to-door type who says, "In order to get this fantastic bargain, you will have to sign up tonight." Don't substitute pressure for persistence.

Instead, you might ask, "Is there anything else you would like to know in order to help you consider this plan?" Or, "When could I check back with you?" Better still, "Can I check back with you in a week?"

If the door is still open a crack, you will probably know it. Perhaps the audience will ask for a copy of your visuals. (Aren't you glad you brought a hard copy? You will be even gladder if you have gone a step further and turned your visuals into a nice little booklet with a typed narration.)

One technique in selling is called the "Ben Franklin Close." In it, the salesperson lists all the reasons why it's a good buying decision on one side of the paper, and asks the prospect to list the reasons why it isn't on the other. The object of course is for the prospect to be unable to list any reasons for not buying, thus leading to a quick close. Although this technique has some high-pressure overtones, it can be useful if you see you are not going to be able to "close the sale." For example, you can fill in the plus side, leaving the minus side blank, and ask for a chance to check back in a few weeks.

A friend of mine in the advertising business says he never tries to confront the customer with a yes or no decision. He feels most people find it more comfortable to make either-or choices. With the either-or path, the presenter can take the customer "down the beam" through a series of electives to a yes decision. Selling a single ad approach is a lot tougher than asking the audience, "Do you prefer this or that?"

If you still leave without an answer, review why you didn't get one, make the necessary adjustments, and follow up. Don't underestimate the power of persistence. In many forms of selling it takes at least five calls to get an order. And in some, five years may even be required.

Sometimes you will have a great idea and it just won't sell. If it doesn't sell in Indianapolis, save it for Fort Wayne. Another time, another place, another audience, and it may become the greatest idea since sliced bread.

Keep your chin up. Keep trying. Remember some of the things talked about here. As a result you won't have to knock your competition; you'll beat the hell out of them!

CHAPTER SEVEN

Practice
Makes Perfect

THE SCENE IS Denver's Stapleton Airport. Not much can be seen through the cockpit windows except the swirling snow and the runway lights just beyond. Clearance received, the jet lumbers forward as the first officer advances the throttles. V_1 . . . V_2. The aircraft is rotated. Lifts off. Everything is normal—for a short while. Then the signals come. Loss of power from number two. Icing. The stick shaker warns of an imminent stall. The turn and bank indicator begins to roll over, and the altimeter winds down crazily until it suddenly stops at zero. Silence.

The cockpit door swings open. "Cuppa coffee, anyone?" asks the instructor, and a discussion ensues with the two pilots who have just "crashed" the simulator. Their conversation centers on what might have been done differently in a real-life situation and ends with an encouraging "Oh well, practice makes perfect," from the instructor.

Practice makes perfect in presentations too. Some experts recommend practicing a talk ten times before you give it. I wouldn't disagree, but I would like to differentiate among the terms practice, dry run, and rehearsal:

- *Practice* is something you can do alone, going over the talk "in front of your bathroom mirror" or into a tape recorder.
- *Dry run* is your first attempt in front of live people—some associates or members of your family.
- *Rehearsal* is that final runthrough which will simulate the actual presentation as closely as possible.

There will be more on each of these terms later. But first a few words on their importance.

Many people don't take pains in preparing their presentations. And their sloppy presentations are an insult to the audience who must suffer through them. I've sat next to these individuals on airplanes as they arranged their slides and lamely cracked, "Don't want to peak too soon!"

On the good side, I've seen preparations for major corporate presentations start four months in advance. In another case, I've seen an engineering manager and a manufacturing manager interlace their presentations so that one would not be a repetition of the information covered in the other. The two of them practiced together every day at lunch for two weeks, so that the result would be a smooth conversational dialogue.

How much time should you spend practicing? Chapter 1 suggested that the length of your talk multiplied by the number of people in the audience is a fair amount of preparation. Or, if that doesn't seem adequate, allow *one hour of preparation for every minute you plan to talk.* Take heart. Keep in mind that you've already accounted for many of those hours during the planning, organizing, and developing process. Also, you'll be breaking up the remaining hours into separate sessions, starting with practicing on your own.

PRACTICING ON YOUR OWN

As you read over your presentation you'll find little things that will make it clearer, sharper, and more colorful. You'll find new angles from which to approach your subject. You'll start polishing those rough edges. You'll develop new and better ways of saying things. And you'll begin to feel comfortable with your material.

Earlier, I mentioned practicing in front of your bathroom mirror, and I put it in quotes because of the number of "bathroom mirror" jokes on the lecture circuit. But why not in front of the mirror? Or in the shower? Or while riding to work? You can practice almost anywhere. Practice a little bit every day to avoid last-minute cramming.

Initially you'll be practicing with the script you've prepared. As you read the script, try to read it with your ear rather than your eye. Better still, read it aloud, underlining those words or phrases you want to punch up. Put in slash marks for pauses. Put parentheses around softer items. Knock out any tongue twisters. You may be able to handle "Peter Piper picked a peck of pickled peppers" on the printed page, but it's tough to do it in front of an audience.

Now find a tape recorder and record your presentation. By now I'm sure most of you have heard a playback of your voice. The first time we are exposed to the sound of our voice most of us are somewhat shocked and don't like what we hear, not necessarily because it sounds bad, but simply because it's so different from what we hear inside our own head.

Once you've gotten over this "Hey, is that really me?" aspect, you can lean back, close your eyes, and listen. Listen for changes in volume. Listen for changes in speed. Listen for changes in tone. Every speech instructor or book warns against speaking in a *monotone*. Concentrate on that word as it appears on this page: Drop the *e* and add a few letters and you have *monotonous*.

A good musician could probably listen to a talk and convert it to sheet music by marking the pace, volume, and tone. Words like *good*, *high*, and *expensive* would be slightly higher on the scale than their neighbors; *bad, low,* and *cheap* would be lower. Some words (e.g., *other, impossible, uncomfortable*) would be stretched out for emphasis. Generally, tempo would be linked to intensity. Slow passages would be done in a softer voice and faster passages would be louder. Delivered properly, the talk would truly be music to the audience's ears.

Getting back to *your* talk, how did it sound? Harmonious or discordant? Most likely somewhere in between. Rewind the tape. Take out the script. Push *play*, and mark those passages that sound off-key. Change—replay—change.

With some tape recorders you can do a pretty good job of dubbing in the new material right over the old. The results may be a little bit patchy, but you'll have the added psychological advantage of wiping out the bad and replacing it with the good. This will also help you get away from relying on your script.

FOUR WAYS TO GIVE YOUR TALK

You are almost ready for your dry run, but first there's an important decision you have to make, which will become increasingly important as you get closer to the actual talk. The question is: "How do you plan to give your presentation?" The four basic approaches are:

- Reading
- Memorizing
- Impromptu
- Extemporaneous

Each has its advantages and disadvantages, so the question is which one will work best for you. Above all else, you should pick an approach you will be comfortable with.

To Read or Not to Read? That Is the Question.

There are times when you must read a talk. For example: when there are legal implications; when the press is present and you must be quoted accurately; if you are a high-level executive, where someone else prepared the speech and you haven't had much time to review it; or because you are *absolutely* sure you can not do it any other way.

Why all these provisos? Well, quite simply, because reading a speech is not a good way to capture your audience. I know a few authorities will take exception to this, but most of them earn their livings as professional speech writers and deal with a clientele quite different from the average person reading this book.

The talk that is read to an audience is usually a downer. Shortly after, "Good morning, ladies and gentlemen," the speaker's eyes leave the audience and shift down to the typewritten page. And, for the most part, the eyes stay down until the speaker reaches, "Thank you. Are there any questions?"

In brief, speeches that are read:

- Can insult the audience (they could read it to themselves better and faster).
- Sound artificial (the unnaturalness may be taken as insincerity).
- Are usually not tailored to the particular audience (certainly they lack flexibility to follow the lead of the audience as reflected by questions or interruptions).
- Need lots of practice to do well (they may not be the timesaver many people think they are).
- Represent indirect communication (the "authority" is in the script rather than in the speaker).

In spite of the foregoing, you may still be determined to read your talk. My job now becomes one of helping you look like you're not reading it.

If you decide to read a prepared speech, be sure you've "thought it out" thoroughly in advance. Otherwise, you'll just be reading something, with the chance of making a gross error. Think about what you are going to say, what it means, and how you are going to say it.

A "read" speech should be *read*, and *read*, and *read again* before it is ever presented. You must know a speech so well that you only have to look down occasionally. Otherwise you're trapped behind the lectern. This minimizes eye contact, and thus minimizes rapport.

Written humor or personal incidents are hard to handle in a read speech. Learn the gist of the story, not the words. Then wing it. Don't just see the words, see the images the words represent.

Most of us have seen Walter Cronkite on TV. (Cronkite was once cited as the most trusted man in America.) Cronkite "read" but it didn't look like it. You've got a lot more time to prepare than Cronkite did on the evening news, so theoretically you should be able to do better. Cronkite did have some other advantages such as his God-given talents and a teleprompter, so you're going to have to do some extra work to make up for that.

A good typing job can help make up for the lack of a teleprompter. Chapter 4 gave you some ideas on how to type your script. Here are some tips on how to mark it:

- Use colored pens for visibility.
- Put slash marks where you want to pause.
- Write "slow" between paragraphs.
- Use large, colored asterisks for slide changes.
- Underline for emphasis.
- Enlarge unusual punctuation (e.g., exclamation points or question marks).
- Circle words or phrases that need to be tied together.
- Mark gestures.
- Box passages you can memorize so you can give them looking up at the audience.
- And, having said all this, don't overmark. You could get lost.

In some cases you may be supplied with a prepared speech written by your organization—perhaps at company headquarters a thousand miles away. Commonly referred to as "canned" talks, these presentations attempt to match every speaker and every audience. It's like equipping every baseball player on a team with the same type of glove or the same size bat, or using the same lineup regardless of the ballpark or the opposing pitcher. Don't be afraid to modify a "canned" talk (without changing the content, of course) to make it *your* speech. If they wanted all the presentations to be the same, they should have hired a famous star and made a movie. Finally, never apologize for having to read it, and never refer to the script as having been prepared by someone else. Never say, "According to what it says here . . .," or, "The figures they gave me. . . ."

If you are going to read your talk, try these techniques:

- Try to look up as much as you look down. When you pause at the end of a paragraph, get that next sentence so you can give it looking up.
- Read as little as possible. Wing it on short, familiar passages. Slide your thumb down the side of the page at a pace that will enable you to glance down and find the right spot.
- Talk naturally, even if it means an occasional "tha" for "the" or "ah" for "a."
- Turn up the volume. (When your head goes down your chin constricts some of your throat muscles.)
- Place the script as high as possible on the lectern. If you had it typed on legal-size paper, using only the top eleven inches, good. If not, tape a strip of cardboard or a pencil on the lectern. The higher you place the script, the higher your eyes and voice will be!
- Don't lean on the lectern; it's for notes to rest on, not you. Picture a sign on it that says "Wet Paint."
- Let the audience know you're not a clothing store mannequin with a recording inside. Gesture. Step away from the lectern to field questions or repeat key ideas.
- "Hide" the manuscript. Have it up there in advance so that your listeners won't think, "God, do we have to sit through all that?" as you walk toward the lectern. (When I go to my dentist, I never see the novocaine needle, and I like it that way.)
- Don't staple your pages or turn them over. Slide them to the left and you'll avoid the hourglass effect mentioned in Chapter 4.

Memorization—The Robotic Approach

Memorized talks suffer from some of the same disadvantages as read talks. Memorizing is another form of reading—reading from within. Instead of the speaker's eyes being cast downward, they're turned inward like Little Orphan Annie's. Or as Pogo used to say, "All blunk out." They're turned inward because they are searching the speaker's brain for the next word or phrase that's supposed to come out, and when they don't find it—"Th-th-th-that's all f-f-folks."

You probably won't have the amount of time it would take to get a long talk down cold. Nor are you likely to give that talk enough times to make all that effort worthwhile. Furthermore, memorizing eliminates any spontaneity, resulting in a canned talk. "Was that live or on tape?" may be a great slogan for advertising recording tapes, but it's a bad question to leave in an audience's mind.

Impromptu Speeches

Impromptu speeches are given on the spur of the moment without any previous thought or preparation. They call for some pretty fancy tap dancing, and the only things that can help you are your own God-given talents, experience on the particular subject, and expertise gained in previous presentations.

Obviously, impromptu talks will take on an informal, conversational, flexible, and (if the speaker has everything under control) relaxed air.

Impromptu speaking is a special skill that is seldom seen. The best impromptu speeches I have ever given have been to traffic cops. The best impromptu speech I ever heard was by Dr. Gordon Lippitt of Organizational Renewal, Incorporated in Washington, DC. Dr. Lippitt was a poor man's Jonathan Winters as he grabbed a few markers and began drawing diagrams while presenting his topic. I was so impressed I went to hear him a few weeks later. As a matter of fact I drove through a snowstorm to see what kind of impromptu talk he would give this time, and he gave essentially the same "impromptu" speech I had heard previously. At first I felt as though Lippitt might be putting something over on his audiences. Later I realized what a good speaker he actually is. He has the skill to mix in stories, illustrations, and examples spontaneously. The correct term for what he did is "extemporaneous."

Be Extemporaneous; Go with the Flow

An extemporaneous speech is one that is well-planned, thoroughly rehearsed, but *not* memorized word for word. Therefore it has all the advantages of an impromptu speech and none of the disadvantages of a read or memorized speech. You may have written the talk out as part of the mental process in preparation, but that script is not up there on the lectern, nor have you memorized it. What is up there are a few notes on your opening and closing, some catch phrases or key statistics, and a listing of the five or so main points you want to make in the order you want to make them. All of which you probably *have* memorized anyway. (Memorizing your opening and closing is a good idea to make sure they go smoothly, but in between you will be winging it.)

The benefits are enormous:

- This type of presentation allows you to adapt instantly to different circumstances.
- No matter how many times you give the presentation, it will have an air of spontaneity.
- Audience involvement and interaction are encouraged and can be handled without disruption.
- Your talks will be more dynamic and more interesting.

The audience will sense all of this and stay with you more easily. You'll be at one with the audience instead of merely spouting out read or memorized words. The more they feel you are talking with them, reaching into your own gut for the next thought, the better your talk will be received.

Asking speakers without experience to adopt this approach may be like asking the lame to throw away their crutches (the manuscript) without a trip to Lourdes, but be brave. The extemporaneous talk can be easier than you think.

First, you must have done your homework, but that's the case in any presentation. And the more homework you've done, the greater your confidence will be. Besides, you're the expert. Otherwise someone else would have been asked to give the talk. So try it. Give the extemporaneous talk a try at your dry run, relying on your script only when necessary. Chances are you won't be one hundred percent satisfied, but stick with it. Use the tape recorder. Listen to it several times. Try it extemporaneously again at your dress rehearsal. Then make your final decision. Once you pull it off, you'll never go back to reading or memorization.

One of the biggest concerns in giving an extemporaneous talk is the fear of leaving something out. But that's not as bad as it seems. So you leave something out. Who's going to know? You will, of course, but the audience doesn't know what was supposed to be there. Chances are it's not really that important anyway, and if it is you can work it back in during the summary. Or, perhaps a confederate (or anyone else for that matter) will take notice and bring it up during the questions and answers.

In addition to brief notes on the lectern, there are many techniques to help you remember key points. If you're using flip charts, you can pencil in "stage whispers" along the side on which you will be standing. These are notes written lightly and small enough that only you can read them. They provide a safety net, there in case you need it. Viewgraph presentations provide an opportunity to put your notes directly on the viewgraph frames.

There are other techniques to help you remember the order of your talk. Some speakers like to picture a totem pole or stack of "groceries" and progress from top to bottom or vice versa.

A very real concern in an extemporaneous talk is that it will fall far short of (or run over) its allocated time. If you've timed your dry runs and dress rehearsal, the former should not be a problem. Nor should the latter if you not only time your runthroughs, but also keep a watch up there on the lectern. (But keep in mind that one peek every five minutes ought to be enough.) Also, you can have a compatriot in the back of the room signal you at the halfway and five-minutes-left marks.

THE DRY RUN

You are now ready to try out your ideas on others. Supposedly, humanity's greatest achievement is our ability to transmit ideas. At the same time, our greatest illusion is that we are transmitting the ideas we think we are, all of which becomes obvious in the dry run. *Everyone* hates dry runs. But, please, don't skip this step. If you do, you'll regret it!

A week or more before your talk, gather a few of your business associates, members of your family, or friends who have volunteered to review your presentation. Tell them what you hope to accomplish when you give the talk to the real audience, and who that audience will be in terms of backgrounds, education, and interests. Tell them how much time you will have. Ask someone to keep time as you do the dry run of your talk. And ask them to role-play as the intended audience and ask questions that might occur to them. Then give the talk, and as you do so, show rough sketches of any visuals you plan to use in the finished presentation.

If there are no questions, ask for them. And be prepared to wait until some are forthcoming. Don't forget how important it is to practice answering potential questions that may arise during your real presentation. Frequently the questions and answers are more important than the talk itself.

You will also be questioning your volunteer audience. Were they able to follow your talk? Did the benefits come across? Did you say anything you shouldn't have? Did you accomplish your stated objective? If they were giving the talk, what would they do differently? How did you do on the allocated time? Were there mispronunciations?

An error in pronunciation can have the same effect on an audience as scraping your fingers across a blackboard. It distracts them and may lead the audience to question your education and intelligence. Right now your pronunciation is probably ninety-five percent correct. But you need to work on that other five percent. Are you saying *fill um* for *film,* or *bag* for *beg*? Notice that we are not condemning accents. Accents can add flavor to a talk. (Indeed one major spice company selected *Accent* as a trade name for a flavor enhancer.) Your accent makes you different from the next speaker and adds interest to your talk.

Non-native speakers face particular challenges in this area. While their accents may make them more interesting, they must exercise care not to have their message missed or misunderstood. With more and more foreign-born technical professionals joining American corporations, communication has become an increasing concern. General Motors Research Laboratories is one of many corporations that have sponsored special speech training for their foreign-born professional employees.[23] Books that will be of help to speakers with this problem are listed in the Suggested Reading section of this volume. For those who need it, a little extra effort will improve both intelligibility and confidence.

Dry runs are usually horrible, but that's good! They give you a chance to repair defects that weren't visible when you were practicing alone. Just one word of caution: Groups that review presentations are sometimes referred to as "murder boards," implying the hurt they can inflict. To avoid this situation, impose a few ground rules before giving your dry run:

- Select individuals who will give "constructive" criticism.
- Ask your volunteers not to interrupt the presentation for analysis or critique of a particular point. ("Real-life" questions are welcome.)
- You're interested first in what they liked, and second in what they would do differently.
- Since you're interested in perfection, no point is too small to mention.

Lick your wounds. Take every comment seriously, but don't feel that you have to incorporate them all. (If you do, you will find yourself creating a camel—the animal that was supposedly designed by a committee.) If time permits, consider scheduling another dry run.

FINALLY, THE DRESS REHEARSAL

You have now reached the third and final step in the practice/dry run/rehearsal cycle. With all the effort you've put into the first two, there may be an inclination to skip this step. Don't do it! *There is always a rehearsal. Unfortunately, it is sometimes in front of the real audience!* A professional performer would never think of appearing without rehearsing. Why should an amateur?

This chapter began with a flight simulation where every possible step had been taken to duplicate actual conditions. So it should be with your rehearsal. Try to hold it in the same place, at the same time of day, and using the same equipment as your actual talk. No point is too small, even what you plan to wear. After all, this is a dress rehearsal!

Now That You've Considered Their Ears, Go to Work on Their Eyes

In addition to capturing the interest of your audience's ears, you'll want to be capturing their eyes as well. Chapter 5 talked about all the various types of visual aids you could use to support your talk. Whatever type you picked, one thing will always be true: *YOU ARE YOUR MOST IMPORTANT VISUAL.* You and what you are wearing will be in the audience's view far longer than any of your visual aids.

Now, while there's still plenty of time to make adjustments, ask yourself, "How am I going to look to that audience?" Your clothes are the frame. You are the picture.

The fundamental rule is dress for the audience. In some situations that might mean a hardhat and workshoes. As a general rule, it usually doesn't hurt to look affluent, but never dress flashily. Conservatively well-dressed is the goal. Ten minutes after you've gone, the audience should have forgotten what you were wearing. But if they were asked, they should agree that you were well-dressed. Usually that means conservative dress and solid colors. Save the checked pants for the golf course. John T. Molloy, author of *Dress for Success*, has made a career out of studying the impact of dress on business situations. In his book, he claims to be able to rate the success of sales personnel simply by observing how they are dressed.

Are your clothes out of style? How about your hairstyle? Even eyeglasses have become a fashion item for men as well as for women. Being drastically out of style can make an audience think you haven't had a new idea in ten years. How old is what you'll be wearing? Might this be a good time to purchase some new items? You'll probably be doing it before the year's end anyway.

I realize that some groups could care less about what you wear. And, I admit that the best talk I ever heard was given by an individual who couldn't afford a suit. But there are occasions that demand a certain level of dress, and for them I reserve a dark blue number I refer to as my "bank loan suit."

Women, of course, face their own problems in this area. Most of them are meticulous in their dress, yet quite a few complain of not being taken seriously by some of the males in their audiences. One young woman who voiced this concern was, unfortunately, presenting mixed messages to her listeners. Her dress, jewelry, and hairstyle were suitable for a disco, but not for a speaker's platform.

Another woman who works in research and development dresses as sloppily as she can. Needless to say, this too is a distraction. The "I'm just one of the good old boys" approach doesn't work for male *or* female speakers. The books suggested in the Resources section at the end of this book will give women some help in this area, especially when you add in two considerations: the type of person you are, and the type of organization you are representing.

Many organizations have their logo made into a lapel pin, and members of those organizations are expected to wear it proudly. One such company is Westinghouse, where former chairman Douglas Danforth had the slogan "You Can Be Sure . . . If It's Westinghouse" shortened to the single word "Sure," and made into lapel pins. And woe betide you if you walked into corporate headquarters without one. An executive assistant I know always carried a few extras in his briefcase, just in case. Unfortunately, he wasn't along the day one of the vice presidents from an outlying location hit town without a lapel pin. Noticing the omission, Danforth asked, "Harry, where's your 'Sure' button?" Without missing a heartbeat the visiting VP replied, "Gee, I don't know. I must have left it on my pajamas."

Timing—Be Sure to Quit While You're Ahead

The moment you begin, the meter starts ticking. And with each tick you're depleting your audience's supply of interest. You want to be sure to finish your talk before your listeners finish with you. Don't press your luck—keep it short. And if you finish early, use the extra time for questions and answers, not filler. You can spoil your entire presentation by dragging out the ending and introducing extraneous material. Know how and when you will close, and how you will make your exit.

Are time allotments sacred? Of course not, but if there's an established agenda, it becomes a "contract" between you and the audience. When you don't stick to the schedule, you're breaking the contract. Running over just before lunch or at the end of the day certainly won't win you any audience awards. Conversely, the speaker who runs out of time and then has to change slides so quickly you can't read them, and skips the closing, looks equally bad.

To prevent this, practice your timing during the dry run and dress rehearsal. Have a colleague signal you when there are five minutes, three minutes, and one minute remaining. It's nice to know that there are five minutes left, but it's even nicer to know where you should be at that point. Be sure to have these checkpoints marked in your script or on your visuals. With this approach you'll probably be able to stay within thirty seconds of the desired time.

Rehearse Using Your Visuals

It's amazing how much time speakers will spend preparing visuals and then neglect to try them out until it's time for the actual presentation. When you give your presentation, you will be interacting with your visuals, and you want everything to go as smoothly as possible. That takes practice. Here are some things to look for now:

Charts

- Be dynamic. Are there any opportunities to write or draw on charts as you talk?
- Will the progressive disclosures work? (Don't use too much tape to secure the coverups.)
- Do you see any use for a second easel to show more detail, to keep some visual showing while presentation continues on the main chart pad, or to record comments from the group while the presentation progresses?
- Could you use a few blank charts to cover an impromptu discussion?

- When you're ready, bind (staple) all of your charts together as a single unit for alignment and to prevent individual sheets from slipping out of the gripper. Finally, add stage whispers, those *lightly* penciled notes written at an angle on the side you will be working from.

Overheads

- Is it better to use a pen or pencil as a pointer on the projector or do you want to move away from the projector toward the screen to get your body out of someone's way? (The latter is usually, though not always, preferable.)
- Would it help to tape a cardboard "stop" strip or an empty frame to the top of the projector to serve as an alignment guide?
- Is there sufficient table space to separate the stack of unused viewgraphs from the used stack?
- Can you change viewgraphs easily and handle progressions smoothly? (Some experts recommend turning the lamp off during changes. Others place an index card, with tape serving as a hinge, over the projector head and flop it back and forth as a light valve. And some merely push the old viewgraph aside quickly as they move on to the next. The smoothest I have seen consists of placing the next viewgraph on top of the previous one and then quickly sliding the old one out of the way while holding the next in position.)

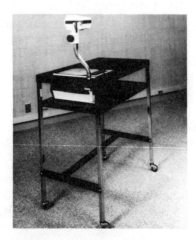

**Special table designed to house
overhead projector (3M Model 39)**

**Lightweight, portable overhead projector
(3M Model 6202)**

- Should you have some blank viewgraphs and transparency pens on hand in case the need arises to improvise?
- Should you consider putting stick-on "Smileys" in the upper right-hand corner of your frames to quickly show you right-side-up and to remind you to smile?

Slides

- Do you have your slides already loaded in a tray with your name on it so you won't have to waste time when you get there and possibly load some incorrectly? (How to load slides will be found in Chapter 8.)
- Are any of your slides poor quality? Is there any way you can work around using them?
- Are any slides on the screen too long? Would inserting a blank slide help?

Rehearse the Questions and the Answers, Too

You've already gotten started on this technique as part of your dry run, but be sure to build it into your dress rehearsal as well. No one can predict exactly what questions your real audience will ask, but your reviewers can probably come close by framing some questions around areas of concern, possible misunderstandings, and so on.

Study Chapter 10 for tips on how to field questions. Before you hold your rehearsal, let the reviewers know you want questions during your talk. Then ask for more at the end, and wait until you get some.

WATCH WHAT YOU SAY

As mentioned earlier, practicing with a tape recorder can improve the sound of your talk. Today video recorders are becoming more and more common, providing you with an opportunity to check both sight and sound. If your organization doesn't have one, a friend may, or (if budgets permit) there are rentals available. Video playback can give you just as valuable a critique as your volunteers.

Changing Times asked executive trainers Jack Franchetti and associate George McCartney what they thought about video replays:

> Short of a professional consultant, there's no better way to take that crucial step back and get an audience's eye view of yourself. Try it next time you prepare a presentation. Record yourself doing a dry run, then play it back. If you were in the audience, would you like what you

Videotaping rehearsals provides an "instant replay" for analysis.

see and hear? Would you pay attention? Would you learn something worthwhile? If you can say yes to all those questions, you're on your way.[24]

With video you can check:

- Gestures.
- Eye contact.
- Body language.
- Interaction with visuals.
- Voice.
- Maddening mannerisms.

These last afflict all of us to a certain degree. Some involve the voice, such as the frequent interjection of "ah," or the more modern (and more irritating) "y'know." Both of these bad habits can be the result of failure to pause at the proper place, or the compulsive need to keep on talking. Pauses help you and they help the audience. Your audience can think about what you've been saying; you can think about what you're going to say. But don't pause indiscriminately— make it at the end of a particular point.

Other maddening mannerisms involve the body, as in the case of a heel-toe rocker; or the hands, which might be tugging at a tie, nose, earlobe, earring, or each other. What a pity to have the hands form a distraction when they could be making meaningful gestures.

What to Do with Your Hands While Your Mouth Is Busy

Make your hands work for you, not against you. As you view the videotape, where are your hands? Are they *both* thrust into your pockets, jangling your keys and change so much that the mike is picking up a sound like a Good-Humor truck? (One hand in an empty pocket is okay, *occasionally.*) Are your hands clasped in front of you in the figleaf, or "God I feel naked up here," position? Behind you at parade rest? Or, are they tucked into crossed arms, signifying closed-mindedness? Are they grasping the edges of the lectern so tightly that your knuckles have turned white? (Instead, try one hand resting loosely on the lectern and the other used for effect.)

If any of these postures make you so comfortable that you can't go on without them, your audiences will have to learn to live with them. But keep in mind that they are all unnatural positions. To find your natural hand position, stand in front of a full-length mirror and raise your arms straight out to each side until they reach shoulder height. Now just let them drop. They'll slap against your hips, bounce around, swing a little, and come to rest in a *natural* position. Try this about a dozen times until you become comfortable. (You might want to alert your family members in order to head off snide remarks.) Now you've got a basic stance from which to start gesturing.

Assume a natural position and gesture when you have something to say with your hands. For example:

Gesture	Message
Point	Shows direction; makes a point
Palms up	Giving or receiving Asking for help
Palms down	Rejecting
Palms facing audience, fingers up	STOP!
Chopping palm	Division
Clenched fist	Strength, anger
Shaking index finger	Warning
Nodding head up and down	Approval, positive
Shaking head side to side	Disapproval, negative
Changing sides on platform	Shift in subject
Moving toward audience	Meeting of minds, receptiveness

You're trying to capture your audience physically as well as psychologically and intellectually. Gestures can do that for you. Imagine the added effectiveness of a speaker shaking his head while stating, "Pilots *don't* like that." Even a raised eyebrow can be a gesture showing excitement over an idea, regardless of whether it's natural or contrived.

A few more thoughts on gestures:

- If you're using slides in a partially darkened room, gestures will not be quite as important during the talk. However, they can still be used during the question-and-answer portion.
- Don't attempt gestures until you get any nervousness under control.

- Don't make your gestures too theatrical—the audience will spot it every time.
- Don't repeat gestures too often. (Bobbing your head up and down repeatedly will make you look like one of those spring-necked dogs in the back seats of cars.)
- Get the timing right.

Don't be like the preacher who, giving a sermon, said, "When the call comes from up there (pointing up), I'm going to be ready to go." (By then his arm had dropped and he was pointing down.) His congregation broke up with laughter, leaving him wondering why.

Gestures can be language without the spoken word. Some years ago, as Louise Fletcher accepted the Oscar for her role as the head nurse in *One Flew Over the Cuckoo's Nest,* she closed with a brief thank you in sign language for her deaf parents. It was the most touching part of the evening. You might even want to turn the sound off during your video replay to see how your gestures fare. Another technique is to put the recorder on fast-forward. Watching yourself do an impersonation of Charlie Chaplin is always good for a chuckle. Unless, of course, nothing moves. Then you've got a real problem.

The "Eyes" Have It!

Once I asked a leading executive what was the most important presentations skill he had ever mastered. The man was an excellent speaker, and had even appeared on network TV. So I was really interested in his answer. His reply, with just a little bit of tongue-in-cheek, "Learning to walk backwards." What he was referring to, of course, was avoiding turning his back on the audience and losing eye contact. (Within a few days after writing this chapter, I saw him leading a group of VIP's on a tour of his laboratories. He actually was walking backwards!)

In presentations, good eye contact can be a plus for both the audience and the speaker. Obviously, it makes the audience feel they're being talked to sincerely and honestly as human beings the speaker cares about. For the speaker, eye contact increases effectiveness—and if done properly, it can also make the speaker more comfortable.

Good eye contact is more than just having your head up, looking at the forehead of someone in the first row or over the heads at the back of the room. Good eye contact is picking out an individual in the audience and talking *to that individual* until you come to a pause, shift in subject, or some other breakpoint—and then shifting to someone else.

Here is where the speaker comfort factor comes in. All through our lives we engage in one-on-one conversations, a much less frightening activity than talking publicly. Now you have a chance to do just that with a larger audience. Start with someone you already know in the audience, or with someone who at least looks friendly. Then move on to someone else. And don't neglect those people sitting in the corners. In those really tough presentations, eye contact can reduce a one-on-one-hundred situation to one-on-one.

Some speech classes use an exercise where everyone in the audience stands or keeps their hands in the air until they feel the speaker has established eye contact with them individually. You might imagine your audience doing the same.

I know one high-level executive who had a bad habit of "checking his shoeshine" in the middle of his talks. Not only would his head go down, but it would stay down for a considerable amount of time. At first the audience would assume he was searching for a thought, then they would wonder whether he was being completely honest with them, and finally they would lose interest. Fortunately, someone had the guts to call this to his attention and he corrected the problem—greatly increasing his effectiveness as a speaker.

Eye contact (or the lack of it) should be evident from watching the videotape, particularly if you are using visuals. How good a view of the back of your head did you get as you moved to the screen or charts? I've seen quite a few videotapes of speakers carrying on long conversations with their visuals rather than with the audience. Pretty amusing in a dry run or dress rehearsal, but not so funny in real presentations.

By now you should be so familiar with what's on your visuals that you shouldn't have to read them to yourself; and the type should be large enough so that you shouldn't have to read them to the audience either. If you are using a pointer, look at the visual just long enough to make sure it's pointing to the right spot, then regain eye contact with the audience.

We started this particular topic by talking about an executive who learned to walk backward to improve eye contact. You might want to apply this technique by counting the number of backward steps you need to take from the lectern or the overhead projector to the screen.

Interaction with Your Visuals

In addition to avoiding talking to your visuals instead of the audience, there are a few other don'ts you can watch for on your videotape:

- Did you hide your visuals from the audience? Did your body block anyone's vision? (This is particularly a problem with viewgraphs.)
- Did you change any visuals too quickly?
- Did you interrupt your speech to handle aids? (Make the transition from visual to visual by saying a few lead-in words as you make the change.)
- Did your visuals and narration combine to present the same point or were there any mixed messages?
- Did you insult your audience by reading the visuals to them?
- Did you credit them with supernatural powers (show them a complicated visual while you engaged in equally complicated narration), or were you just trying to give them a choice as to which one to follow?

One other thing: All your visuals should be in final form for the dress rehearsal. But if you're missing one, don't try to *tell* the audience what it looks like, show them. Show them the butcher-paper chart or quickie viewgraph you prepared for the dry run. If it's a slide that's missing, insert a clear blank that you've written on with a transparency pen to give the main idea. Trying to explain missing visuals will throw your timing off and lead to other problems.

A Few Pointers on How to Use One

While I don't recommend the use of a finger, it's often better than many of the distractions caused by the use of pointers. Rather than use the pointer to give Papal blessings, practice your golf swing, or simply rap the charts or screen as a not-too-subtle way of saying, "Wake up, stupid," there are two simple rules for using pointers:

1. Point to something long enough so that everyone in the audience has had a chance to locate it. (Three seconds should be long enough.)

2. The rest of the time, put the pointer down or keep it out of the way at your side.

Other points on pointers: It never hurts to have an extra one or two located strategically so you don't have to walk halfway across the room to fetch the one you just put down. One good place is in the roll-up portion at the bottom of portable screens.

By now, we've all seen the collapsible pointer. (Sometimes being used to give accordion lessons à la Judy Tenuta.) The latest craze is the collapsible pointer with a small red light in the tip that comes on when it's extended. Available through your local stationery or advertising specialty supplier, or from Ozburn-Janesville/Autopoint (1209 Plainfield, Janesville, WI, 53545-0497; (608) 754-0317) for around $11. Check it out.

Other Benefits of Video

By now I'm sure you are sold on the benefits of video, but there are two more points I should highlight.

First there's the use of video to practice the eyeball-to-eyeball, one-on-one type of presentation where there's bound to be a lot of interaction. Find the right person to role-play the other individual and go at it. Perhaps you'll want to try this role-playing with a series of individuals—one each day.

Second, there's the use of video as a confidence builder. Sound strange? I hope you didn't expect to look like a television personality on the video playback. For one thing the lighting wasn't that good, and the camera was an inexpensive model. Besides, there wasn't any makeup. Seriously, aside from the star image, most people's presentations look pretty good on TV. The little mistakes that you know were there didn't show up (the audience doesn't see most mistakes either), nor did that little bit of nervousness. True, there were a few mechanical items and some of those maddening mannerisms, but you'll take care of those next time.

Finally, don't ignore TV and radio broadcasts. You learned to talk by imitating your parents, and you can learn to talk better by imitating those who do it as part of their professions. Watch how politicians, radio newscasters, and religious leaders use their voices to sustain interest. Tell yourself, "This person's good, and I'm going to learn at least one thing that I can use in my own talks." C-Span TV offers a tremendous opportunity to see both the good and the bad.

ANALYZING YOUR TALK AND THOSE OF OTHER SPEAKERS

If there is a golden rule for analyzing other people's talks (and your own), it is *Build on strengths before you tear down weaknesses.* People in the behavioral modification field refer to this as positive reinforcement. Immediately after a dry run or dress rehearsal of your presentation, you want feedback from your volunteer observers and, if you have one, the video camera. You want to know:

1. *What did I do right?* That way you can do it more often. Use and reuse those things that work best for you. Build on your skills.
2. *What did I do wrong?* You need to be aware of areas for improvement. Don't worry if you can't completely eliminate a shortcoming. Look for ways to reduce it little by little.

Oral feedback from your review team is fine, but written comments are a good addition. On page 128 you'll find a presentation analysis form used in various presentation courses. Side A, at the top of the page, is completed as the presenter gives the talk and serves as a checklist for further discussion. (Notice the equal emphasis on strengths versus weaknesses.) Side B, below, covers a number of standard speech items and is quickly transformed into a series of bar charts simply by putting a horizontal line in each column at the appropriate level.

The form has many advantages. One is its anonymity. Although we hope your reviewers are not going to write criticisms they wouldn't have the nerve to tell you, there are situations where a written point may be more tactful, such as where a fairly large group is present. Second, the form can save time, since reading it is quicker than sitting through an oral review where there are a large number of reviewers. The third, and most important, advantage of the form is its permanency. Collect the forms and save them. They can be looked at later as further preparation for this presentation or some future talk.

At Jack Franchetti Communications, Inc., (JFCI), a quality firm in both speech/presentation skills and media training, it's recommended that presenters practice against an "eye/ear" chart. This is an easily developed analytical tool that actually becomes your coach. All it takes is an index card and a videotape recorder.

First, draw up two columns on the index card. Label one *Eye* and

PRESENTATION ANALYSIS

Presenter _____

Topic _____

Date _____

"I particularly liked..."	"If it were mine to do, I would..."

Presentation analysis form (Side A)

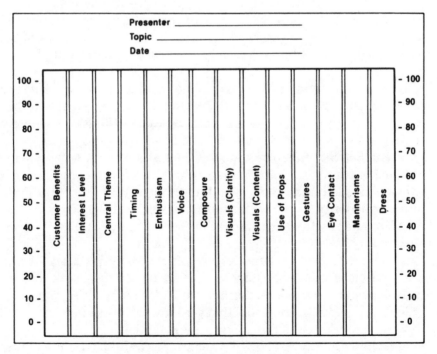

Presenter _____

Topic _____

Date _____

Presentation analysis form (Side B)

the other *Ear*. Then list the features your audience will see and hear when you address them. Here's a sample chart:

Eye	**Ear**
Gestures	Inflection
Eye contact	Pace
Body motion	Pause
Head motion	Tone
Facial expressions	Volume
Hands	Pro-/Enunciation
Posture	Ums, Ahs, You knows . . .
Dress	Jargon/Acronyms
Grooming	Simple words/Sentences
Swaying	Humor

JFCI points out that two facets are important to the success of any presentation: the message and the manner in which it's delivered. While your message may be of primary concern to you, don't overlook your manner. *How* you deliver your message determines the impression you'll leave with your audience. And remember, often successful presentations depend more upon the impression than the message itself.

This is where the eye/ear chart comes in. It's designed to help you make an impression that will ensure that your audience retains your message.

Now you're ready to go on camera.

Record your speech. Then play it back against the points on the eye/ear chart in order to determine what kind of impression you will make.

For instance, did you have too many gestures? Your head motion and facial expression: are they natural or stiff? Will your clothing make a positive statement for you?

The inflection of your voice: is it natural or forced? Did you use jargon or acronyms known only to a select few in your audience? How many times did you say "um" or "ah" or "you know"?

Check yourself against all the points on the chart. If you are pleased, chances are your audience will be pleased too. In this way, you'll make a positive impression.[25]

A FEW LAST WORDS

This has been one of the longest chapters in this book, and in real life it will be one of the areas where you should spend the most time.

You now have the confidence that comes from having done your homework. You know you can give the talk because by now you have already done so at least three times (and watched or heard it replayed three more).

You are now ready for the real thing. Surprisingly, it may be easier than your dry run and rehearsal. At least the audience won't be waiting to say, "If it were mine to do I would . . . ."

• CHAPTER EIGHT •

Check
Your Rigging

WITHOUT A DOUBT, the greatest group of tightrope walkers in history was the Wallenda family headed by its patriarch, Carl. And, perhaps their greatest exploit occurred during a rehearsal one day at Madison Square Garden in New York City. With the entire troupe up on the wire on bicycles and balancing poles, a maintenance man inadvertently turned off the main power switch leaving the family in total darkness forty feet above the arena floor. Summoning all the calm he could, Carl reassured his sons and daughters that things would soon right themselves, and fortunately he was correct.

Once I had the opportunity to see this great man in person. Despite his advanced years, Carl Wallenda still cut an impressive figure. But as imposing as he was, it was something he was doing that made a bigger impression on me. Here was the boss, the star, the patriarch, checking out the tautness of each wire in the myriad that connected to the main wire he would be walking on. It occurred to me that he could have told one of the roustabouts to do it, or asked a family member. But he had a good reason not to. They weren't going up on that wire—he was!

And so it is with talks and presentations. The next few pages cover all the things you need to check out ahead of time to make sure your performance is flawless. Many of them are minor and mechanical, and your audience may never notice; that is, of course, unless things go wrong. When that happens, you may or may not be as fortunate as the Wallendas were at Madison Square Garden.

When I cover the importance of checking your rigging with groups of meeting planners, I like to ask, "How many of you have ever been trampled by an elephant? . . . Nobody, I dare say. Well then, how many have been stung by a bee? Almost all, which just goes to prove it's the little things that can hurt you!"

Your attitude might well be, "I'm not a janitor or projectionist! I've got other things to think about. Let someone else handle the details." Not an unreasonable attitude except for one thing: you've got a vested interest in how well the presentation goes. It's *your* countless hours of research, writing, and rehearsal that have been invested—not the janitor's. And it's you and your reputation standing at the lectern—not the projectionist's.

Clearly, if you care about how you look and how well you communicate, the responsibility for the preliminary arrangements rests with you. Take a look at some of those important little things you need to do in advance of your talk.

BE AN EARLY BIRD

Given advance warning, most problems can be avoided in time. A week or so before your presentation you should be checking any printed material you plan to hand out and any props or models you plan to use. Are your visuals ready? Has the necessary projection or other audiovisual equipment been reserved? Has the audience been notified as to time and place? Has the meeting room been set aside?

If possible, visit the room a week in advance. If you're using visual aids, you have both a good reason and a good excuse for doing this. Check seating, electrical outlets, and switches. Measure distances and screen size to determine the focal length of the lens you'll need. Where are the doors? (It's pretty obvious that you'll want them in the back of the room where late arrivers or in-and-outers won't disrupt your talk.) If you should happen to meet the custodian while you're there, offer a few kind words along with a diagram of the desired setup. This can work wonders later on.

Hopefully, wherever you speak you will have some help from local people in making suitable arrangements. But don't count on it! You can't walk in five minutes before you're due to go on and expect all to be in order. It just doesn't work that way. Murphy's Law makes sure of that. Plan to arrive about an hour before your audience is due. And make sure the chairperson, custodian, projectionist, and other appropriate people know you plan to arrive early so that:

- You'll be able to get into the room.
- There will be someone there to help you. (If in doubt, take a friend.)

- Others who are involved won't be operating on a last-minute rush.

Spend that hour checking all the mechanical aspects of your presentation. There's almost always something that needs to be done. And if, miraculously, all is to your satisfaction, then use part of the remaining time to glance through your script once more, and the rest to relax for a few moments and get in tune with the room. But before you relax, be sure you've covered *all* the bases!

WILL THE AUDIENCE BE COMFORTABLE?

Audience comfort generally revolves around two factors: heating and seating. Adjustments to the heating or air conditioning will take time (particularly with the newer locked thermostats that only the custodians or maintenance personnel can adjust), so proper temperature is one of the first things you will want to check for. If the room has only been open for a few minutes, it's understandable that it will be too hot or cold, but check the air coming out of the vents to make sure things are headed in the right direction.

Don't underestimate the importance of this obvious item. It could ruin your entire presentation. In Philadelphia, I once had the misfortune of giving a series of talks in a storeroom where the only heat was from plug-in, resistance-type electrical heaters. The wiring system in the room was so old that every time I added a slide projector, the load created by the heaters blew a fuse. Faced with this either-or situation, you can probably guess which option my frozen body selected.

In terms of seating, keep in mind the old adage, "The brain can only absorb as much as the buttocks will endure." Having an uncomfortable audience because of poor seating can provoke just as much negativism as poor temperature control. Chances are you will be severely limited in what you can do in this area, but here are a few suggestions:

- If you have any say about the room selected, consider the seating (along with ceiling height, overall dimensions, layout, screen location, etc.).
- If the meeting is important enough, perhaps better chairs can be substituted from another room.
- Remove any surplus seats (or stack them in the back of the room), culling out any seats that are damaged or of a different style.

Perhaps the biggest latitude you will have is in the arrangement of the seating, and this is no small item.

SEATING ARRANGEMENTS

If you're talking to a large audience in an auditorium, obviously there's not much to be done about arrangement. Auditorium seats can be "roped off" (with a roll of masking tape) to force a less-than-capacity crowd closer to you. In some auditoriums, this roping off effect can be enhanced by turning off the lighting in distant sectors.

Smaller groups and small rooms offer many options. Tailor the seating arrangement to fit the size of the group, the nature of your talk, and your personality. Various arrangements can stimulate or inhibit discussion. Here are a few you might want to consider:

Theater Style

Theater style offers the greatest number of seats in the smallest space. You might want to consider this setup for any group numbering over fifty, particularly if room size and screen size are limited. The lack of tables is disadvantageous in that your audience will have difficulty taking notes. They will also not have anything on which to rest their elbows. And row upon row of seating may block the audience's view of you and/or your visuals, unless some sort of elevated platform is provided. Most formal theaters feature a stage, but if one isn't available, you can build your own out of "risers" if they are available from the maintenance personnel.

Classroom Style

While this setup won't handle as many people as the auditorium style because of the addition of tables or desks, it is still quite efficient in terms of capacity. The position of authority remains up front, which may be desirable. Classroom setups promote teacher/student discussion, but inhibit group discussion.

Classroom style is good for groups of thirty to fifty or more. At the higher end you might want to arrange the rows with a slight curve or slant (curving toward the speaker, as shown on page 135).

Solid Square

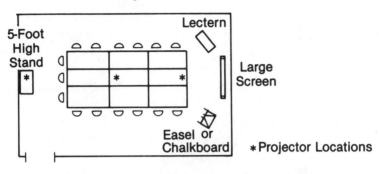

Classroom or "Amphitheatre"

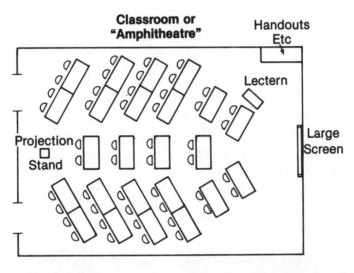

U-Shape/Outside Only

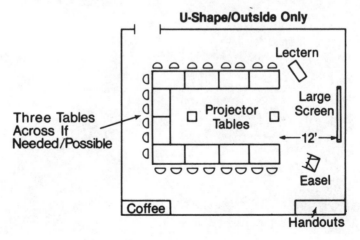

Standard seating arrangements

U-Shaped Seating

Perhaps the best arrangement wherever both audience and room size allow, U-shaped seating is ideal for groups of fifteen to thirty. Attendees can all see each other, promoting group dynamics. Yet, the source of authority lies in the open end of the U presided over by the speaker and the visuals. This setup also allows the speaker to step into the audience by entering the open end.

When butting the tables together to form the U, it's generally better to put those forming the sides outside those forming the base of the U. This will provide a broader open area where room width allows. It will also provide a little more room up front for the speaker and the visuals.

Hollow (or Solid) Square, Board Room, or Circled Chairs

These circular arrangements are good in situations calling for shared leadership or teamwork. Theoretically, every seat is equal. This arrangement is excellent for groups up to a dozen. The tighter the circle, the less formal (and easier) the discussion will be.

U-shaped seating promotes dialogue, as does
"lights-on" projection capability of overheads

Offset Seating

This arrangement places the projector at the front corner of the audience instead of at the center. Its value lies in presentations involving overhead projection. It avoids the situation where the speaker has to step aside after placing each viewgraph on the projector so that the speaker's body will not block anyone's view. Careful setup and experimentation will be required to make this setup work to maximum efficiency.

Other Seating Arrangements

There are many other possibilities. For example, there's a V-shaped arrangement with the speaker at the point of the V. (No doubt who's the boss here!) There's also a T arrangement for banquets. In a long room with a low ceiling and a large audience you might consider placing the lectern along the side wall, flanked by a screen on each side set at an angle toward the opposite corner. (Screen, lectern, screen, and wall would then form a trapezoid, with the wall being the longest side.) Although this requires duplicate projection equipment and visuals, it can greatly improve visibility of both speaker and visuals.

Of course the best way to ensure arriving at an arrangement that will suit your purposes is to send a sketch ahead of time whenever practical. Some rearrangement is always possible upon arrival, but finding people who want to move furniture early in the morning or after the sun has gone down can be pretty difficult.

If you're at all technically inclined, try to draw your sketch to scale. Standard collapsible tables measure either 8 feet or 6 feet long by 15, 18, 24, or 30 inches wide. You'll want 3 feet between rows. Try to leave at least 12 feet between the front row and the wall for yourself, your screen, the lectern, chalkboard, easel, and a table for handouts; indicate their position. Also indicate any projector stands or tables, plus tables for coffee or other refreshments.

When locating projectors, keep in mind that the cooling fans in some slide projectors are fairly loud. Therefore, it's a good idea to locate them behind your audience rather than between you and your audience. This will require a little extra room in the back, an elevated stand or two tables stacked atop one another, the right type of lens, and a remote-control extension long enough to reach the lectern, but it's well worth it in terms of reducing the noise and other distractions. Whatever the setup, never plan on placing your projector on the same

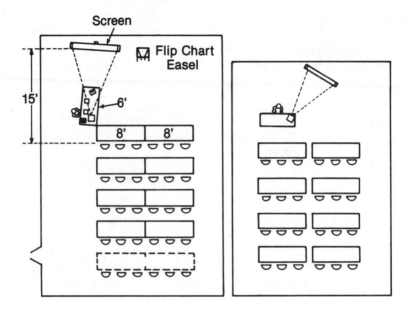

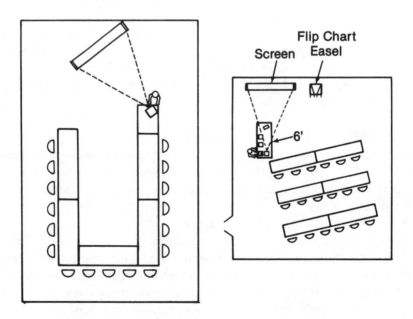

Offset seating arrangements for overhead projection

table where people will be sitting. The slightest jiggle by anyone will make the image jump several inches on the screen.

Now, having drawn all of this, add a list of required items at the bottom of the page or on an accompanying page. If available, add water service (a pitcher and glasses on a tray with a cloth liner) and tablecloths for a touch of class. (Green, blue, or pastels will do nicely. Avoid white and red unless you serve breadsticks.) Ashtrays should, of course, be available and clean. (More and more larger meetings are being divided into smoking and nonsmoking sections, with some companies barring smoking altogether.)

As mentioned earlier, having seating arrangements spelled out in advance will certainly save a lot of time. If you are unable to do so, or nobody paid any attention to your arrangement, do what you can in the time available and move on to the other critical items. Key among these is the projection equipment.

PROJECTION EQUIPMENT

There are two things you will want to know as soon as possible about your projection equipment:

1. Is it there?
2. Does it work?

If you think these questions sound a little ridiculous, you've never had anyone say, "Nobody told me that we needed to order a slide projector." Nor have you ever been wiped out by a burned-out bulb left in a projector, or found that the lens or some other critical component was missing. P.S. If the bulb in a slide projector is going to fail, it will usually do so when the projector is first turned on. So, turn it on a little early and leave it on (without a slide on the screen; insert a blank if necessary).

Be sure to project at least one of your visuals to see that:

- Your visual fills the screen without spilling over, and all letter-ing is as large and easy to read as possible. (The larger the screen, the better.)
- The image is positioned as high on the screen as possible, help-ing people to see over the heads of those in front. (Four-and-one-half feet from the bottom of the visual to the floor should be adequate. Using only horizontal visuals will also help.)

- The projector is focused properly.
- Images are rectangular. (If keystoning occurs, can it be reduced by tilting the top of the screen outward or pulling the bottom back?)
- None of the seats will have an obstructed view when you are at the lectern or overhead projector.
- Seats in the front row are not at too sharp an angle to the screen.

Unless you are really pressed for time, run through all your visuals for a quick review and make sure:

- The remote control is working properly.
- Nothing has been damaged in transit. (Slide frames can sometimes pop apart.)
- Everything is in the right order. (Not so much a problem with slides carried in a tray, unless there have been last minute changes—always a concern with viewgraphs.)
- Everything is right-side-up. (There are eight possible ways to project a slide or viewgraph, making the odds seven-to-one against you if you leave it to chance. I once saw a speaker try more than eight times and still not get it right!)

It's really very easy. With slides, merely hold the slide above the tray, looking in the direction the projector's beam will follow. Now, when the slide is in the correct reading position, invert it as you "dunk" it into the tray. (See the illustrations below.) Viewgraphs are even easier. If they are placed on the projector so they read correctly as you face the audience, they will read correctly on the screen.

Correctly loading slides in tray

LIGHTING

As part of your projector check, you will also want to familiarize yourself with the room's lighting controls. Does the room have a dimmer switch? Fantastic! A single off-on control spells trouble.

You can show viewgraphs in full light, but a slight dimming would be better. Slides will require some additional dimming, perhaps down to the level where people can see well enough to take notes. Movies will require even more dimming, but should not be shown in total darkness. With all of these, make sure the ceiling lights don't create any "hot spots" on your screen.

There are some things you can do with those lighting controls. If the room has a dimmer, experiment to find just the right level. Then put a piece of masking tape on the wall or knob, marking the correct position so that you (or an associate) can return to it quickly.

No dimmer switch? Check to see if there are two on-off switches. If so, you are probably in luck. Each should control one-half of the room. Just leave the half where the screen is located turned off. Occasionally, you'll find two switches that work a bit differently. I once found two switches, each of which controlled every other bulb in a series of 150-watt bulbs spaced across the ceiling. At that wattage, having either switch off didn't make an appreciable difference. Ingenuity, however, coupled with a quick trip to a local store and a borrowed stepladder, saved the day. I substituted seven-and-one-half-watt bulbs throughout one of the circuits, thereby providing two (actually three if you want to be technical about it) levels of light, not unlike three-way bulbs.

But what if there is only one single wall switch? In that case, try to borrow some auxiliary lights to leave on while you turn out the overheads to show your visuals. A few table or floor lamps will do nicely. Or you can make that trip to the store again and pick up some nightlights. Get enough to plug one into each of the outlets.

Why all of this fuss about lighting? Well it's certainly more than just the fear that your audience might fall asleep if it's too dark. You want them to be able to take notes, see you (and vice versa), and feel comfortable asking a question.

There is one other aspect of lighting that should be touched on: windows. In addition to presenting a distraction, windows without drapes can present a lighting problem that is virtually impossible to overcome—unless you're willing to wait until dark. I once saw 500 people, intent on seeing a movie, head to a cafeteria where a handful were frantically trying to paste brown paper over thousands of square feet of windows because no one had alerted the janitorial force or checked to see that it had been done ahead of time. Another time, I went to England to give a slide presentation to a proposal team. It was a nice trip. Unfortunately, their quarters were new, and the blinds hadn't been installed. Fortunately, for some reason—probably uncertainty about available equipment—I decided to take viewgraphs as well as slides.

Learn to expect the unexpected!

GETTING THE FEEL OF THE "STAGE"

Once you've covered seating arrangements, projectors, and lighting, you should be up at the front of the room checking all the other details.

If there actually is a stage, practice climbing the stairs and moving around on it. I once almost walked (fell would have been more like it) off the front of a stage, which is one of the purposes of footlights and yet another good reason for not turning the house lights down too low.

Does the lectern have a light on it? Does it work? (The first time you try to look down at your notes is *not* the time to find out.) Does it contain any other light controls? Do you have any props or handouts to place inside the lectern? (The shelf under the lectern can be used to hide all sorts of things, not the least of which is a glass of water.) Where is the slide advance button? Is the height of the lectern adjustable? Some have pegs for adjustment, others operate electronically. A few lecterns come equipped with timers, but beware of the mechanical variety that are so noisy they can be heard in the third row.

Microphones

For any audience larger than fifty, you'll want to consider using a microphone. Over one hundred it's a must. Yes, I know they can hear you in the back row, but you're also breaking their eardrums in the front row. And if you're soft-spoken, you *really* need a microphone.

Microphones are delicate. Treat them with care. Despite their rugged appearance, they are the most sensitive element of any public address system. If nothing else, *never* blow into a microphone to test the system. Scratch the microphone lightly or snap your fingers in front of it to check it out. Better still, try a few "Test . . . one . . . two's" or a portion of your talk.

The basic rule of microphone use is to ignore it entirely and speak to the audience in a comfortable voice. Overcome the tendency to talk louder. With a well-adjusted public address (P.A.) system, you could talk forever without straining your vocal chords. It's also acceptable to ask your audience if they can hear you if you sense there are problems, then adjust your voice according to the response. Finally, don't stand too close to or lean into the mike. When you're too close, you can hear yourself through the P.A. system. Pull back to a position where you can't hear yourself through the system. That's about where you should be. (Eighteen to twenty inches should be about right.) If it's an uncomfortable position, then lower your volume (voice or amplifier) for the same effect.

Note that the mike works with your mouth, not your eyes. If it's positioned so high that it's aimed at eye level, lower it.

Lavaliere microphones give you greater freedom of movement—they're smaller, and easier to ignore. They are also a little trickier to use. The ones that attach with a clip are easy enough. Those that use a lanyard around your neck can present problems, the first of which occurs when the speaker attempts to slip the loop over his or her head without unhooking it. Usually the loop is too small, resulting in mussed hair, glasses knocked askew, and a lot of mike noise, including audible grunts as the speaker tries to force the loop down over the ears and nose.

The secret, of course, is to unhook the loop, which leads to the second problem. Not knowing exactly how to rehook the loop, speakers strain their necks, heads askew, so they can see what they are doing—a next-to-impossible task—all of which is usually unnecessary. Most lanyards operate on the ball-and-hook principle. The ball is at the free end of the cord, and the hook is part of the bracket that holds the cord to the microphone. Holding one in each hand, the speaker need only place the hook over any part of the cord and then slide it down the cord until it engages the ball. Voilà! Whether attached by clip or lanyard, the lavaliere mike should be positioned over your *sternum*. (That's just above the solar plexus, not what you nautical types are thinking.)

Most lavaliere mikes are omnidirectional, thus *clothing rustle* can become a problem. To minimize this, grab the cord at arm's length and tuck the loop under your belt or into your waistband. If you are wearing one, your jacket will hide it. Now, body movement causes no cord or mike movement, hence no background noise. There's one other advantage: this technique provides an early warning when you literally reach the end of your rope, and prevents you from hanging yourself on stage. Think of the background noise that would cause!

Cordless mikes solve all of these problems, but the systems are more expensive and can be a problem if security of information is important.

If you are using a cordless or lavaliere, remember to leave it up there for the next speaker. If you forget, the lavaliere will certainly remind you.

Two final notes about the P.A. system:

1. Other than turning it on, try not to mess with someone else's system. The result can be trouble. Public address systems are often customized or may be preset for another (perhaps more important) event scheduled after your talk. If at all possible, have someone familiar with the system control it, or at least show you how.
2. If for any reason the sound system acts up during your talk, pause until it's fixed or turn it off and rely on your voice power. "Feedback," that ringing or squealing that has the same effect on the audience as scraping your fingernails across a blackboard, is to be avoided at all costs..

Modern sound systems are much more reliable than those of a few years ago. You may never have to use one, but if you do, don't become its slave. Try to forget it's there.

WHEN IT SNOWS, ROLL OVER

No, I'm not suggesting that you skip your talk. These are just two of the things that can happen to you if you plan to show a videotape. Auditorium systems are not as simple as the one you have at home. If possible, have a trained audio-visual specialist handle it. If not, make sure they tell you how to do it, show you how to do it, and then watch as you do it. After they show you the equipment works with *their* tape, try it with your tape.

Building in an extra half-hour to your arrival time is good insurance when video is involved. I've seen a lot of different problems arise in this area; most were solvable with luck or people who knew what they were doing. One that wasn't occurred in Chicago where a speaker arrived early and found the equipment on the fritz. "No problem," said the rental company. "You've got plenty of time, we'll bring another." And they did, much to the relief of the speaker, who went on to other things.

The old equipment was rolled out, the speaker began her talk, and everything went fine until she pushed the *play* button and found out that her tape was still in the old equipment, which was by then in a truck heading across Lake Shore Drive.

NOW'S A GOOD TIME TO START YOUR DIET

Watch what you eat and drink before speaking. Powdered doughnuts can make a mess out of a dark blue suit. But beyond that, avoid big meals. Digesting food takes energy. Cut back to one half of what you might normally eat. Skip the carbonated sodas; they can cause pressure in your chest. (If you must, pour them so that most of the gas is released.) Another reason for skipping the sodas is that cold drinks tend to close your throat. So forget the ice in that water glass on the lectern. Try hot tea, to open your throat. (No one will laugh as long as you hold the cup normally.) Add lemon to open your nasal passages. No alcohol!

THE SPEAKER'S CHECKLIST

The previous paragraphs covered most of the major factors in checking your rigging. The table on pages 146–147 recapitulates these along with other odds and ends. You might want to make a copy to take with you on the day of your talk. Hopefully it will keep you from ever having to tell your audience, "Sorry, I didn't think of it" when something goes wrong, which is like saying you didn't think they were important enough.

If your position is such that you have someone who will do all this for you, so much the better. But remember, if the bad dog gets out, you will be the one standing in the yard.

I recently sent a very competent crew of audio-visual people to a hotel to set up a ballroom for a speech to be given by a high-ranking executive to a group of 400 people. They were to set up the projectors, stage, drapes, P.A. system, and so on, and they did so flawlessly, in record time, as I knew they would. Despite my confidence in them, and despite the fact I was on crutches after a recent knee operation, I went along because if there were any complaints, I would take the hit. For the most part all I did was get the hotel to throw the previous group out when they ran 45 minutes over, and then sit on a chair in

THE SPEAKER'S CHECKLIST

Room
Reserved in advance.
Floor plan sent in advance.
Temperature and ventilation.
Coat racks in "secure" location.
Clean up in advance.
Six square feet per attendee?
   (Auditorium style) Ten square feet
   per attendee? (Classroom)
Excess chairs removed.
Will corner seats in front row be able to
   see screen clearly?
Adequate clear space up front for you
   and equipment.
Divide large groups into smoking and
   non-smoking (or ban smoking).
Close blinds to eliminate distractions.
Must windows be blacked out?
Build speaker's platform with one-foot
   risers for larger groups.
Wastebasket, trash container.
Tape door latches for silence during
   late arrivals.
Table for handouts, etc.
Disconnect phone. Alert operator.
U.S. and state flags if appropriate.
"Do not enter" signs on doors near
   front.

Breaks
Refreshments scheduled.
Table for coffee, etc.
Wastebasket.
Restroom locations.
At least one break for every 1 1/2 hours
   (more frequently in afternoons).

Place Settings
Name tents, pencils, pads, water,
   ashtrays.
Broad felt-tipped markers for name
   tents (one for every three
   attendees).
Agenda for longer meetings.
Rolls of mints or candies.

Projector(s)
Who will supply projectors?
Tables or stands supplied.
Plugged in, aligned, and focused.
Any light fixtures in the way?
Lenses dust-free.

Spare bulbs on hand.
Takeup reel available for movie
   projector.
Extension cords taped to floor, outlets,
   and table legs.
Electrical circuits adequate to handle
   full load plus coffee urn, etc.
Remote control working properly.

Projectionist
Has marked script or cue sheet.
Has signal light or headphone buzzer.
If green, yellow, and red timing lights
   are used, agree on schedule.
Small light available for projectionist.

Sound
Mike and speakers working.
Practice putting lavaliere mike on.
Feedback problems?
Check levels and set if required.
Do you want talk recorded?

Lighting
Adjustable?
Levels checked out and marked.
Who will work the lights?
Will auxiliary lights be required?
Windows adequately draped.

Signs
Room location sign in lobby or hall.
Meeting title on room door.
Message board for day-long sessions.
"Quiet Please—Meeting in Session."

Easel/Chalkboard/Markerboard
Fresh pad.
Fresh markers, varied colors.
Erasable markers for markerboard (not
   permanent).
Chalkboard clean.
Colored chalk.
Eraser.

Lectern
Light working?
Timer working? Noisy?
Water nearby.
Signal to projector/projectionist.
Pointer available.

THE SPEAKER'S CHECKLIST (cont.)

Props hidden.
Script or cue sheet ready.
Height properly set.
Does it block anyone's view of screen?

Handouts
Arranged in order.
Conveniently located.
Evaluation forms or surveys.
Current reprints.
Where do you want handouts?
When will you distribute?
Agenda at each place.
Certificates of completion (training).

Screen
Large enough for readability.
High enough for visibility. (Bottom

of screen should be 4 1/2 feet
   above floor.)
Fill screen with image.
Does image keystone?
Any hot spots from overhead lights?
Offset for viewgraphs?

Visuals
In correct order.
All right-side-up.
Extra blank viewgraph sheets.
Transparency pens.
Movies or videotapes advanced to
   proper start.
Sound levels set.

the middle of the room hoping the double dose of Extra-Strength Tylenol would find its way to my knee. However, about ten minutes before the doors opened for our show, I made the one contribution that made it all worthwhile. Everything was perfect except there were no U.S. and state flags on the stage. We came that close to having the M.C. say, "I pledge allegiance to the wall . . . ."

THE SPEAKER'S EMERGENCY KIT

Although I was never trampled by an elephant in my speaking career, I did get stung by a lot of bees—so many that I was tempted to assemble an emergency kit that would take care of any possible difficulty. The contents are listed on pages 148–149 and I offer it to you as a once-in-a-lifetime opportunity to avoid those once-in-a-lifetime disasters. As you can see, the total contents would fill a three-suiter. If you're a professional meeting planner, get the model with wheels on it and take the whole nine yards. (Have you ever seen the inside of a paramedic's truck?) If you're an occasional speaker, pick a few items that you think will do you the most good. Someday you may have a chance to say, "Boy, am I glad I brought that!"

EMERGENCY KIT FOR PRESENTATIONS

Paper towels
Small box of pushpins
Plug adapter (3-prong to 2-prong converter)
Extension cord(s)
Extension for slide projector remote control
Roll of masking tape
Small roll of transparent tape on dispenser
One box of assorted markers
One dozen manila file folders (When open to 19 by 12 inches they
    make a good emergency chart.)
Transparency pens for writing on viewgraphs
One box of transparencies
Soft chalk (white and colored)
Hand towel
Wet napkins
Eraser
Two collapsible pointers
Four nightlights (for rooms having only off-on lighting)
One 8 1/2 by 11-inch meeting pad (with pen)
One pocket-sized memo pad (with pen)
One pack of 3 by 5-inch index cards
One calendar
Assortment of stomachache, headache, and cold or allergy relief
    medications
One box of throat lozenges
Various sizes of company logos
One corporate telephone directory
Small slide viewer or magnifying glass
One-half dozen translucent sheets that slides snap in and out of
    easily (in case major rearrangement or sorting is required)
Matchbooks with company logo
White-out (for whiting out errors)
Single-edge razor blade
Scissors
Pocket knife
Two large clips (to hold charts in case easel is broken)
One dozen blank black slides
One dozen clear slides
Pocket flashlight
Cricket (for slide change where no other signal is available)
One dozen envelopes with stamps

EMERGENCY KIT FOR PRESENTATIONS (cont.)

One express-mail or package service envelope and form
Small bulb for lectern
Small bottle of lens cleaner and tissues
Headcleaner for VCR
Small bills, for tips
Projector bulbs for slides and overheads
Important FAX numbers
Shoeshine packs
Thirty pieces of 8 1/2 by 11-inch white card stock to fold in half for
    name tents
Stick-on name badges
One dime (for removing jammed slide trays)
Small American flag (in case you are accused of "flag waving")

WHAT TO DO WHEN EVERYTHING'S UNDER CONTROL

The last thing that needs a little mechanical adjustment is *you*. Now is the time for that trip down the hall to straighten your tie, brush your hair, or whatever. If you tend to speak with your hand in your pocket, then empty the pocket of coins, keys, or anything else that will jangle and distract the audience. Also remove pens from outside coat or shirt pockets where they might cause a visual distraction. If you are to be introduced, go over the material with the chairperson—not only to catch any possible errors, but to force a rehearsal.

For some, this is a good time to relax, practice your mantra, or at least do a little deep breathing. For others, this is a time to get fired up, just as some football players do. In general, I would recommend the former for the less experienced speakers who might need to get some nervousness under control, and the latter for the old pros who may be a bit blasé.

Eve Zibart researched this area and wrote an interesting article for the *Washington Post*. According to Eve, here's what the stars do.

> Operatic soprano Renata Tebaldi had to have a portrait of her mother on her dressing table . . . Roger Daltry of "The Who" runs in tight little circles backstage, around and around and then right out onto the stage . . . Jazz-rock bassist Stanley Clarke indulges in a personal kind of meditation . . . Country superstar Loretta Lynn has to go off

entirely on her own . . . Tenor Joe Bonsall of the Oak Ridge Boys does calisthenics . . . Jim Lehrer (of the "MacNeil/Lehrer Report") says, "I must get up. *I get up.* The adrenalin flows . . . the alternative is just too horrible."[26]

Ah, I think the audience is arriving. Since you've got everything under control, it's a great opportunity to meet a few of them. They'll be impressed, and you won't feel like you're talking to a group of strangers.

CHAPTER NINE

It's
Showtime

SOMEWHERE, WHAT SEEMS a hundred or more miles away, you hear the words, ". . . and now, it brings me great pleasure to introduce . . . ." Or, the voice more likely says something like, "Joe here has an idea that might increase productivity in the assembly area, and I asked him if he would go over it with us." At this point all the attention to detail in the previous chapters will begin to pay off.

Whatever the introduction, within a few moments it will be your turn to be doing the talking to that "sea of upturned faces" that Sir Walter Scott wrote about. This chapter will take you through that experience, pointing out a few tips you can use the next time you do it for real.

BATTLING THOSE BUTTERFLIES

Everybody experiences a certain amount of anxiety when talking to a group. It's natural to have a higher pulse rate before starting a speech, because your adrenalin is flowing. It's an unfamiliar situation and you may feel somewhat out of control. Even the stars who will perform tonight on Broadway face this experience. They never know for sure what the response is going to be. So, the trick is not to eliminate nervousness, but to control it. There's nothing wrong with having butterflies in your stomach. It's when they get out and flutter around the room that hurts. Here are a few ways to keep them from escaping:

- Remember, you're the expert—even if your listeners all out-rank you. If you didn't have something worthwhile to say, you wouldn't have asked (or been asked) to talk.
- Remember all the time and effort you've put into preparing. Knowing that you've done your homework should instill confidence.
- Remember that everyone in the audience (at least everyone who "counts") wants to learn from you, and wants you to succeed.
- Practice diaphragmatic breathing. Stand or sit up straight and provide more push from your diaphragm. Essentially this means taking deeper breaths. It pumps oxygen into your system and gets more oxygen to your brain. It also clears your lungs of stale air. (Most of us use only the top third of our lungs.)
- Loosen up. Before taking off in an airplane, the pilot wiggles the controls to make sure everything is going to work. Speakers should do the same thing. Don't sit there tight-jawed.
- Keep telling yourself, "I'm glad that I'm here, and I like what I'm doing . . . I'm Glad That I'm Here, And I Like What I'm Doing! . . . I'M GLAD THAT I'M HERE AND I LIKE WHAT I'M DOING!!!"—*Even if it's a lie.*
- Be yourself. Nobody expects you to be a movie star or William Jennings Bryan. Remember all the rules, but do what's natural for you.

Still bothered by butterflies? It could be worse. You could have gypsy moths. They not only flutter around, they eat a hole in your stomach.

If you're still a little nervous, think of it this way. We practice "public speaking" every time we talk to someone. So pick out somebody who looks friendly and get ready to start talking.

THE HANDOFF—INTRODUCER TO SPEAKER

When you've been introduced, you should acknowledge the introduction. In a small group, a simple "Thank you, Sharon," with a bridge into the talk, such as, "You know, Sharon's right . . . " may suffice. With a larger group you might want to use the same words, but add a handshake as you pass each other on the stage or exchange places at the lectern. This provides both verbal and visual acknowledgment.

You may get an offbeat introduction such as, "It's been said that today's speaker needs no introduction. And if that isn't true I'm in one hell of a fix, 'cause I've never heard of him." If so, you might want to try a riposte used by former Vice President Mondale. "Let me thank you for that wonderful introduction. Of all the introductions I've every received, that was certainly the most recent!" Or you may get an overzealous introduction that goes on and on, in which case your opening remarks might be, "And, in conclusion . . . ," or, "Are there any questions?"

When you're introduced, look like you're happy and anxious to get started. Be close at hand, not in the back of the room. Rise promptly, move forward quickly. When you reach the lectern, pause briefly and survey the audience. You've captured their attention, now hold it with good eye contact.

Start with a smile, even under pressure. Some experts say, "Smile until they smile back at you." When there's no smile, the audience withdraws.

NOW YOU'RE READY TO START, BUT IS THE AUDIENCE?

With larger groups there may be some housekeeping details that need to be taken care of, such as:

- *Calling for a stretch break.* Suppose they've been sitting there through an invocation, dinner, the Pledge of Allegiance and "God Bless America," recognition awards for almost everyone in attendance, and finally it's your turn. Even though the schedule may not call for one, you had better call for a stand-in-place stretch break. A few mild aerobics can be your best possible opening. You can start with, "Gee, it felt good to stand up. Why don't you join me for a moment?"
- *When "Please be seated" doesn't work.* Maybe they've just had a break and they're reluctant to reassemble. With small groups this usually doesn't cause many problems. Normally people will take their seats when asked. In larger groups, the mere process of finding the right seat and sitting down can take a fair amount of time, leaving you or the M.C. at the mike with nothing to say. Instead of just standing there or getting waspish, try a little humor. "They must not be able to hear me, I can't believe they're ignoring me" or, "If you don't sit down I'm going to start taking names."

- *Filling the front rows.* You're about ready to give your talk, but everybody is sitting in the back rows, with no one up front. If you ask them to move, no one may, leading to mutual embarrassment. The secret is to ask portions you want to move to stand up. THEN ASK THEM TO COME UP FRONT. Then thank them, and tell them why you did it (you like to be close to your audience, it makes you feel better and makes you a better speaker, etc.).

Hopefully, a chairperson or M.C. will take care of all these problems and also give you a good introduction, leaving you free to concentrate on your talk.

THOSE CRITICAL FIRST TWO MINUTES

The audience is sitting there wondering, "Who is this guy (or gal)? I certainly hope she (or he) is good." Or, despite your introduction, their thoughts may still be outside the room. They may need a short warm-up period to "erase" a previous presentation or some of the cares of the day. Put them at ease.

Recently I saw a particularly effective opening useful for foreign-born presenters who, while they speak English, do so haltingly with a heavy accent and would be more at home with their native tongue. In this case the speaker was a native of China who, when introduced, launched into a rapid-fire recitation of Chinese which certainly caught everyone's interest. After a few seconds he paused, translated his opening, and said, "Obviously it would be much easier for me to give this talk in Chinese. However, it is for your benefit that I will attempt to do it in English. Please then, excuse my accent." This opening put both the audience and the speaker immediately at ease.

Here's an opening Dave Davies, a physical chemist working on a new product line for 3M, used in seeking $20 million from his corporation's executive operations committee:

> Good afternoon. What I'm here, gentlemen, to ask you for is approval for the expenditure of $20 million. Now to request approval for $20 million in this kind of product area is really a fairly simple issue, for my mind. There are three questions:
>
> - Can we make it?
> - Will someone buy it?
> - And can we make a decent margin on it?

But I think we'll spend most of the time analyzing in depth the financials. (He then went on to give his agenda, and asked) Is this agenda acceptable to you gentlemen?[27]

Let me make a few points concerning his opening. "Good afternoon" may seem like a throwaway line, but it gives you a chance to say something *strongly* to test your voice, and it gives the audience a chance to respond. "Gentlemen" can't hurt either. Notice that he asks for the order ($20 million) right up front, says it's fairly simple, but he's not going to dodge the tough financial issues. As a matter of fact, he's going to spend most of the time on it. (Would they let him get away with anything less?) Having three points is nice. Anybody can remember three things. Expressing them as rhetorical questions is also good.

The agenda is the "Tell 'em what you're going to tell them" part. It gives them a menu of what's to come. And, asking if it's acceptable to them (again, "gentlemen") is another nice touch. Once you get them saying "yes" they hopefully will continue.

The presentation went on from there, with the speaker demonstrating his credibility as a result of having really done his homework. Did he get his $20 million? You betcha!

Some other sample opening remarks were given in Chapter 4, and no doubt you've incorporated a variation of one of them into your talk. Above all, keep your opening brief. Then lead with your ace, the main reason you are there. Convince your listeners in that next minute and everything that follows will become a confirmation.

Whatever you do, don't give in to the old, "Let's everybody stand up and introduce ourselves" opening sometimes used as a time filler by novices with nothing better to say. For any group of over ten people, it becomes long and boring. Even with smaller groups it can make the introverts uncomfortable and/or encourage the extroverts to steal the meeting.

And, finally, *never make excuses!* I know you didn't put phrases such as "I didn't really have much time to prepare this talk," or, "I'm not much of a public speaker," in your script when you wrote it. Don't succumb to the temptation to use them now. Be positive.

How to Energize Your Audience—The AMP Formula

An ampere is a unit for measuring the strength of an electric current, and its abbreviation—AMP—provides a convenient acronym for remembering three things that can electrify or energize your audience:

- *Appearance* has a subliminal effect. It includes not only what you are wearing, but your stance (head up, shoulders erect for a confident, alert appearance) and poise (confidence and assurance). Remember, you are your most important visual.
- *Movement* can energize your audience despite the fact that they are sitting still. Don't get locked behind the lectern like a department store dummy. Move sideways, or out toward the audience, to signify a new point or to answer a question. Move over to your visuals to point out a specific item. Don't hide your hands. Use them to make some of the gestures you practiced in Chapter 7.
- *Personality* can best be shown by a slight smile. If the situation warrants a broader smile, go ahead. Smiling at an audience will make it easier for them to like you. As part of that smile, make sure you establish eye contact with your audience, showing you are interested in them as individuals.

It's amazing how much of an impression you will make on your audience in those first two minutes. I once did some consulting work for an organization interested in screening employees as potential spokespersons. The initial screening (to be followed by additional training) was based on a two-minute introduction. Hundreds of people were screened. I picked out ten evaluations that I thought might be helpful (see page 157). As you scan through them, pick out those assets you want to copy and build on, and be aware of the liabilities (set in *italics*) you want to avoid.

En Theos—"God Within"

The Greek *en theos,* meaning "god within," gives the root for the word *enthusiasm.* I like to think of it as a god-like spirit that lies within each of us, waiting to be tapped. Of course various speakers are capable of varying levels of enthusiasm, and different speaking situations call for different approaches. This is *not* to suggest that you try to imitate the announcer on television who does the "It cuts, it chops, it dices, it slices" commercial, or John Moschitta, the guy with the machine-gun mouth for Federal Express ("Pittsburgh's perfect, Peter. May I call you Pete?"). Enthusiasm is much more than talking loud and fast. However, you *should* let some of that god-like spirit within you come out in the form of movement, gestures, and vocal variety. (Some speakers even have enthusiastic eyes.) As a result, your audience will know that you are interested in what you have to say. Chances are they will be, too.

SPEAKER EVALUATIONS

Speaker	Pluses and Minuses

1. Told of personal experience. Got away from lectern. Inspirational message. No loss for words. Lots of "you's" and "your's" in talk. Could be quite good with more experience. Called others by name. *Ending was somewhat abrupt.*

2. Gestured. Message had meaning. A fun person. Handled needling well. Praised group. Good accent added interest. *Sometimes vague. Needed to be more specific.* Good closing message.

3. *Audible sigh. Parade rest position. Needs work on eye contact.* Good smile (when it's "on"). Told story from real life. Cited magazine article. Used rhetorical questions. Conversational style. Easy to listen to.

4. Historical facts interesting. Good smile. Obviously a happy person. *Used notes.* Personal glimpse showed us a very open, honest person. Likable. *Spent too much time looking down.* Otherwise at ease.

5. Got off to fast start. Winning personality. People will like her. Determination shows. Used repetition for emphasis. *Needs to avoid "rock-a-bye baby" position.* Discussed common problem shared by others. Talked directly to individuals.

6. Two favorite positions: *Hands in pocket and figleaf.* Good appearance and voice. *Needs to slow down a little.* Mentioned others in group by name. *A little too static. Locked behind lectern. Needs work on eye contact.*

7. Good, modern appearance. Lively eyes/eyebrows. *Told good joke, but what was the point?* Expressed pride in work. *Too commercial (unnatural) at times.* Smooth transition into wrap-up.

8. *Nervous? Voice pitch changes. Shouldn't have ended with, "That's all I have to say." Needs to be more lively.* Did pose challenge for group action (i.e. "asked for the order"). In general, quality improved with time. *Maintain better level throughout. Warm up?*

9. Sounds like a believer! Proud of work. At ease. *Needs more gestures. Work on eye contact.* Well received. *Too many "ahs."* Very lively.

10. *Both hands in pockets.* Interest in family and job transfers to audience. Mellow voice. Good speaker. Has tough job. Mentioned people who inspired him. *Ran out of gas at end. Should have stopped sooner.*

HOW TO TELL IF YOU'RE LOSING THEM

I wish someone would invent a monitoring device to measure the vital signs of an audience. It would have to measure more than just breathing and heartbeat—that would only tell us if they were still alive. It would have to measure hearing, sight, attention, interest, understanding, body comfort, excitement, and a host of other functions. Such equipment would be a milestone in the development of better speakers and, possibly, better audiences.

In the meantime you will have to rely on the oral and visual feedback currently at your disposal. Orally, you can tell a lot about your listeners from the questions they ask (or the lack thereof) and the arguments they pose. Good eye contact will tell you even more. Here are some danger signals to look for:

- They start lighting up cigarettes.
- They start looking around the room or at their watches (or worse yet, shaking them).
- Nodding does not necessarily mean agreement. It may merely mean they're still listening—or worse.
- Yawns, fidgets, dozing, and loosening of ties are all sure signs to look for. When everybody reaches for the water pitcher at the same time, you're in trouble.
- Watch for that glazed look. It's called "taking an excursion" or "going down Route 350."*
- Worst of all is the door at the back of the room opening and closing as your audience trickles away.

Be at one with your audience. Stay tuned in to them with both your eyes and your ears. React. What do you do? You can't drop to your knees and pray! But you can:

- Repeat any complicated ideas, downshifting to a lower gear if they appear not to understand.
- Turn on more steam, tell a story, ask a question, stop talking, show something, give the audience something to do, talk to specific people. Use their name tents or badges to work in their names.

---

* The number 350 results from subtracting the rate of speech (150 words per minute maximum) from the rate at which an audience can think (500 words per minute or more). Thus, the 350 represents an excess capacity that can lead to daydreaming or other extracurricular mental activity.

- If a sailor isn't getting the right wind, a different tack is tried. "Let me depart from this prepared address to tell you about . . ." can be magic words.
- Some people in the audience bring their bodies, but leave their minds at home. Jolt them! Get them to do something—call for a show of hands. ("How many of you have actually seen a welding robot?")
- Review your main points (or preview the next ones) with a fingertip enumeration to either give them a second shot or alert them to what's coming.

If boredom is going to strike, it usually hits an audience in the second half of a presentation. Keep in mind that boredom isn't always entirely the speaker's fault. When you give your presentation, chances are you may be speaking to an audience that has had a long, tough day and is now breathing second-hand air in a smoke-filled room.

Although boredom may not be your fault, you're the one who's stuck with it. When their eyes start to droop and their stomachs start to growl—quit. Better yet, before that happens, quit while you're still ahead!

AVOIDING SIDETRACKS AND OFF RAMPS

There are other ways to lose an audience. First there are the sidetracks or tangents you may be tempted to take as you elaborate on a point in which you are particularly interested. Then there are mechanical breakdowns or other errors. And finally there's that horrible feeling of watching your audience disappear down an off ramp while you attempt to cruise merrily ahead on the main route.

Typical off ramps include such distractions and interruptions as:

- Late arrivals or early departures.
- Telephones ringing or messages brought in.
- Maintenance personnel or gardeners at work within sight or sound of your meeting.
- Side meetings or talkers.
- And, possibly, meeting monopolizers, hecklers, or even drunks.

Never ignore an interruption. You've already lost the audience's attention. Acknowledge the interruption, then proceed.

In some cases, you can even turn an interruption into an asset. Let's suppose someone walks in late. Whatever you do, avoid the temptation to crack a joke. (They may have been in an accident, had some family problems, or been hit with some other misfortune.) Instead, show some concern and offer to quickly review the material covered so far. In addition to giving that individual some extra attention, you're providing a summary for the entire group—particularly those who may have been on an excursion. And, of course, you've smoothly handled the interruption. This technique is particularly valuable if some VIP is going to be late, since it allows you to proceed without waiting an undue amount of time.

Early leavers are a different matter. Hopefully, they will exit at the break, or sit in the back and go quietly. If they pose a distraction, some comment is in order. "Sorry you have to leave us. I'll give you a call tomorrow (or please call me)." Or, less seriously, you might say, "I didn't realize this talk was so moving"* as a good response.

Suppose the coffee arrives in the middle of your talk and it poses a distraction. Pause. Thank the person who brought it, mentioning, "It's good to see it here early." Then continue with, "We'll be taking our coffee break in just a few minutes, but first let's take a look at . . . ."

Dr. Herb True, a renowned speaker who works out of South Bend, Indiana, tells of giving a seminar in a hotel and being interrupted by a maintenance man who came in carrying a stepladder in order to change a light bulb, explaining, "I get off at four, and if I don't fix this now, it won't get fixed."

True's immediate inclination was toward anger, but instead he controlled himself. Remembering some of his own advice for handling interruptions, he said, "Gee, that's great. You know, that darn flickering bulb has been bothering me all day, and it's good to see someone take such an interest in his work. As a matter of fact I'll mention this to the assistant manager on my way out tonight." (And, to himself, he added, "You bet your sweet bippy I'll mention it.")

By now the maintenance man had departed, and True, gloating a little, explained to his class that he had just given us a demonstration in how to handle interruptions. But, no sooner had True finished than the maintenance man came back in to change another light bulb. In the two years he had been working at the hotel, this was probably the first time anybody had fed his hunger for respect, recognition, and appreciation, and he wanted another "warm fuzzy."

Telephones are worse than maintenance men. Having a telephone in the room is asking for interruptions. Have it disconnected

---

* You can also use this one if someone's chair tips over.

if possible. And ask that any messages be taped on the outside wall near the door unless they are absolutely urgent.

Side meetings and talkers present yet another distraction. You can afford to ignore them for a little while. Next, try silence and a stare—waiting as long as necessary. Eventually you may have to address them with one of the following:

- "It seems we're missing something. Would you care to share that with the rest of us?"
- "Roland, Jane has a good idea over here, let's give her a chance." (During questions and answers.)
- And finally, "Gentlemen (or ladies), could we have one meeting *please!*"

One of the best people at handling distractions I know of is Bill Sears, head of a management consulting firm in San Francisco. Bill is meticulous in this area, even to the point of stipulating crushed ice in the water pitchers rather than those noisy cubes. Once after listening to all his advice, a group of us attending one of his seminars conspired with the hotel staff to set him up for a series of distractions and he handled them all beautifully—the message brought into the room, the dishes crashing in the kitchen, even the vacuum cleaner next door. Only when the hotel manager walked her dog in one side of the room and out the other side did Bill catch on, pause, and shaking his head, moan, "You bastards."

HOW TO HANDLE A HECKLER

Eventually you may run into a "bastard" in your audience in the form of a heckler or a drunk. Notice that by heckler I'm not referring to someone who simply has a different opinion to express, but to someone who threatens to take over the meeting.

Don't let them do it. Let them arrange their own meeting and gather their own audience. Give them a chance to express their views, but not to deliver a "political" tirade. During questions and answers, insist on questions, not statements. And insist on one question at a time. Open forum meetings in the civic sector frequently require patient listening to emotional arguments that sometimes border on personal abuse. Keep your cool. Don't lose control by playing the other person's game.

You are much more likely to run into meeting monopolizers than you are hecklers or drunks. Monopolizers usually tip their hands by asking more questions than the rest of the group combined. Once after I gave a report-writing training session for the Society of Technical Communications, the chairman told me, "Your seminar was great, and I particularly like the way you handled old 'so-and-so'." "Who?" I replied. "You know," he answered, "you really put him in his place on all those 'smart' questions." Well, to tell the truth, I *didn't* know. Yes, one individual had asked a lot of questions, but I had tried to treat them as honest questions and answer them to the best of my ability. And this would still be my choice if I were to run into the same situation tomorrow.

The only exception might be if the same individual continued to ask a lot of really stupid questions. This happened to me one day in Pensacola, Florida. An individual had asked a series of pretty dumb questions, and I had handled them in a normal fashion. But it was apparent to me and the rest of the group that he just liked to hear himself talk and would engage his mouth without having his mind in gear. Obviously an advanced case of foot-in-mouth disease. Finally, I was talking about the disadvantages of read talks and said, "To borrow some terminology from the streets, a read talk is a downer. The head goes down, the eyes go down . . . ." The audience was composed of young people familiar with the term "downer," but he chose to interrupt in mid-sentence with, "Wait a minute, do you expect us to give talks on street corners?"

Perhaps it was being stopped in mid-sentence that did it! While I paused to recollect my thoughts, my mind did a flashback and I said, "You know, this reminds me of my boyhood, growing up on the farm. I knew I wasn't cut out to be a farmer. Actually I wanted to be an electrical engineer, and I spent most of my time fooling around with gadgets I had invented. One was an electric flyswatter that I hooked up for my father's prize mule.

"Well, I wasn't cut out to be much of an electrical engineer either. Never could remember if it was $E = IR$ or vice versa. As a result, I electrocuted that poor mule.

"Now my father had a terrible temper, and I was really afraid of what he would do to me when he came out to the barn and found the dead mule. I knew he'd be looking for me. Well, he discovered me cowering behind the woodshed, which shows there were a lot of things I wasn't very smart about.

"Surprisingly, instead of being enraged, he was very calm. I think my mother may have had a chance to talk to him first. He merely said, 'Son, I know you meant well, but that was a terrible thing you did to that poor mule, and *one of these days that jackass may return to haunt you.*'"

Looking up at the group, I then added, "And I think *today* is the day."

That stopped the incessant, inane questions from that individual without inhibiting questions from the rest of the group. As a matter of fact it served as an icebreaker and they got more involved. Later I apologized to the individual, and still later I asked one of the more senior speakers what she would have done. Her reply: "Next time don't apologize."

Actually, the first time I heard the jackass story it was used by a stand-up comic to quiet a drunk in the Poconos. A quicker, more effective method is to ask the inebriate to repeat the statement or question. Usually he or she will have some difficulty doing so, which may be enough in itself. If not, it will give you a little more time to think of a comeback.

Whether it's a heckler, drunk, or monopolizer, keep in mind that the audience will invariably be on your side. They're just as irritated by the irrelevant interruptions are you are.

WHAT TO DO WHEN THINGS REALLY GET OUT OF HAND

Letitia Baldrige covers meetings, conferences, and seminars in her book on executive manners and gives this tip on how to handle a particularly unruly audience:

> I will never forget being present in a meeting of two sharply opposed factions. The chairman, a senior executive, had trouble keeping order as managers argued vehemently on two sides. Finally he rose from his chair and walked over to the light switch on the wall. Suddenly fifteen emotionally upset executives were plunged into total darkness. There was no sound in the room; it was as though a cool wet blanket had been wrapped around a steaming room interior. A few seconds later, the chairman switched on the light. It worked. The discussion continued in a calm, rational way; the disagreement was settled, and the meeting came to a close.[28]

IF DISASTER STRIKES REACH FOR A LIFE PRESERVER

Anyone who knows the first thing about boats would never think of going out in one without a life preserver. As a speaker there are a few life preservers you need to have handy at the lectern.

The first is a glass of water. Chances are you won't have any trouble with your throat, but better to have a glass of water up there just in case. It certainly beats running down the hall gagging.

Another life preserver is a brief set of speaker's notes with the main points you plan to cover and a few pertinent statistics. A single 8½ by 11-inch sheet should suffice. The sample sheet below shows how one can be constructed. Notice that its division into three parts allows it to be folded easily, aiding its concealment if carried to the lectern. I use this type of life preserver on a 1¼-hour presentation entitled "You, the Talk, and the Audience," and it serves me quite well.

The beginning of this chapter talked about every speaker having butterflies in the stomach and ways to keep them under control. But suppose a few get out and fly around the room where people can see them? If this happens, you want to make sure that they are at least flying in formation.

The speaker can't paint over mistakes like an architect, or bury them like a doctor. But chances are your mistakes aren't that serious. Every speaker makes mistakes, and usually the audience doesn't notice.

——— OPENING REMARKS ——— (Main theme, its importance, your credentials, etc.)		
TOPIC A	**TOPIC B**	**TOPIC C**
Major Point — Logic or Supporting Evidence — Supporting Evidence — Supporting Evidence — Supporting Evidence Major Point — Logic or Supporting Evidence — Supporting Evidence — Supporting Evidence — Supporting Evidence Major Point — — — —	Similar to A	Similar to A

Single-sheet speaker's notes

If your memory runs out or you get going too fast and leave something out, forget it. Or, if it's really important, stick it back in with an "Oh, by the way . . ." or remember to cover it in your wrap-up.

What do you do if you turn a chart too early? According to Bill Sears, if you even touch the chart go ahead and turn it if at all possible. Don't call attention to mistakes by going back to correct them.

Sears also has some good advice on what to do if an annoying wrinkle begins to develop along the top of your charts as you flip them. Take a moment to straighten it out with a tug on the back of the chart, or if the wrinkle still won't come out, pull at the corners. Otherwise you will have an irritant both to yourself and the audience that will, if left uncorrected, get progressively worse with the turn of each new chart.

Usually, you can avoid this problem altogether by "rolling" the charts rather than flipping them. That is, grab the lower corner of the chart and pull it upward along the outside edge of the pad so that the opposite corner is doing approximately the same thing. Then "roll" both corners over the top of the easel at the same time.

What if you push the slide change button too early or if you push it and nothing happens? If you are too early, try not to go back. The audience won't know there's a problem until you call their attention to it. If you pushed and nothing happened, try again (a little firmer) before you check for a malfunction. If there is a malfunction, determine whether it can be fixed quickly. If not, call for questions while someone else looks into it, or let the audience take a break while you do.

If you are working with a projectionist, don't be too fast to cry wolf. If a slide comes up too early, try to move on in your narration. If one doesn't come up right away, give the projectionist a chance to catch up before you press the signal a second time. Otherwise you may wind up with two slide changes.

Don't raise hell with the projectionist or anyone else if things go wrong. Keep calm. Be a gentleman or a lady. Disasters are only disasters when the speaker lets them become so.

In 1964, when Governor James A. Rhodes of Ohio and President Lyndon Johnson attended the 160th anniversary of Ohio University, Governor Rhodes intended to say, "This venerable institution." Instead he proclaimed it, "This venereal institution."[29] Touching, very touching. If something you inadvertently say breaks up the audience, try to enjoy the laugh along with them.

PACING YOURSELF

In order to get your talk off on the right foot, start on time. If you feel you must delay, keep it under five minutes at the very most. Why punish those who are prompt in order to accommodate latecomers? If late arrivals cause a distraction, you can recapitulate as explained earlier.

The only thing more important than starting on time is finishing on time. Have an associate in the back of the room signal the time remaining. Finish a few minutes early and leave your audience wanting more. I'm convinced that there is a special corner in hell where long-winded speakers are forced to endure an eternity of public television membership drives. The mere thought of it should help you keep your talks short.

If you don't enforce self-discipline regarding time, the audience will by tuning you out. And remember that time is more critical for a VIP audience. Reestablish how much time is available before you start, and be ready to readjust. If you've grabbed their interest, they'll keep it going beyond the "official" time with their questions. *Don't rush them at this stage.* The end of their questions will tell you when to say thanks.

What if you are part of an agenda, and one or more previous speakers have run over, and the chairperson has allowed them to use up a major portion of your time, perhaps backing you up against lunch or the end of the day? Since the moderator didn't take charge earlier, you must do so now. One speaker I know faced this problem by starting his talk with, "And in conclusion . . ." and then gave his summary. A better approach would be to negotiate a new contract, reaching an agreement with your audience before you start. Basically, they have two choices:

1. You will give your talk, making up whatever time possible, but recognizing the schedule will run at least _____ minutes over.
2. Recognizing that their cumulative experience is no doubt greater than yours, you can offer an open discussion of their interests, problems, or suggestions, with you serving as moderator and "tailgating" with (inserting) portions of your prepared talk where appropriate. Promise to end on schedule.

Their politeness may predispose them in favor of the first alternative, but if you get a chance, sway them toward the second. You may not get an opportunity to show all your visuals or make all your points, but synergism may ensue, making the end result much more effective. You may even become a hero!

THAT BIG FINISH

Chapter 4 covered interesting endings for your presentation, and presented the speaker who, with a tone of relief, suddenly says, "Thank you," and abruptly sits down. Remember, there's nothing wrong with thanking your audience, but it ought to be a little more elaborate. And the fact that you've come to the end should *not* be a surprise reminiscent of the old camping song, "I guess you think this is the end. Well, it is."

The closing is really the time for the big finish. Step forward to meet the audience and launch your summary or wrap-up. "Now that I have finished presenting my case, let me stress one fact . . . ." Then restate your chief benefit. Are you sure they know what you want them to do? Do they know why action is important now instead of later? Did you "Ask for the order?" After the question-and-answer session you might acknowledge their comments warmly. Use, "I appreciate your sharing your ideas with me . . . ."

STANDING OVATIONS ARE SOMETIMES EASY TO GET

I hope the end of your talk is greeted with applause, and that the applause is based on content, not merely on the fact that it's concluded. If your presentation was really outstanding you may even get a standing ovation. (Spontaneous standing ovations are rare, but you can usually get one for someone else or a committee fairly easily by subtly suggesting it—particularly if the audience is large and has been sitting for a long time. Try it.)

Maybe you will merely get a thank you or a nod of the head. Whatever. Giving a good presentation is its own reward, knowing that you have sold yourself and your ideas.

CHAPTER TEN

Questions and Answers: The Speaker's Dessert

"QUESTIONS AND ANSWERS are the speaker's dessert?" you ask. Well, there's more to that analogy than just the fact that questions and answers follow the main course. Like dessert, questions and answers add something extra, something special that can be sweet and satisfying, something to look forward to. Indeed, in many cases, the question-and-answer session can be more important than the presentation itself.

However, instead of looking forward to questions and answers, some speakers dread the session. They feel it will wreck their presentation. Good speakers should look on questions as an opportunity. They should cast aside the W-R-E-C-K and concentrate on the R-E-C—seizing an opportunity to Repeat, Emphasize, and Clarify.

Certainly, having an audience ask questions does pose a degree of risk. Just as soldiers are sometimes killed in battle after an armistice has been signed, so speakers can be hit by a "stray bullet" after their ending. But the benefits of questions and answers far outweigh the risks. Don't pass up this opportunity to start a dialogue, do additional tailoring, and provide more details that your audience wants to know.

"ARE THERE ANY QUESTIONS?"

All of us have heard speakers finish a talk by asking this question. Frequently it's followed by a microsecond pause before the speaker says "Thank you," and sits down. What the speaker is really saying, internally, is, "Thank God it's over!"

What a missed opportunity! Don't let it ever happen to you. Dialogue is what presentations are all about; it's what separates them from reports and proposals or formal speeches. The question-and-answer session provides feedback on your ideas. Despite any misgivings you may have, you *want* questions. Here are some ways to make sure you get them:

- As part of your introduction, the chairperson should announce that questions will be welcome. And, if the chairperson forgets, you should make the announcement. You might even elaborate a little to drive the point home. Tell them you're looking forward to the Q & A portion. Ask them to jot down any particular items they would like to discuss further.
- At the conclusion of your talk, the chairperson can provide a smooth transition between the main body and the Q & A portion by thanking you and then asking for questions. If there isn't a chairperson or M.C., you should thank the audience, pause, and then ask for questions. In either case it usually helps to alert the audience to how much time is remaining. ("I see that we have ten minutes remaining. Are there any questions?")
- Be prepared to wait for that first question. Just because it doesn't pop up immediately doesn't mean it isn't out there. Perhaps someone in the audience is thinking about how to phrase the question. Most speakers are uncomfortable with silence at this stage, but you can let that silence work on the audience instead of on you. Ten seconds at this point may seem like an eternity. Put it to good use. Use it to rest.
- If no questions are forthcoming, you have a decision to make. Turn them loose or keep trying? Ask yourself, "Is there more to be gained?" If the answer is "yes," a little prodding may be in order. One technique is to state, "Well, if no one wants to ask the *first* question, would someone like to ask the *second*?" This usually will break the ice. Another technique is to turn the tables on them, "Well, if you don't have any questions for me, I have a few for you. Did you all understand (or agree with) the portion of my talk dealing with . . . ."
- Many times, getting questions is like getting olives out of a jar—after the first one, the rest come easily. You can get the questioning started by planting one in advance with someone you know in the audience. Or, if this seems somewhat underhanded, merely get someone to promise they will ask a question of their own choosing. Tell them how important the Q & A portion is, and ask them to help get things started if need be,

or to hold their question until a lull in the Q & A and ask it then to keep things going.

WHY AUDIENCES ASK QUESTIONS

A few of the many reasons audiences ask questions are: for attention, to test you, to help you (or sometimes to hurt you), to seek help, to show how knowledgeable they are, to make their own points with preambles to their questions, to lay the groundwork for a second question, for approval, and to just hear themselves talk. Usually questions are asked to gain information. Whatever their reasons, it's not the rationale behind the question but how you handle it that's important.

HANDLING QUESTIONS

After you have had a chance to study the following suggestions on how to handle questions, you'll feel a lot more comfortable with the Q & A session. Further reinforcement will occur each time you practice—so get started.

Receive All Questions Cordially

How you handle questions is most important. Never react as though someone is trying to put you on the spot. Don't be defensive. Don't assume that the questioner is your adversary. Instead, assume that the question is being asked because you are the expert and the audience is seeking your help. Respond with introductory phrases such as: "I'm glad you asked . . ."; "That's a good question . . ."; or, "Many people are concerned about that . . ."

Don't show impatience with a question you've already covered in the main body of your talk. The fact that it was missed earlier may be as much your fault as theirs. Instead, use the question as an opportunity to repeat, emphasize, and clarify. Calling attention to the fact that they "obviously weren't listening" won't win you any Mr. Nice Guy awards with any of the members of the audience.

Be Sure You Listen Carefully

Listen actively. Be alert and attentive. Listen for tone of voice, emphasis, and inflections—but above all, listen for content.

Make sure you understand the question. Ask for clarification if necessary, or clarify it yourself by restating it for the benefit of those who may not have heard it. Lack of attention or the size of the room may cause half your audience to miss the question, particularly if the questioner is in the front half of the room with his or her back to most of the audience. Restating a question will also give you an opportunity to modify any "inflammatory" words in the original. Restating or asking for clarification gives you time to think about your answer.

Don't Shoot from the Lip

Grammar school has left all of us with a Pavlovian passion to answer questions as quickly as possible to show how smart we are and gain the teacher's approval. Speakers suffer from this same passion, and sometimes will be so quick that they supply the right answer, but to the wrong question. In other words, the answer is on the way before the question has been heard (or at least understood). Or, they find themselves trapped by comments they may regret later. The result is called foot-in-mouth disease, a result of putting your mouth in motion before your brain is in gear.

So try to avoid instantaneous answers. Audiences can be irritated by smugness or the rehearsed "party line." A very slight pause—counting slowly to three—is enough. In that time you can decide:

- Why was the question asked?
- How does this fit my objectives?
- How can I condense my answer?

Remember that you want your customer (or employees) to start talking. Don't cut them off in midstream with a quick answer.

Answer with a KISS

The KISS formula—Keep It Short and Simple—also applies to your answers to questions. We've all heard answers that were so long we forgot what the question was. There's no need to make another speech. During Q & A, audiences tend to be dubious of any high-blown language or catch phrases.

Keep your answers brief (but not just "yes" or "no," which would stifle dialogue). Think of a short, to-the-point answer, perhaps supported by a reason or example.

Make your point immediately. Think in terms of a newspaper article where the headline tells the story, followed by more detail. How much detail will depend on the depth of interest (and expertise) of the audience and any time constraints you may be facing. Thirty seconds should be enough.

You might even extend the KISS formula to KISSS, with the third s standing for *singular*. Keep it short, simple, and singular. Avoid multiple-part answers that become confusing.

However, you should have additional supporting material available for questioners who request or demand it. This can be in the form of a single sheet or even a three-ring binder containing in-depth statistics you would not be expected to remember. Or, it can be in the form of additional slides or viewgraphs you "hadn't planned to use but brought along anyway because they were available." In either case you will have to be sufficiently familiar with the material to find it quickly and discuss it intelligently.

Case histories, statistics, statements by experts, and first-hand observations can all come in handy.

Let's suppose you represent the National Park Service, which has decided to reduce the thirty-six-hole golf courses at Haines Point in Washington, DC, to a twenty-seven-hole layout.* The forty-five acres gained will be used to eliminate traffic problems, and to add 150 parking spaces, six ball diamonds, and additional picnic areas. Sounds well and good, but you run into opposition from a group of retired and elderly golfers who favor the nine holes being converted because the shorter fairways suit their game.

Thus, the East Potomac Golf Association is formed, letters are written, personal appeals are made to congressional representatives, petitions are circulated, and strong criticism is leveled at the Park Service. You have the job of answering the opposition's questions at public meetings and in the media.

Well, working the foregoing statistics into your answers would help. And having some more ammunition available would certainly come in handy. For example, suppose surveys showed golfers make up only sixteen percent of the people using the park, but the thirty-six holes occupy sixty-five percent of the land.

As to the particular nine holes selected for conversion, these nine offer an opportunity to construct a new road that would connect with existing roads and relieve congestion.

---

* *Based on an actual situation as reported by Joe Pichirallo in the* Washington Post.

Then you could add that the decision was not made lightly. Over two-and-one-half years were spent studying alternatives, city and federal planners were consulted, and public hearings were held.

Finally you might add that the Park Service will try to meet the needs of the senior golfers by realigning the fairways on one of the three remaining courses.

As a result of having done your homework, you and the Park Service come away looking a little bit better in the eyes of the general public.

If You Don't Know, Say So

No one likes to be hit with a question to which they don't know the answer. We don't like to admit that we just don't know. But, the consequences of bluffing, guessing, or faking an answer are much worse.

I was once in a meeting where the speaker was queried concerning the costs associated with a certain approach. He sighed and disdainfully replied, "Peanuts." This was quickly met by a second question, "And would you mind telling us exactly what peanuts are selling for this year?" And so, the speaker finally admitted he didn't know—in this case to his plant manager.

Wouldn't it have been much better to say, "I don't know the cost of that particular item, but I'll have it for you before you leave today"? In this case you've demonstrated candor, indicated that you know where to find the answer, and established a time limit for responding.

Sometimes you can throw a question back at the audience, asking their opinions. After all, the sum of their collective expertise may well outweigh yours. This increases dialogue and may flatter the audience. I've used this technique frequently on the seminar circuit. Many times the answer I got from the group in Detroit made me look like a whiz the next week in Des Moines.

If you've done a thorough job on your homework, you'll be able to answer ninety percent of the questions. Rehearsing potential questions may raise that percentage even higher.

Rehearse the Questions and Answers

At first, the thought of rehearsing potential questions and answers may strike you as ridiculous, abhorrent, or both. But it can make a lot of sense. The Q & A session can often be more important than the presentation itself. In these cases, rehearsing questions and answers not only makes sense, it would be stupid not to. Indeed, I have seen rehearsals where more time was spent on questions and answers than on anything else. Most organizations, however, sadly neglect this area.

Why rehearse the answers? So that you can deliver them with machine-gun rapidity? Of course not. Instead, you are preparing your ammunition. Finding those areas where more backup data will be required. Anticipating objections. Here's one question you had better be ready to answer: "What's your confidence level . . . ?" It's frequently asked by upper management, and a hesitant answer can write *finis* for your proposal.

How many times have you found yourself thinking, "Gee, I should (or shouldn't) have said . . ." That's what such a rehearsal will provide, an opportunity to take a second look at your answers. And, if you are taking that second look via video tape, here are some things to look and listen for.

Watch Out for Eye Contact

Look directly at the individual asking the question as long as she or he is talking. You want your entire attention focused on the person talking and what is being said, and you want the questioner to know it. During the initial phase of your answer, maintain that eye contact. But as you get into more detail, feel free to break that contact and shift to others. (This will help avoid a series of followup questions resulting in the possibility of a dialogue between just the two of you.) Always return to the individual who asked the question initially. Does the questioner look satisfied, puzzled, or angry? If appropriate, rephrase your answer or ask if you answered the right question.

Stock Phrases Worth Studying

If you're using a video tape to record your practice Q & A session, listen to the tone of your answers. Did you choose your words carefully? Did you sound credible? Pompous? Antagonistic? Hurt? Here are some examples of good approaches:

- "I'm sorry I missed getting the point across. I should have stated that more clearly." (Instead of, "You missed my point.")

- "Your point is well taken."
- "Let me clarify that a bit." (Instead of, "You don't understand.")
- "I didn't mean to slight that."
- "Am I glad you asked that question."
- "Bear with me one more second."
- "If this were a true/false test, the answer would be easy. But it's going to take more than that."
- "Did I answer the right question?"

It's tough to agree, yet disagree. If a questioner asks, "Wouldn't it be possible to . . . ?" try, "Well, it would if you include . . . , however . . . ," instead of, "Naw, that won't work!" Be careful of "Do you understand (or follow) me?" and "OK?" and "You know?" Many people will suspect a subliminal "stupid" implied therein.

Body Language

The importance of appropriate body language—particularly the position of your arms—is as great as it was at the start of your presentation. Various books on body language state that crossed arms are a sign of being closed-minded or of rejection. Do you have your arms crossed as you answer questions? You may merely be cold or have them crossed for personal comfort. But those in the audience who have read about body language—and even those who haven't—may reach other conclusions.

Do you find your head dropping down as you think, or find yourself shifting from foot to foot? The likely impression there is uncertainty and shiftiness. If necessary, rest your chin on one hand, with the other across your chest. The impression now changes to one of contemplation.

These tips all deal with routine questions. Most will fall in this category, and you shouldn't have too much trouble handling them. But *when* you want questions to be asked is another problem you'll have to face.

WHEN DO YOU WANT QUESTIONS?

Of course, you always want questions. But you have some degree of control over whether they will be asked during your presentation or saved until the end. The choice depends on a number of factors. Your own style and what you are most comfortable with will help you decide. The type of audience will play a role. With extremely busy executives, a question you can't answer in the middle of your presentation (e.g., "How much will this cost?" or "Has it been budgeted?") could effectively end the presentation right there. The type of visuals used will also have an effect. (For example, a slide presentation with its darkened room discourages questions.) So will your time limitations and subject matter. If you are developing an extremely complex idea that requires continuity, you may not want questions during your presentation. Otherwise you probably will, because questions provide an opportunity to establish rapport and find out if you are reaching the group.

Be sure your audience knows at the outset whether you want them to ask questions during your talk or to hold them for the end. And if you are serving on a panel, the audience should know whether questions will be accepted after each speaker or should be held until everyone is finished.

Questions during the Presentation

Generally, this is the better approach, particularly with a small audience. It gets the audience involved, gives you feedback, and maintains the timeliness of both question and answer.

Just as a radar sends out a pulse and listens for a return, be sure that you go into the "receive" mode occasionally. Don't always be transmitting. Be alert for questions. Nothing is more embarrassing than having a hand raised, missing it, and keeping right on talking. Better eye contact and pauses will prevent this from happening.

If you entertain questions during your presentation you will occasionally run up against one that is premature; that is, one that involves a topic you will be explaining in a few more minutes and the answer should be forthcoming. Politely table these and thank the questioners. Congratulate them for mentally moving faster than your dialogue. Tell them they are about three slides (or whatever) in front of you and you'd like to defer the question until you reach that point. Then, when you do, make sure their questions are answered.

Questions after the Presentation

Although answering questions after your talk can make a tidier presentation, it has some drawbacks. The chief one is that this portion of time is very important to you and you want to end on a high note. Leaving it to questions and answers could result in your ending on a bad question, a bad answer, or both. Instead, you want a big finish. To accomplish this you may want to reserve time for a summary after the questions to make sure you don't end on a downer.

RECOGNIZING WHEN YOU ARE BEING PUT ON THE SPOT

Don't lull yourself into thinking this is going to be an uncontroversial presentation to a friendly audience. True, 98 percent of audiences *are* friendly. But it can be a big mistake to take it for granted. I once showed up to give an "ain't life grand" presentation, only to find out the audience wanted a guillotine demonstration wherein I was to play the lead role. The person who asked me to speak gave no such indication. (I like to think he didn't know.)

If only I had put some feelers out, asked more questions in advance. I might have found out an ambush was being planned.

I should point out that this was the only time this ever happened to me. Obviously, it left its mark.

Sometimes you may face hostile audiences, particularly if you work in the public arena. Watch out for questions that are prefaced by, "With all due respect . . ." and for the questioner who faces the audience to ask a question. That's usually tantamount to, "Let's get this guy (or gal)!"

Types of Loaded Questions

Chances are that you'll never be put on the spot by being asked the old, "When Did You Stop Beating Your Wife?" question. But there are a number of equally perplexing questions that can catch you off guard if you are unaware of the techniques behind them. These loaded questions have become a favorite tactic of radical groups and some members of the press. As a result, a number of consulting firms offer training programs designed to teach CEOs, politicians, and other leaders how to handle them. One of the better firms in this field is Jack Hilton, Incorporated. Here is a summary of their advice on various types of loaded questions and how to handle them.[30]

The A or B Dilemma is a no-win situation. The questioner asks, "I find it outrageous that your organization has . . . . Is that due to greed or ineptness?" Or the question is "Is your company more interested in profits or the public?" or, "Which is nuttier to deal with, Country X or Country Y?" When you find yourself faced with this type of dilemma, don't opt for the lesser of two evils. The world isn't all black and white. Who says the answer has to be A *or* B? It can be C or D or E. You should answer the three questions posed above as follows: 1) "Well, of course it's neither . . ." 2) "Obviously we are interested in both . . . " 3)"Neither, and I think that's a poor choice of words . . . ."

The Irrelevant Question can be a trap set by someone trying to stir up controversy. Let's suppose you are "Mr. Wonderful" representing the Boy Scouts of America and a questioner asks you how you feel about marijuana. Don't react to the stimulus by saying, "Well, in my own personal opinion . . . ." This won't work because you are a spokesperson for the Boy Scouts and your personal opinion is irrelevant. Your answer should be: "The Boy Scouts of America has no written position on marijuana, but we encourage boys to obey the laws; *all* the laws." Thus you have taken the initiative and are free to go on to make whatever point you wish.

The Absent Party Question puts you in the role of answering for someone else. Examples might include: "Do you think the President's stand on _____ was politically motivated?" or, "Why are people like Senator Mugwump out to get you?" Here your answers would be, "I can't speculate on his motives," or, "I really can't guess at that, your guess is as good as mine," or, "Why don't you ask him?" And, if appropriate, you might add, "I can, however, tell you what I would have done (or what I think he should have done) . . . ," thus seizing the initiative.

The Inconsistency Trap involves being reminded of how you voted the last time, or your role in establishing a previous policy. Don't steadfastly defend old outmoded policies. Only fools never change.

The Hypothetical Question usually involves a "what if." Indeed, it may include three or four "what ifs." Your best bet is probably to reply, "There are so many 'what ifs' (or, There is such a big 'what if') in that question that I think it's entirely too speculative for me to try to answer." If you elect to respond at all, feel free to put your own conditions into the record, and they can be equally "iffy." In fact, you may want to highlight the remoteness of the possibility by accentuating the if. "Well, *if* such and such were to happen, and then *if* . . . , we might have . . . , but only *if* . . . , and finally *if* . . . , so you see, *if* . . . ." Or, once again, you have a chance to turn the tables with, "I think that your question assumes a situation that . . . . But let's consider . . . ." Again, take the initiative.

The Loaded Preface isn't a question, it's a setup or thinly veiled attack. In this situation the questioner starts with an inflammatory comment such as "Given the deservedly low regard for . . ." or, "Since you big manufacturers get together to set your prices . . ." or, "Do you mean to tell me that your agency, which has raped our environment, also . . ." and then goes on (perhaps at length) to ask an unrelated question or maybe even couples the loaded preface with an A or B dilemma. The tendency is to ignore the emotional preface or gloss over it in order to get to what you perceive as the real question. Don't do it. Since the preface has set the tone for the audience, you have to challenge it. Try, "I'd be very pleased to answer your question, but first I'd like to address your allegation." Or, "If you're going to include a speech in your question, I'm going to include a speech in my answer. First . . ." Having taken care of the loaded preface, you can then go on to the rest of the question. (But try to do this without stooping to the gutter tactics of the questioner or you may lose your audience.)

All of these loaded questions present you with an opportunity to take the initiative and continue to score points of your own. And here's how Jack Hilton recommends doing it.

Going from Defense to Offense

In handling tough questions, you want to be as positive as possible, switching the flow from the negative question to a positive answer. The technique for doing this is called bridging. Bridging consists of using transitional statements that take you from where you are to where you want to be:

- "Obviously, we have a difference of opinion, but let's not waste time arguing on that. What's more important is . . . ."
- "I can understand where you might have gotten that impression, but I couldn't disagree more. Let me point out that . . . ."
- "Quite the contrary. Perhaps you're not aware of . . . ."

Then try to follow these with three or more positive points you can work into your answer. Go for the knockout! To do this you must be ready with objectives of your own. You have to have more than just your speech in your pocket. And that's where rehearsals or courses like Jack Hilton's come in handy.

Other Ways to Defuse Nasty Questions

In addition to bridging, there are other ways to defuse nasty questions. Watch out for labels (high impact words) in the question, like: failure, overrun, poisons, delays, swindle, slippage, pain, price-fixing, pollution—particularly any words that might be associated with a civil or criminal offense. Then restate the question for the audience without the zingers, and follow up with a positive reply.

You can also question the questioner. If you don't know why a question was asked or you think it may be a trap, ask for clarification. This will give you time to think and make it obvious to the audience what the questioner is doing.

Sometimes humor can be effective in these situations if the audience is in the right mood. If you are talking to a group that disagrees with you, but is not angry or openly hostile, you might try, "I feel about as welcome as a leper at a skin lotion convention." Or in response to a tough question, "When *he* tells you to go to hell, you're anxious to get started." Or, "I feel like a human target for a near-sighted knifethrower." Or, "I didn't come here to cuss, I came to discuss."

Above All, Stay in Control

Very few presenters can win their case by losing their cool. Be patient and kind. Agree with questioners—up to a point. If you must attack, attack the idea and not the questioner. "OK, so you're opposed to nuclear energy. Let me tell you a few things I'm opposed to—strip mining, air pollution, inflation caused by high prices for foreign oil, oil spills, etc."

Those of you familiar with Transactional Analysis will do well to keep the principles of the Parent-Child-Adult process in mind. A petulant, childish question can lead to a scolding, parental answer and vice versa. Try to keep the dialogue on a calm adult-to-adult level—or at least your side of it.

The table on page 181 lists strategies suggested by Reddy Communications and the RCI Consulting Group for handling adversary confrontation.

ETHICAL STRATEGIES
FOR ADVERSARY CONFRONTATION

I.   Be Audience-Centered

It is highly unlikely that you can convert your opponent, so your information and arguments should be developed with the audience in mind.

A.   *Analyze your audience*—direct arguments to their attitudes and interest. Don't dwell on minor technical details.

B.   *Stay within the audience's frame of reference*—simplify the language. Don't assume technical "know how."

C.   *Avoid "fighting" with your opponent*—getting into "one-on-one" verbal battles only creates a competitive, win-lose situation.

II.   Advance Your Position

It is imperative that you counter questions raised by your opponents about the points you advocate. There are a variety of techniques for countering an opponent's attack, such as:

A.   *Disassociate*—separate any negative comparisons between your company and other companies, events, or organizations, that are not relevant.

B.   *Give to get*—acknowledge minor problems to win major points.

C.   *Selective response*—when an adversary raises multiple issues select the one with which you feel most confident and respond to it.

D.   *Buying time*—ask questions or request further clarification to give yourself time to think.

III.   Refute Your Opponent's Position

Invalid arguments or assertions by your opponents must not go unchallenged. Such fallacies can be exposed with techniques like:

A.   *Hyperbole*—exaggeration for effect.

B.   *Flat denial*—deny inaccurate statements. (This is a good technique for "getting the floor.")

C.   *Directive questions and statements*—leading questions or statements in order to guide the discussion into your strong suits and your adversary's weak suits.

D.   *Play it out*—show the consequences if your adversary's position is accepted by extending it or creating a scenario.

IV.   Control the Time

Your goal should be to control 60 to 70 percent of the time in discussion to allow your arguments enough development. Time control is aimed not at simply "holding the floor," but also to insure enough time to effectively state your case.

A.   *Interrupt*—closed-end question or statement to gain the floor.

B.   *Tag team*—maintain control by turning the discussion over to your teammate so that he may add to it or provide further development.

C.   *Issues list*—have a list of key issues prepared for use during lulls in the discussion.

HANDLING THE LONG-WINDED QUESTION

Often such questions come in multiple parts, and many good speakers jot down brief notes to make sure they don't miss anything. Indeed, the audience may have forgotten parts of the question. So it might be helpful to restate the main parts with, "Let me see if I can summarize that a bit."

If the questioner is really rambling, try for a graceful cutoff. (The audience will most likely be with you.) Give the questioner a chance to run out of breath, and when there's a pause, summarize the question. Anticipate the ending, supply an answer, and move on. After a particularly long, involved, multi-faceted question, you might try, "Was there anything else?"

If the question is tangential or the answer is extremely involved, you might say, "That's a good question, but I wonder if the entire audience is sufficiently interested to warrant discussing it now. I'll be around later so that the two of us and anyone else who's interested can get into it. Are there any more questions on . . . ?"

NONQUESTIONS

Sometimes you will be faced with statements disguised as questions. "Do you think these factory workers really want early retirement?" is a clue that you are about to hear what the questioner thinks. Perhaps the questioner is making a "political" statement or merely wants to show how smart he or she is. That's OK. Accept such questions. You might even ask such questioners for more detail or their own views. Then amplify or refute what has been said with points of your own.

QUESTIONS YOU DON'T HAVE TO ANSWER

Some questions are clearly out of place, but come up as a result of thoughtlessness or an attempt to embarrass the speaker. For example, unless your salary is a matter of public record, it's nobody's business but your own. You can feel free to dismiss such questions with "I think that's a rather personal question and irrelevant to the subject under discussion. Could we have another question please?"

Don't be trapped into giving an "authoritative" answer to a question dealing with something outside your responsibility or competence. You need only say, "I'm sorry I can't answer that, the question is outside my area."

There are many other reasons why you would elect not to answer a particular question. For example, the matter may be in litigation. Try to give your audience an idea why you choose not to answer—particularly if that audience includes members of the press.

AND IF THE PRESS IS PRESENT

Years ago, there must have been a movie where the star rushed through a crowd of reporters saying, "No comment. No comment." Obviously the phrase made such an impression it's still being used today, even though in today's world, "No comment" often translates into *guilty as charged.*

Instead of saying "No comment," tell why you can't answer:

- It's in litigation.
- It's being studied and the report is due on _____.
- It's outside your area of expertise.
- You simply don't know.

Keep in mind that news is a business. Therefore it involves competition. Sometimes this results in a touch of sensationalism, especially where sensitive issues are involved.

Listen *carefully* to questions from the press. Many times their questions won't appear in the printed or broadcast version, only your answer will. So, if there is a "bad" choice of words in the question, don't repeat it in the answer. Remember that the *real* audience is not the reporter, it's all those people out there. So keep your objectives in mind. Also, keep in mind that newspeople are always newspeople. That includes at the club, on an airplane, and *after* they say, "Hey, that was a great interview." Finally, remember that in order for something to be "off the record" or for "deep background purposes," you will have to make it clear *before* you make the statement.

Remembering all this while a microphone is thrust in your face can be quite a challenge. But perhaps these tips will help you tap dance through any media minefields you might encounter. Hopefully you will never face this type of grilling. Instead, you may be actively seeking media coverage to publicize your talk. Providing it's on a newsworthy subject, you may very well be able to get some press and possibly local TV coverage as well. Here's how:

- About two weeks before the talk, send a summary to news outlets. Be sure to include a "hook" that will get them (and their audiences) interested.
- Two days before, follow up with a phone contact.
- If anyone expresses interest but can't make it, try to arrange a separate interview—perhaps at breakfast or lunch.
- Print copies of your talk as a handout or a mailer.
- If your organization has a public relations department, ask their help.

With a little luck you may be able to multiply your exposure a thousand-fold or more.

CHAPTER ELEVEN

PC Graphics: An Aladdin's Lamp for Presenters

LOOKING BACK on the thousands of presentations I have sat through, the most forgettable were those marked by poor visuals. Particularly the typewritten viewgraphs that you couldn't read—or if you could, they were as dull as a public-television fundraiser. What better way to tell your audience you simply don't care about them!

True, most of us aren't artists and don't have access to one we can afford. But we can't get away with that excuse anymore. There's a professional art department right inside our personal computers.

More than 15 years have passed since the advent of the desktop computer, and at least 20 million American homes have PCs used in business functions. Close to three million PCs are being used for graphics. That's a threefold increase since 1984, when the first edition of this book was written.

If you're fortunate enough to already have a PC, you can do limited graphics for design and analysis. But the visuals have very low resolution. They look jagged and rough, and you probably wouldn't want to use them in an important presentation to your managers or customers. You need to import that data into a special presentation graphics program. With one of these software programs you'll be able to sharpen up your data and enhance it with clip art, 3-D effects, shadow areas, and other techniques that Lotus 1-2-3 and other data analysis programs can't match. Nothing else short of a professional artist at your disposal can give you the business quality (if not boardroom quality) that these programs provide.

If you don't have a PC, or access to one, I'm not suggesting that you should rush right out and buy one. You'll want to do a lot of reading first and some talking to PC owners. (This chapter will get you

Courtesy of Hewlett-Packard

A typical setup for producing computer graphics

started.) When you're ready to make your move, here's what you'll find: Within an hour you'll have your PC set up on your desk. Within another few hours you'll be able to pull down easy-to-understand on-screen menus, push the appropriate buttons, and watch your commands being carried out.

Lesson disks and workbooks contain sample figures and exercises that will give you keystroke-by-keystroke direction. Scads of training courses featuring small classes where everyone gets a computer to work at are available at community colleges, in many corporations, and at local computer stores.

Some of the things you will be able to do include:

- Word charts—Probably 70 percent of all visuals fall into this category, which includes bulleted lists printed in different fonts and perhaps drop shadows and clip art to customize.
- Data graphs—You can convert those large printouts that no one reads into exciting visuals that will impress your audience.

Courtesy of Hewlett-Packard

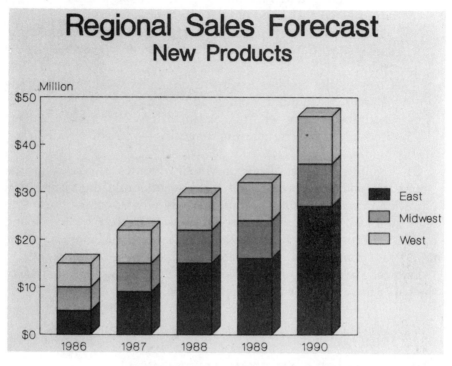

Courtesy of Computer Associates International, Inc.

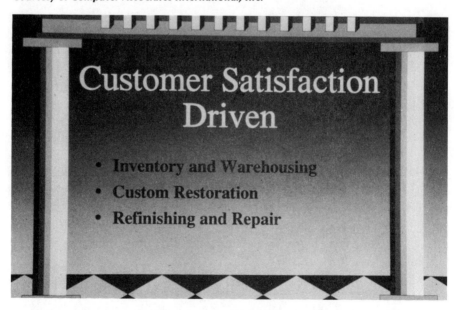

Typical visuals produced on a PC

Summarizing and illustrating important data is becoming a natural step at the end of every data processing run.

- Simple charts—Bar charts, pie charts, and other creations from spreadsheet data, with a title and, perhaps, a piece of clip art added.
- Complex charts—Three-dimensional effects with overlapping columns, freehand drawings, advanced color, "the works."
- Diagrams—Flow charts, organization charts, process or product cycles, engineering diagrams—you get the idea.

Once you design the visuals on your PC you can make them into overheads, slides, or prints. You can also integrate the visuals and narration into a script or handout. It's only when you see these systems in action that you can appreciate how easy they are to use and how much they can do for you. Not the least of their benefits will be to increase your visibility and credibility within your organization.

Let's take what I hope will be a very user-friendly look at some of the hardware and software involved.

WHAT YOU WILL NEED IN THE WAY OF A COMPUTER

The good news is you won't need a mainframe. The bad news is that the old Osborne that your Aunt Millie offered to bring you from her attic won't work either. But a lot of relatively inexpensive computers will. An IBM-PC or an IBM-compatible such as Compaq would be a nice place to start. And there are many others. Because of its standard graphical user interface, the Apple Macintosh produces excellent graphics and offers some advantages over the fundamentally text-oriented PC. Devotees of each are about equally divided. The Mac–PC debate is a raging controversy at one San Diego company I'm familiar with. The vice presidents and marketing troops prefer Macs, while most engineers use PCs. Strongpoints of each machine are:

Mac—Easy to learn. Consistent, intuitive interface. No 640K memory barrier.
PC—Power, speed, variety, lower cost, more peripheral choices.

Shortly before this book went to press the two moved closer together when Microsoft Corporation unveiled its nifty new Windows

3.0 software, bringing advantages of the Apple Macintosh to IBM compatible users.

We will cover both but, admittedly, lean toward the PC.

If you're thinking about buying a PC, the first thing to do is list all the things it will be used for. *Then go back over the list and rearrange it in the order of importance.* There's no sense paying for niceties you'll never use.

Before we move on to some nitty-gritty, just four thoughts:

1. Buying a computer is a lot like buying a boat. You can start with a dinghy and work your way up to another Trump Princess as your navigation skills and fortunes improve. In computers, upward mobility is driven by two factors: expansion and obsolescence.
2. Read up on the subject: a good overall book, such as *Computers Today* by Donald H. Sanders (McGraw-Hill, Inc., 1988), and the current issues of *PC Magazine, PC Week,* or *PC World.*
3. Talk to your friends who are users. People who know PCs are very eager to share their knowledge. But watch out. There are so many choices out there that even a computer scientist can get confused. Friendly advice can be subjective and sometimes misleading.
4. The folks in the showrooms can also be very helpful, but watch out for one who says, "Trust me." (Most personnel in PC stores are trustworthy, but most are also PC enthusiasts. Their standards are different from the first-time PC buyer's. You need to make sure you're getting a system that meets *your* needs, not a "neato-whizbang" setup that costs twice as much for functions you'll never use.)

HOW TO DECIPHER THE NUMBERS IN THE ADS

Have you been looking at computer ads in magazines and newspapers and understanding only the numbers that start with a $? Well, here's a little help.

If you see 80286 or 80386 (or merely 286 or 386), it refers to the microprocessor used in the system. The 286 is a 16-bit system. That is, it can handle 16 bits of data at a time. The 386 has a 32-bit microprocessor. The higher the bits, the greater the data transfer speed. Personal computers of the 1970s were only 8-bit systems. IBM introduced its revolutionary PC AT in 1984, with an 80286. Compaq introduced the first 386-based PC in 1986. You'll need a minimum of 286 to get going. The 386 chip is becoming the standard. Computers with 386 chips can also use virtual memory, which makes large-image storage and fast image manipulation possible.

A recent arrival, the 386SX chip, fits in as a "tweener" between the 286 and 386. It has 32-bit processing with 16-bit data paths, and because it performs better than the 286 and costs less than the 386, it's rapidly becoming the standard for home PCs. In the January 8, 1990 issue of *PC Week*, Jim Seymour discussed the rapid rate of change:

> The Intel 386 and 386SX chips will very soon become recognized as the baseline processors for office computers. The market for older 286 designs, despite a sales surge over the last year, will collapse like a punctured tire, as buyers realize they're investing in yesterday.[31]

And, now there's a data-intensive (but expensive) 80486 chip available.

The Apple Macintosh series uses chips from Motorola numbered 68000 (16 bits) and 68030 (32 bits).

Another number you'll see in the ads will have MHz or megahertz behind it. That's how many millions of times the processor will cycle between instruction and execution in one second. The faster it cycles, the faster you get your work done. (Theoretically at least; there are other factors, such as the number of left thumbs you possess.)

Dodge may build their trucks RAM-tough, but the RAM in the computer ads stands for Random Access Memory—the primary storage of your computer. It's a thousand times faster to access data in the primary storage of a computer than it is to go to a disk operation. (Even when you're counting in nanoseconds, time is money.) Systems can be expanded by plugging a board with additional RAM chips into a slot. That's what the ads are talking about when they say "expandable to . . . ." They're expandable up to the point where you run out of slots.

The software programs we will be discussing later call for RAM between 384K and 640K, although 512K is frequently recommended and in one case 1MB. Most programs recommend a hard disk drive and some require it. (Hard drives have better access speeds and more storage size than floppy disks. Graphics eat space.) Some programs will operate on DOS 2.0; others require 3.1 or later. (DOS, or Disk Operating System, is the software that controls the overall operation of the computer. You'll need to insert a DOS disk in order to "boot up" the system, or have DOS installed on the hard disk.) You must fit the program requirements to the machine.

The two most important elements for graphics are the video screen and the display card (adapter) that drives it.

The graphics adapter, which determines the quality of the graphics viewed on any microcomputer screen, is a board that you buy with your computer. It must work with your monitor. In general, five types are used. They're arranged on the list below to go from lowest to highest resolution (more dots). The more vertical and horizontal dots on the screen, the smoother the picture and the better approximation of what you will get when you move off screen and use an output device. You can get better resolution off screen than on, but you want to strive for WYSIWYG (What You See Is What You Get). Here are the types of cards:

- CGA (color graphics adapter)—An older, general-purpose adapter. Limited to two modes: 640×200 pixel two-color and 320×200 four-color. (A pixel, picture element, is an individual dot on the screen.) Usually used with standard color display (SCD).
- MCGA (multicolor graphics array)—An extension of the CGA. Two additional modes: 640×480 two-color and 320×200 256-color.
- EGA (enhanced graphics adapter)—Six modes. Can be used with enhanced color display to generate 640×350 16-color mode. Makes color displays palatable but is nearing obsolescence.
- VGA (video graphics array)—More resolution and more colors than the EGA. Provides all the modes of the others and a 640×480 16-color mode. Plus 256 colors at 320×200 resolution. (Notice that color and resolution are a tradeoff.) Makes color displays worth savoring.
- Super VGA—800×600 resolution. Most users won't see or use the difference.

For convenience, most displays are listed as monographic, CGA, EGA, or VGA—or by their pixel ratings. VGA is today's video driver of choice. It is the graphics standard in the world of IBM and IBM-compatible PCs.

Keep in mind that the type of video display used can limit the on-screen resolution of your adapter and vice versa. For example, a CGA provides a resolution of 640×200 pixels and can display 16 colors. Thus, it cannot display any of the modes that use more than 200 raster lines. However, Enhanced Color Displays (ECD) provide 640×350 pixels and can choose 16 displayable colors from a palette of 64.

Therefore, in shopping for displays it is important to find a good match of monitor, adapter, and software. The pictures you see will be limited by your weakest component. Using a higher resolution display or monitor with a basic CGA adapter would not buy you anything.

Analog displays such as those on the IBM Personal System/2 can vary the intensity in infinitesimal degrees so that more colors and subtler gradations can be displayed. The total palette of such displays contains more than 256,000 colors. For a guy like me who can't get his socks to match, that's pretty awesome.

Before Moving On . . .

The $64,000 question has always been, "Should I buy now or wait for the next major advancement (or better yet, a drop in prices)?" Weighing costs versus benefits, I would say, "Buy now." There's another question: Should you pay more for the latest and greatest, or shop the fire sales for equipment with one foot in the grave? The key to buying software and hardware is: Don't get stuck with an orphan! Sale items may soon be obsolete or nearly so, but there's no guarantee new technologies will catch on either. (Anybody out there want to buy a Beta VCR or videodisk player?) Play it safe! Buy new but established and accepted hardware and software.

Also, keep in mind that it's a good idea to buy your PC from a store that offers help with problems, not from some "warehouse" that offers low prices but no support. Otherwise you may find yourself driving your sick PC to the regional service center.

The bottom line for a serious home user today is that it may be suicidal to buy any machine that does not have a minimum of a 386SX chip, 640K RAM, 30MB hard disk, and a VGA color display. Furthermore, the machine should be expandable up to 4MB RAM and still have slots available for peripherals such as a modem, a printer, extra memory, and a mouse (a point and click device that positions the cursor on the screen and lets you draw and select options).

SOFTWARE—THE KEY INGREDIENT

The hardware we have been discussing so far (and will return to) refers to the mechanical, magnetic, electronic design, structure, and related devices of a computer system. Software is a generic term for the programs, data, and routines. Without minimizing the former, it's the latter that brings computer graphics to life.

Software products deliver word charting, drawing tools, clip-art libraries, hardcopies and projection visuals, and even monitor-based slide shows.

The world of graphics software has a number of continents and subcontinents. There are programs specifically designed for artists, and programs for engineers or scientists. Although there is some overlap, we will be concentrating on a third category—business graphics.

There are dozens of good business graphics packages to pick from. Chart-Master (along with its teammates, Diagram-Master and Sign-Master, in Ashton-Tate's Mastergraphics Presentation Pack) was an early leader. In October 1989, *PC Magazine* reviewed seven of the leaders and singled out Freelance Plus and Harvard Graphics for special mention.[32] A month later, *PC World* matched these two packages against two from the original comparison and three others and came to essentially the same conclusion.[33] The table on page 194 lists various PC graphics software programs and their requirements. Any of the manufacturers would be happy to provide more information on their products. Some offer self-running demo kits and sample outputs. Bear in mind that these were the programs available at the time of writing; suppliers you speak with may have information on more recent packages introduced after we went to press.

Macintosh has set the pace for graphics. For Mac users, Persuasion from Aldus is the clear winner. (Microsoft's PowerPoint; Cricket's trio of Draw, Graph, and Presents; and Symantec's More II rate honorable mentions.) Persuasion's system configuration calls for an Apple Macintosh Plus, SE, or II; a hard disk drive; and one 800K drive. A PC version of Persuasion is now available, and its many features make it worth a look.

Keep in mind that these comparisons have become a yearly special feature for most computer magazines and, given the way programs are developing, you'll want to check out the latest issues before putting your money down.

Los Angeles Times columnist Lawrence J. Magid cited William Coggshall, president of the market research firm Desktop Presentations, as stating that about 2.1 million desktop presentation programs have been sold for IBM and IBM-compatible computers while Macintosh users have bought about 500,000 programs.[34] Most software programs currently list at $495, but their street (or mail order) prices are considerably lower.

After loading your software, the steps in the process include:

- Entering the data (data import)
- Chart selection (format) and modification (editing)

PC GRAPHICS SOFTWARE AND REQUIREMENTS

Package	Manufacturer	Requirements
Applause II	Ashton-Tate Corp., 20101 Hamilton Ave., Torrance, CA 90509. (213) 329-8000; 1-(800) 437-4329.	512K RAM. DOS 2.0 or later. Two disk drives. Hard disk recommended.
CA-Cricket® Presents	Computer Associates International, Inc., 10505 Sorrento Valley Rd., San Diego, CA 92121.	640K RAM (1MB rec.). DOS 3.1 or later. Hard disk. IBM AT, PS/2, or compatible. Windows 2.1.1 or later. Window runtime is provided.
Gem Presentation Team	Digital Research, Inc., Box DRI, Monterey, CA 93942. (408) 649-3896; 1-(800) 443-4200.	384K, DOS 2.1 or later. Hard disk drive.
The Graphics Gallery Collection	Hewlett-Packard, 19091 Pruneridge, Cupertino, CA 95015. 1-(800) 752-0900.	384K RAM. Two floppy disks (at least one high density). 512K RAM and hard disk recommended. DOS 2.1 or later. CGA, EGA, VGA.
Graph Plus*	Micrografx, 1303 Arapaho, Richardson, TX 75081. (214) 234-1769; 1-(800) 272-3729.	512K RAM (640 rec.). DOS 3.0 or later. Hard disk and mouse recommended.
Harvard Graphics	Software Publ. Corp., Box 7210, Mountain View, CA 94039. (415) 335-2000.	512K RAM. DOS 2.0 or later. CGA, EGA, VGA, MCGA, or Hercules Graphic display. Two 3 1/2″ disk drives or hard disk.
Kinetic Words, Graphs & Art	Kinetic Presentations, Inc., 250 Distillery Commons, Louisville, KY 40206. (502) 583-1679.	512K RAM (640K rec.). DOS 2.1 or later. CGA, EGA, VGA or Hercules Graphic display. Hard disk. Digitizing tablet and mouse supported.
Lotus Freelance Plus	Lotus Development Corp., 55 Cambridge Pkwy., Cambridge, MA 02142. (617) 577-8500.	640K RAM. DOS 2.1 or later. Hard disk.
Perspective Junior*	Three D Graphics, 860 Via de la Paz, Pacific Palisades, CA 90272. (213) 459-7949.	640K RAM. DOS 2.0 or later.
SlideWrite Plus*	Advanced Graphics Software, Inc., 333 W. Maude #105, Sunnyvale, CA 94086. (408) 749-8620.	390K RAM. DOS 2.0 or later. Hard disk recommended.
35mm Express	Business and Professional Software, Inc., 143 Binney, Cambridge, MA 02142. (617) 491-3377; 1-(800) 342-5277.	256K RAM (512K rec.). DOS 2.0 or later. Two disk drives.

*Has features for scientific as well as business presentations.

- Type selection
- Adding art
- Enhancements
- Output.

Data entry or import involves taking all those numbers from the spreadsheets and feeding them into the graphics package. Fortunately you don't have to do it by hand. Data-driven charting allows you to generate charts directly from spreadsheets, data base files, and/or the keyboard. As you enter your data, charts develop almost automatically. As a matter of fact, some programs use "hot linking" so that any change made to an underlying spreadsheet updates the chart automatically.

Now you're ready for *chart selection*. What will it be? A bar, pie, or line chart? Or a mixed bar/line? Perhaps a scatterplot to show the correlation between different distributions. Once you pick the type of chart that best suits your needs, your software package will pick the title, typeface, colors, and so on, and will autoscale the X and Y axes.

Most people don't really want to design their own charts, they just want to get charts. That's where style sheets and templates come in: They let you see the finished chart (either in documentation or on the screen, or both) as it will appear rather than make you pick and choose all the attributes. For example, you type in the title on the line that says TITLE. Then you select, for example, Helvetica font, 24 point type, and drop shadows. Press ENTER and *bingo*!

How does it look? Do you want to *edit* your chart? Although graphics software automatically selects pleasing colors for each bar, line, and background, to fit within the palette you've selected and to blend well with its surroundings, you can override these decisions if you wish. Also, are any areas too crowded; is there any overwriting; do you want to delete some of the detail?

Text can be entered line-by-line with dedicated attributes such as size, color, justification, typeface (font), boldface, or italics available for each line. The ugly lettering produced by first-generation PCs has been replaced by improved fonts that rival those done by graphics designers. Typefaces include serif, sans serif, and outline fonts that you can size, rotate, reflect, and fill with color and patterns. (You can also buy extra fonts.)

Again, you don't have to be a computer whiz. Almost all commands are visual. You can create by looking and doing; there's no need for reading and memorizing. You can choose picture elements from a menu (programmed choices) or you can draw freehand. Text can be added anywhere you like by positioning your cursor and typing.

In a menu-driven system, text is entered in the word screen and charts are generated on the chart screen. You bring the two together in the picture screen and then enhance the image with drawing tools. Menu-based interfaces are so simple and intuitive that you can become a confident user in a matter of a few hours. The menus guide you through the steps of drawing, rotating, duplicating, and resizing.

Although they are not generally used for word processing or spreadsheets, a mouse, trackball, or other pointing tool is essential for drawing freehand pictures and using pull-down menus on the personal computer.

You can enhance your visuals by adding color, texture, or depth. You might want to enhance a pie chart by making the outside rim a tire (if that's your business) or a bottle cap (if you're in the beverage industry). A few weeks of reading *USA Today* should give you plenty of ideas for this technique.

But Why Reinvent the Wheel?

Symbol libraries in your software program have built-in generic artwork available at the touch of a key. These libraries contain hundreds of graphic aids, signs, icons, pictorials, and applications. And if they're not enough, you can extend this capability with one or more of the separate clip-art packages on the market.

Clip art has been around for years. Its name derives from the practice of thumbing through volumes until the right illustration was found and then clipping it out with a scissors. Now all that is done electronically. But, despite the new ease of retrieval, most of the old drawbacks are still there. Its worst feature is that clip art is usually instantly recognized for what it is—not original. Secondly, some of it is just too "cute." (Watch out for cartoons; you don't want your presentation to look like the Sunday funnies.) However, both these drawbacks can be overcome. As Robin Raskin, contributing editor of *PC Magazine*, pointed out:

> From business presentations to desktop publishing, clip-art images can be a lifesaver for those who lack the time, money, or talent to create custom artwork. Like canned soup, canned art all by itself can be pretty bland. But when blended with a smidgen of design sense and spiced up with other software ingredients, it can be transformed into an appetizing recipe.[35]

Let's say you're in the highway construction industry and you're giving a presentation on the effect of trucks on road surfaces. No doubt your symbol library will have a picture of a truck. Also, let's say you're talking about trucks on highways in Iowa. Find the outline map of the state, superimpose the truck and the map, and you've got a nice piece of interesting art for your title visual or to liven up a word chart. For another word chart you might select clip art of a person standing at a blackboard, pointing to the message area. Put your list on the blackboard, using it and the person with the pointer as an attractive, interesting border. Finally, you might want to liven up your bar charts by substituting clip art for the bars (comparing freight trains of different lengths, or buildings of different heights, or stacks of dollars).

Check *PC Magazine* or similar publications for their most recent reviews and analyses of the leading clip-art packages. They frequently pick winners based on various criteria.

Image scanners (digitizers) that convert art, photos, or text into a digitized map of "on" and "off" pixels, can be used to encode images directly off of a printed page; you can then position, size, flip, or edit them. At the 1989 International Technical Communications Conference I watched an IBM sales representative take a snapshot of his young daughter from his wallet, run a scanner over it, bring it up on the screen—and then proceed to correct her chipped front tooth by flopping the one next to it into position and copying it. I'm sure he wished her trip to the orthodontist had been that easy.

Sound wonderful? It is. But, when using a scanner, watch out for copyright problems. You may (or may not) get by with sneaking a piece of published art or a photograph into an ad hoc internal presentation, but using one in a talk that's going to reach the outside world could put you in serious trouble.

FINALLY, PAYDIRT!!!

Now that we've designed your visuals we can talk about various output devices. These include dot matrix and laser printers, pen plotters, color copiers, cameras, film recorders, slide service bureaus, and electronic presentations. You can output your designs to paper, film (or transparencies), or a high-resolution video screen. More importantly, they can have much greater resolution than an EGA or VGA, and can supply the crisp, clean, business-level quality you and your audience are looking for. Depending on your output device, you can produce your work in color, black and white, or shades of gray.

Most PC owners are reluctant to spend more than 50 percent of the price of their PC on any peripheral. In that price range, you'll probably have trouble finding much in the way of output devices. Most people I know who have their own PCs design their visuals at home and produce them at work. If work and home are one and the same, you'll need to do some tradeoffs. High image quality on the hard copy—not on the monitor—is your goal. You might consider buying a monitor with low to medium resolution and spending the money you save on a better plotter or film recorder.

Regardless of whether you plan to use your own output device or one available at work or at some other location, here's a quick look at what's available.

Dot-Matrix and Laser Printers

Dot-matrix printers have significantly increased the resolution of their graphics output in the past few years. However, they are still mainly used for producing review copies rather than finished art because of their jagged lines and arcs.

Laser printers make presentation-quality graphics feasible because of their speed and higher resolution. The Hewlett-Packard (HP) LaserJet Series gives you 300 dots per inch, 14 fonts, and four pages per minute. It also supports an optional PostScript cartridge with scalable typefaces. A sample output for an overhead is shown on page 199.

PostScript is a device-independent page-description language. Essentially, a graphics software package sends PostScript code to a PostScript printer. PostScript-compatible printers print a page description of a scalable vector language and not a series of dots (bitmaps). Thus, they are very important for graphics users. One of the favorites is the Apple LaserWriter II.

If the built-in type fonts in your laser printer aren't adequate for your needs, you can invest in a cartridge that will boost its capabilities. Pacific Data Products and IQ Engineering offer cartridges for the popular HP LaserJet.

Most software will automatically convert a color graphic to a black and white so that it can be output to a dot matrix or laser printer for producing black-and-white handouts or transparencies. The best software will do shading instead of just crosshatched patterns.

Courtesy of Hewlett-Packard

The Market Center Marketplace
1st Half 1989

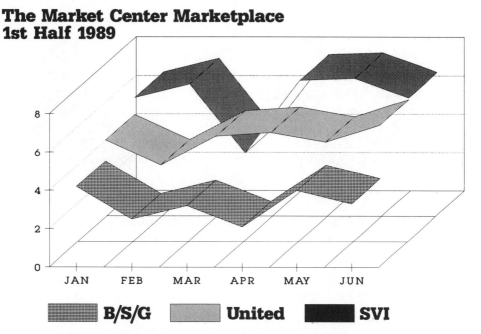

Overhead created using Harvard Graphics and Aldus Page Maker 3.0.
Mastered on the HP LaserJet IIP printer using fonts from Harvard Graphics
and the HP Persuasive Presentation font cartridge.

Pen Plotters

Pen plotters will enable you to produce color overheads which, if
they are not up to boardroom standards, are certainly better than
many I've seen used in business presentations. Results are far superior to those possible on a dot-matrix printer. (See page 200 for a
comparison.) However, pen plotters have a limited number of colors,
they can smear, and they require babysitting to ensure that nothing
goes wrong.

Pen plotters cannot output bitmap graphics like clip art or scanned
images.

Plotters such as those from Hewlett-Packard shown on page 201
are widely used to produce color transparencies generated on PCs.
They feature exceptional repeatability (returning precisely to a given
point so that lines will meet exactly) and will fit on a desktop.

Since overhead transparencies outnumber slides by about three to
one, a pen plotter may be just what you need—particularly if you
don't plan to get too artistic (i.e., three-dimensional).

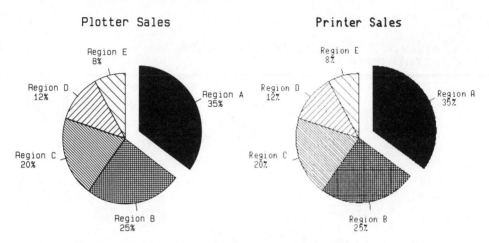

Comparison of visuals from Pen Plotter and Dot-Matrix Printer. (Note: original/actual plotter visual was in five colors.)

Inkjet Printers

Some printers use nozzles to shoot color inks at the paper or transparency. (The process is called thermal inkjet drop-on-demand printing.) Microthermal resistors regulate ink flow to within one drop per $1/25,000$ of a second. Depending on your software's use of color, you can get thousands of shades and hues. Depending on the power of your computer, you can get a full page of color graphics in about four minutes. Hewlett-Packard has two entries in this market, the HP PaintJet ($1,395 list) and the high-volume HP PaintJet XL (at $2,495). QMS ColorScript 100 is another. These wonderful machines are great on both overheads and paper.

Film Recorders

Film recorders consist of a camera and high-resolution monitor built into a separate module that connects to your computer. They allow fairly rapid production of 35mm slides.

Just as a pen plotter draws on paper with ink, film recorders draw on film with light. But instead of getting four colors you can get thousands. However, their price tags place film recorders beyond the reach of most individual users. Only a fairly large organization that

HP ColorPro 7440A. Eight-Pen Plotter from Hewlett-Packard. (HP's slightly upscale 7475A model was cited as *PC Magazine's* "Plotter of the Year" in 1984, 1985, 1986, and 1987, and received *Mac World* magazine's award in 1985, 1986, 1987, and 1988.) The HP 7550A is the top of the line.

needs its slides in a hurry or has to keep them confidential will be able to justify the cost. But don't give up hope, there are more reasonable alternatives.

Slide-making service bureaus such as MAGIcorp are the "Fotomats" of the graphics industry and then some. They use digital film recorders to create very-high-resolution slides in thousands of colors. You can transfer your graphics files to them electronically through a modem, or on diskette using a messenger service, and get finished slides or other presentation media back through an overnight delivery system—for only $8 to $15 per slide. (Prices are lower if you can wait another day.)

Still not confidential enough or fast enough?

The Polaroid desktop PalettePlus can turn any image generated on your computer screen into a slide, overhead transparency (small format: $3^1/4'' \times 4^1/4''$), or print—in two to four minutes! Unlike earlier cameras that mounted directly on the tube face of your PC, PalettePlus memorizes the image electronically and actually can enhance it with a higher degree of resolution. You can also paint your graphics from 72 colors—even with a monochrome monitor. Cost is around $3,000 and includes an image recorder, camera backs, software, processor, slide mounter, and owner's manual.

If that's still too steep, here's your last chance!

The simplest and most economical tool for preparing color slides consists of a 35mm camera attached to a lightproof cone that is pressed against the screen. Results may be adequate where content of the visual and speed of production will outweigh its lower quality.

Electronic Presentations—The Wave of the Future?

In addition to slides and overheads, you can use your PC as a "projector." Called on-screen slide shows, desktop presentations, or (more correctly) electronic presentations, the charts you create are presented directly on a monitor screen, bypassing the need for slides or overheads. Last-minute changes are a snap. Production costs are zilch because the disk itself is the media. Transitions between visuals are built into the graphics software and include smooth fades, dissolves, wipes, and venetian blinds. (Don't overdo the last two—and, completely forget about waterfalls and spirals.)

For a single-viewer sales presentation you can use a laptop; for small groups, a normal PC and monitor. For larger audiences you can use a data projection system that plugs into a PC. Three guns (red, green, and blue) take the computer image and project it onto a large screen. Color and resolution are good, but the equipment is very expensive (it can be rented), nonportable, and finicky. However, watch for this technique to take a big bite out of slides and overheads in the next five years.

Another way to use your PC or Macintosh in a presentation is to project its images using an LCD (liquid crystal display) similar to that used in a laptop computer. Here, an LCD device such as the Sayett DATASHOW® is placed on the overhead projector where you would normally place the transparency. As you press keys on your computer or remote control, data and graphics (and changes) are presented in real time. This setup can be extremely effective in projecting text and numerical values during strategic planning sessions and other interactive decision-making processes where the group assigns weighted values to various alternatives and the computer shows possible results.

Wait, There's More—Animation

There's one more very interesting thing electronic presentations can do: they can team up with your software to produce animation.

Having come this far, it's a relatively short jump to animating your images. The first time I saw this was in 1985 when a friend used his personal computer to put together a program where his word charts were all progressive disclosures, his curves drew themselves, animated figures marched across the screen, and he had sound effects. He did it largely for his own amusement, but his company thought it was so good they used it in a trade show exhibit. That's not surprising; if graphics make a presentation strong, animation can make it even stronger.

A FINAL WORD

Today's PC-based systems excel at presentations that are relatively short and uncomplicated. They are not generally used in large production environments where greater graphics flexibility and access to high-resolution devices are required. Here, engineering or high-end graphic workstations are still the rule. However, the gap is narrowing rapidly, and in some cases has already begun to overlap.

As to the future, it will already be here by the time you read this. Such is the dynamic nature of the field. Two things are certain: It is and will continue to be exciting. And, you will soon be able to do all these things without the red warning light coming on in your wallet— at least not permanently.

Good luck!

Notes

1. Lee Iacocca, *Iacocca: An Autobiography* (New York: Bantam Books). Copyright © 1984 by Lee Iacocca. Reprinted by permission of the author.

2. "A Public Fear," *Health Journal*, Fall 1989, p. 12.

3. William S. Tacey, *Business and Professional Speaking*, second ed. (Dubuque: William C. Brown Co., 1975), p. 102.

4. George Plimpton, "How to Make a Speech," *Power of the Printed Word Series*, International Paper Co.

5. J. Lewis Powell, *Executive Speaking—An Acquired Skill*, revised ed. (Washington, D.C.: The Bureau of National Affairs, Inc., 1980), p. 28.

6. Abridged excerpt from Chapter 17 "To Be Exact" in *How to Write, Speak, and Think More Effectively* by Rudolf Flesch. Copyright © 1946, 1949, 1951, 1958, 1960 by Rudolf Flesch. Reprinted by permission of Harper & Row, Publishers, Inc.

7. Bob Bly, "Plotting Your Course—Storyboarding Your Slide Presentations," *Audio Visual Directions*, October/November, 1981.

8. Courtesy of Dale Carnegie and Associates, Inc.

9. Powell, op. cit., p. 58.

10. Roger E. Axtell, "Interpreters: Avoiding Foot-In-Mouth Disease," *Meetings and Conventions*, January, 1989, p. 177 Copyright © 1989 by Reed Travel Group.

11. Lynne Cheney, "And You, Sir, Have All the Characteristics of a Dog—Except Loyalty." Reprinted with permission from *The Washingtonian*, October, 1984, p. 111.

12. "Looking for the 'Capo d'Astro Bar,'" *Business Marketing*, April, 1989. Copyright © 1989 by Crain Communications, Inc.

13. Peter R. Schleger, "Coping With the Script Review Process," *Training and Development*, May, 1986, p. 87. Copyright © 1986 by the American Society for Training and Development. Reprinted with permission. All rights reserved.

14. Schleger, *op. cit.*

15. Reprinted with permission of Dr. Jerry Tarver, from "Speechwriter's Letter."

16. From *In Search of Excellence: Lessons from America's Best-Run Companies* by Thomas J. Peters and Robert H. Waterman, Jr., p. xviii. Copyright © 1982 by Thomas J. Peters and Robert Waterman, Jr. Reprinted by permission of Harper & Row, Publishers, Inc.

17. Russ Johnston, *The Marplex Digest*, April, 1983.

18. Anthony Jay, *The New Oratory* (New York: American Management Association, Inc., 1971), p. 78. Printed by kind permission of Curtis Brown on behalf of Anthony Jay © 1970.

19. Ibid., p. 79.

20. Specified excerpt (p. xx) from *In Search of Excellence: Lessons from America's Best-Run Companies* by Thomas J. Peters and Robert H. Waterman, Jr. Copyright © 1982 by Thomas J. Peters and Robert Waterman, Jr. Reprinted by permission of Harper & Row, Publishers, Inc.

21. Based on "The Making of An Awesome Speaker" by Peter Johnson, *NSA-Speakout*, January, 1989.

22. Peter Prichard, *The Making of McPaper*, (New York: Andrews, McMeel & Parker, 1987).

23. Sandra C. Browne and Thomas N. Huckin, "Four Problems in Spoken English for Non-native Technical Professionals," *Proceedings of the 32nd International Technical Communication Conference*, 1985, p. RET-73.

24. "How to Wow 'Em When You Speak," *Changing Times*, August, 1988, p. 29. Reprinted with permission from *Changing Times* Magazine. Copyright © by Kiplinger Washington Editors, Inc., August 1988.

25. Used with permission of Jack Franchetti Communications, Inc., 12 Parkwoods Road, Manhasset, NY 11030.

26. Eve Zibart, "Psyching Up; Contortions, Potions and Meditations—How the Stars Get Ready for the Show," *The Washington Post*, August 5, 1979.

27. Used with permission of John Nathan, 535 Boylston St., Boston, MA.

28. Letitia Baldrige, *Letitia Baldrige's Complete Guide to Executive Manners*, p. 194. Reprinted with permission of Rawson Associates, an imprint of Macmillan Publishing Company. Copyright © 1985 by Letitia Baldrige.

29. Foster & Green, Inc. Newsletter, December, 1982.

30. Used with permission. Copyright © 1980, Jack Hilton.

31. Jim Seymour, "Don't Underestimate the Rate of Change in the '90s," *PC Week*, January 8, 1990, p. 11. Copyright © 1990, Ziff Communications Company.

32. Robin Raskin, "Presentations Graphics: The Packages Behind the Presentations," *PC Magazine*, October 1989, p. 95.

33. Richard Jantz and Michael Smith-Heimer, "Polished Presentations," *PC World*, November, 1989, p. 116.

34. Lawrence J. Magid, "Interest in Desktop Presentations Spurs Sales of Software," October 9, 1989; Copyright © 1989 by Lawrence J. Magid, p. 21.

35. Robin Raskin, "PC-based Clip Art: Instant Images," *PC Magazine*, October 17, 1989, Copyright © 1989, Ziff Communications Company, p. 149.

Resources

The following is a list of references and resources cited throughout this book. (Copyrighted material used with permission.)

Books

Baldrige, Letitia. *Letitia Baldrige's Complete Guide to Executive Manners.* New York: Macmillan Publishing Company, Rawson Associates, 1985.

Flesch, Rudolf. *How to Write, Speak, and Think More Effectively.* New York: Harper & Row, 1960; New American Library, Signet Books, 1964 (T2346).

Guth, Chester K. and Stanley S. Shaw. *How to Put on Dynamic Meetings.* Reston, VA: Reston Publishing, 1980. (Available from School Annual Publishing Co., Coshocton, OH 43812.)

Iacocca, Lee. *Iacocca: An Autobiography.* New York: Bantam Books, 1984.

Jay, Anthony. *The New Oratory.* New York: American Management Association, Inc., 1971.

Kemp, Jerrold E. *Planning and Producing Audiovisual Materials.* New York: Thomas Y. Crowell, 1975.

Molloy, John T. *Dress for Success.* New York: Peter H. Wyden, 1975.

———. *The Woman's Dress for Success Book.* New York: Follett, 1977.

Peters, Thomas J. and Robert H. Waterman, Jr. *In Search of Excellence — Lessons from America's Best-Run Companies.* New York: Harper & Row, 1982.

Powell, J. Lewis. *Executive Speaking — An Acquired Skill,* revised edition. Washington, D.C.: The Bureau of National Affairs, Inc., 1980.

Prichard, Peter. *The Making of McPaper,* New York: Andrews, McMeel & Parker, 1987.

Tacey, William S. *Business and Professional Speaking,* second edition. Dubuque: William C. Brown Co., 1975.

Articles

"A Public Fear," *Health Journal,* Fall, 1989.

Axtell, Roger E. "Interpreters: Avoiding Foot-in-Mouth Disease," *Meetings and Conventions,* January, 1989.

Bly, Bob. "Plotting Your Course—Storyboarding Your Slide Presentations." *Audio Visual Directions,* October/November, 1981.

Bombeck, Erma. "Anxiety Over Speaking." *The Evening Capital,* July 11, 1983.

Browne, Sandra C., and Huckin, Thomas N. "Four Problems in Spoken English for Non-native Technical Professionals," *Proceedings of the 32nd International Technical Communication Conference,* 1985.

Cheney, Lynne. "And You, Sir, Have All the Characteristics of a Dog— Except Loyalty." *The Washingtonian,* October, 1984.

Finkel, Coleman. "Meeting Clinic." *Successful Meetings,* January, 1978. (Bill Communications, Inc.)

Foster & Green, Inc. Newsletter, 16 E. Chase St., Baltimore, MD 21202, December, 1982.

"How to Wow 'Em When You Speak," *Changing Times,* August, 1988.

Jantz, Richard, and Smith-Heimer, Michael. "Polished Presentations," *PC World,* November, 1989.

Johnson, Peter. "The Making of An Awesome Speaker," *NSA-Speakout,* January, 1989.

"Looking for the Capo d'Astro Bar," *Business Marketing,* April, 1989.

Magid, Lawrence J. "Interest in Desktop Presentations Spurs Sales of Software," *Washington Post,* October 9, 1989.

The Marplex Digest, Marplex, Inc., Chagrin Falls, OH 44022, April, 1983.

Plimpton, George. "How to Make A Speech." *Power of the Printed Word Series,* International Paper Co., Box 954, Madison Square Station, New York, NY 10010.

Raskin, Robin. "Presentations Graphics: The Packages Behind the Presentations," *PC Magazine,* October, 1989.

Raskin, Robin. "PC-based Clip Art: Instant Images," *PC Magazine,* October 17, 1989.

Schleger, Peter R. "Coping With the Script Review Process," *Training and Development,* May, 1986.

Seymour, Jim. "Don't Underestimate the Rate of Change in the '90s," *PC Week,* January 8, 1990.

Tarver, Dr. Jerry. "Speechwriter's Letter." Box 444, The University of Richmond, Richmond, VA 23173.

Zibart, Eve. "Psyching Up; Contortions, Potions and Meditations—How the Stars Get Ready for the Show." *The Washington Post,* August 5, 1979.

Consulting Organizations

Jack Franchetti Communications, Inc., 12 Parkwoods Road, Manhasset, NY 10030.

Jack Hilton, Inc., 60 E. 42nd St., New York, NY 10165.

National Conference Centers, Coleman Finkel, President, East Windsor, NJ 08520.

Organizational Renewal, Inc., Dr. Gordon Lippitt, 5605 Lamar Rd., Bethesda, MD 20816.

Reddy Communications, Inc. and the RCI Consulting Group, 537 Steamboat Rd., P.O. Box 1310, Greenwich, CT 06830.

W.R. Sears & Co., Management Consultants, Bill Sears, President, 3187 Greenoak Ct., San Mateo, CA 94403.

Team International, Inc., Dr. Herb True, 1717 E. Colfax, South Bend, IN 46617.

A-V Suppliers

Audio Visual Division/3M, 3M Center, St. Paul, MN 55144. The leading marketer of overhead projectors and transparency film. Lettering Systems. Overhead supplies. Screens. Presentation furniture.

Cinegraph Slides, Inc., 11642 Knott Ave., Bldg. #14, Garden Grove, CA 92641. Custom-made original slides for business presentations. The customer writes copy, they do everything else. Catalog available.

Dynamic Graphics, Inc., 6000 N. Forest Park Dr., Peoria, IL 61614-3592. Publishes camera-ready artwork of exceptional quality, including: the Clipper Creative Art Service; Print Media Service; specially themed art packages.

Eastman Kodak Co., Dept. 454, 343 State St., Rochester, NY 14651. Film and Projectors. Publishes numerous how-to booklets.

Genigraphics Corp., Box 591, Liverpool, NY 13088. Computer graphics.

Oravisual Co., Inc., Box 11150, St. Petersburg, FL 33733. Meeting equipment and training aids. Portable and wall-mounted easels. Lecterns. Sound system accessories.

Schwan-STABILO USA, Inc., P.O. Box 2193, 435 Dividend Dr., Peachtree City, GA 30269. Overhead projection kits.

Scott Graphics Inc./Scott Paper, Holyoke, MA 01040. Overhead supplies.

Variatronic Systems, Inc., 300 Interchange Tower, 600 South Highway 169, Minneapolis, Minnesota 55426. (800)637-5461. Poster-Printer enlarges $8\,^1/_2 \times 11$-inch images to 23×33 inches for use as charts or bulletin board posters.

Visual Horizons, "The Audio Visual Department Store," 180 Metro Park, Rochester, NY 14618. Stock and custom slides. Slide mounts, slide files, and light tables. Slide duplicating. Slides made from your PC and modem. Overhead supplies. A-V furniture.

Xerox Reproduction Centers, Xerox Square 862, Rochester, NY 14644.

Computer Graphics

Aldus Corporation, 411 First Avenue South, Suite 2000, Seattle, WA 98104. *Persuasion* software for Macintosh computers.

Hewlett-Packard Co., Box 10301, Palo Alto, CA 94303-0890. Computers, printers, pen plotters, etc.

IQ Engineering, 685 N. Pastoria, Sunnyvale, CA 94086. (408)733-1161 or (800)765-FONT. Cartridges to increase the capabilities of a laser printer.

MAGIcorp, 50 Executive Blvd., Elmsford, NY 10523. (800)FOR-MAGI; (914)592-1244. Slide service bureau.

Pacific Data Products, 9125 Rehco Road, San Diego, CA 92121. (619)552-0880. Cartridges to increase the capabilities of a laser printer.

Polaroid Corporation, Presentation Products Dept., 575 Technology Square-3P, Cambridge, MA 02139. (800)343-5000. PalettePlus electronic imaging for slides, overheads, and prints.

Sayett Technology, Inc., 100 Kings Highway, Suite 1800, Rochester, NY 14617. (716)342-0700. DATASHOW Liquid Crystal Display for overheads.

Other

Dale Carnegie and Associates, Inc., 1475 Franklin Ave., Garden City, NY 11530.

SALLY FORTH by Greg Howard © 1983 Field Enterprises, Inc. Courtesy of Field Newspaper Syndicate.

"Orben's Current Comedy," The Comedy Center, 700 Orange St., Wilmington, DE 19801.

Toastmasters' International, 2200 N. Grand Ave., P.O. Box 10400, Santa Ana, CA 92711.

Suggested Reading

Adams, Corinne. *English Speech Rhythm and the Foreign Learner.* The Hague: Mouton Publishers, 1979.

Angel, Ian. *Advanced Graphics with the IBM Personal Computer.* New York: John Wiley & Sons, 1986.

Barnes, Gregory A. *Communication Skills for the Foreign-Born Professional.* Philadelphia: ISI Press, 1982.

Bland, Michael. *The Executive's Guide to TV and Radio Appearances.* New York: Van Nostrand Reinhold, 1980.

Braude, Jacob M. *Braude's Treasury of Wit and Humor.* Englewood Cliffs, NJ: Prentice-Hall, 1964.

———. *Speaker's Desk Book of Quips, Quotes, and Anecdotes.* Englewood Cliffs, NJ: Prentice-Hall, 1963.

Carnegie, Dale. *The Quick and Easy Way to Effective Speaking.* Garden City, NY: Dale Carnegie and Associates, 1962.

Carnes, William T. *Effective Meetings for Busy People.* New York: McGraw-Hill, 1980.

Davidoff, Henry, editor. *The Pocket Book of Quotations.* New York: Pocket Books, 1952.

Fechtner, Leopold. *5,000 One and Two Liners for Any and Every Occasion.* West Nyack, NY: Parker Publishing, 1973.

Flesch, Rudolf. *How to Write, Speak, and Think More Effectively.* New York: Harper & Row, 1960.

Hilton, Jack and Mary Knoblauch. *On Television! A Survival Guide for Media Interviews.* New York: AMACOM, 1980.

Hodnett, Edward. *Effective Presentations: How to Present Facts, Figures, and Ideas Successfully.* West Nyack, NY: Parker Publishing, 1967.

Howard, Vernon. *Talking to an Audience.* New York: Sterling Publishing, 1963.

Howell, William S. and Ernest G. Borman. *Presentational Speaking for Business and the Professions.* New York: Harper & Row, 1971.

Huckin, Thomas N., and Leslie A. Olsen. *English for Science and Technology: A Handbook for Nonnative Speakers.* New York: McGraw-Hill, 1983.

Jay, Anthony. *The New Oratory.* New York: American Management Association, 1971.

Kelley, Joseph J., Jr. *Speechwriting: A Handbook for All Occasions.* New York: New American Library, 1980.

Kemp, Jerrold E. *Planning and Producing Audiovisual Materials.* New York: Thomas Y. Crowell, 1975.

Kenny, Michael. *Presenting Yourself.* New York: John Wiley & Sons, 1982.

Kenny, Peter. *A Handbook of Public Speaking for Scientists & Engineers.* Bristol, England: Adam Hilger Ltd., 1982.

Larson, Orvin. *When It's Your Turn to Speak.* New York: Harper & Row, 1971.

Lieberman, Gerald F. *3,500 Good Jokes for Speakers.* New York: Dolphin Books, 1975.

Linkletter, Art. *Public Speaking for Private People.* Indianapolis: Bobbs-Merrill, 1980.

Lobingier, John L., Jr. *Business Meetings That Make Business.* London: Collier-Macmillan, 1969.

McFarland, Kenneth. *Eloquence in Public Speaking—How to Set Your Words on Fire.* Englewood Cliffs, NJ: Prentice-Hall, 1961.

Mambert, W.A. *Presenting Technical Ideas.* New York: John Wiley & Sons, 1968.

Molloy, John T. *Dress for Success.* New York: Peter H. Wyden, 1975.

———. *The Woman's Dress for Success Book.* New York: Follett, 1977.

Morrisey, George L. *Effective Business and Technical Presentations.* Reading, MA: Addison-Wesley, 1975.

Olmstead, Joseph A. *Small-Group Instruction: Theory and Practice.* Alexandria, VA: Human Resources Organization, 1974.

Oskamp, Stuart. *Attitudes and Opinions.* Englewood Cliffs, NJ: Prentice-Hall, 1977.

Powell, J. Lewis. *Executive Speaking, An Acquired Skill,* revised edition. Washington, D.C.: The Bureau of National Affairs, Inc. 1980.

Rodgers, Natalie H. *Talk Power.* New York: Dodd, Mead & Co., 1982.

Roylance, William H. *I Shoulda Said . . . A Treasury of Insults, Put-Downs, Boasts, Praises, Witticisms, Wisecracks, Comebacks, and Ad-Libs.* West Nyack, NY: Parker Publishing, 1973.

Samovar, Larry A. And Jack Mills. *Oral Communication—Message and Response.* Dubuque, IA: William C. Brown, 1980.

Sanders, Donald H. *Computers Today.* New York: McGraw-Hill, 1988.

Seldes, George, compiler. *The Great Quotations.* New York: Pocket Books, 1967.

Simmons, S.H. *How To Be the Life of the Podium.* New York: AMACOM, 1982.

Spinrad, Leonard and Thelma. *Speaker's Lifetime Library.* West Nyack, NY: Parker Publishing, 1979.

Sutherland, James, editor. *The Oxford Book of Literary Anecdotes.* New York: Pocket Books, 1975.

Swrydenko, Nicholas and Harvey Wasserman, editors. *The Book of Facts.* New York: Dell Publishing, 1979.

Tacey, William S. *Business and Professional Speaking.* Dubuque, IA: William C. Brown, 1975.

Tarver, Dr. Jerry. *Professional Speech Writing.* Richmond, VA: The Effective Speech Writing Institute, 1982.

Thrash, Artie Adams, Annette N. Shelby, and Jerry L. Tarver. *Speaking Up Successfully.* New York: CBS College Publishing, 1984.

Tufte, Edward R. *The Visual Display of Quantitative Information.* Cheshire, CT: Graphics Press, 1983.

Walter, Otis M. and Robert L. Scott. *Thinking and Speaking.* New York: Macmillan, 1979.

Weiss, Harold and J.B. McGrath, Jr. *Technically Speaking.* New York: McGraw-Hill, 1963.

Williams, William G. *Money-Making Meetings.* Annapolis, MD: Share Publishing, 1982.

Index

Adversary confrontations, 181
Animation, computer, 203
Answers, stock phrases, 174
Anxiety, 1, 151
Appearance, 115, 156
Art, three-dimensional, 70
Audience
    captive, 32
    comfort, 133
    interests and concerns, 14
    participation, 42, 92
    retention, 58, 158
    what you want from, 32
Autotrain, 100

Bar charts, 66–67
Benchley, Robert, 32
Benefits, 4, 99
Block diagrams, 66
Body language, 175
Boredom, 158
Bush, George, 34
Butterflies, 3, 151

Canned presentations, 85, 109
Carnegie, Dale, 37, 89
Cartoons, 70
Chalkboards, 62
Charisma, 86
Charts, 62, 117
Classroom seating, 134–135
Clip-art programs, 196
Clothes, 115
Color, 69

Computer graphics, 81, 185
Confidence level, 102, 174
Consistency, 71
Conversational style, 34
Cost, 92, 99
Curves, 66–67
Customers, assessing needs, 87

Data, analyzing value, 22
Demonstrations, 94–95
Developing talk, 32
Diplomacy, 96
Distractions, 159–161
Dress, 115
Dress rehearsal, 115
Dry run, 105, 113

Editing narration, 50
Electronic presentations, 202
Enthusiasm, 156
Evaluation form, 128
Excursions, 159
Extemporaneous talks, 107, 111
Eye contact, 5, 91, 123, 174

Fear of speaking, 1–3, 151
Federal Express, 100
Figures of speech, 38
Film recorders, 200
Finish, 54, 167
Flexibility, 92
Flip charts, 62, 80, 165
Food and drink, 145
Foreign-born speakers, 114

Gestures, 121–123
Gimmicks, 42

Hands, 121, 156
Harrison, William Henry, 18
Hecklers, 161
Help, where to find it, 19
Horizontal formats, 77
Hostile audiences, 177

Iacocoa, Lee, 2
Ideas, capturing, 20
Impromptu presentations, 107, 111
Index cards, 20, 27
Interruptions, 159
Introductions, 35, 151

Jokes, 39

Kemp, Jack, 54
Kennedy, John F., 51
King, Dr. Martin Luther, 26

Lalophobia, 2
Laser printers, 49, 198
Length of talk, 17
Lighting, 141, 163
Lincoln, Abraham, 6, 40, 86
Lists and tables, 61
Liquid crystal displays, 202

Management approval, 52
Maps, 17, 64, 197
Materials checklist, 146–149
Meeting rooms, 16, 134
Memorable presentations, 37, 58
Memorized talks, 107, 110
Metaphors, 38
Microphones, 142
Mistakes, how to handle, 164
Models and mockups, 63, 82
Monopolizers, 159
Monotone, 107
Movement, 156
Movies, 63
Multi-image presentations, 74

Narration, writing the, 33
Non-native speakers, 114
Notes, 164

Objectives, 10–11
Opening remarks, 35, 154
Organization
  index cards, 27
  reviewing, 30
  types of, 24
Outlines, 7, 27
Overheads, 62, 81, 118, 136–138, 141

Pacing yourself, 165
Pen plotters, 199
Perfection, 5
Personality, 155
Persuasion, 87
Photography, 70
Picture words, 37
Pie charts, 61, 64–65
Planning, 9
Pointers, use of, 125
Positive approach, 85, 97
Posture, 121, 156
Practice, 105
Preparation, 6
Press, handling the, 183
Printers, 198
Progressive disclosure, 72
Projection equipment, 139, 146, 165
Props, 63, 82
Publicizing your talk, 183

Questions and answers
  defusing nasty questions, 177
  during or after presentation, 175
  going from defense to offense, 179
  hostile, 177
  long-winded, 182
  practice handling 119, 173
  questions you can't answer 173, 182
  rehearsing, 119, 173

Read talks, 44, 107–108
Reagan, Ronald, 40
Rehearsal, 105, 115, 173
Research, 7, 21
Results, 102
Review and evaluation
  narration, 50, 127
  organization, 31
  storyboards, 28
  visuals, 77
Room checklist, 146–147

Sales strategies, 89
Schematics, 66
Scott, Sir Walter, 151
Scott, Willard, 2
Scripts, 48, 109
Seating arrangements, 135
Selling, 84
Semantics, 95
Shortness, 53
Side meetings, 159, 161
Similes, 38
Simplicity and sincerity, 53–54
Slide-making services, 82, 201
Slides, 62, 74, 119, 140
Smile, 153, 156
Socratic approach, 98
Soft-sell approach, 91
Software, 192
Stage, 142
Stage fright, 151
Stage whispers, 113
Statistics, 39
Storyboards, 28, 76
Strength, 53
Symbol libraries, 196

Tape recorders, 106
Teleconferencing, 63
Thank you's, 56, 167
Theater style seating, 134, 135
Thesis screen, 23
Time allocations, 7, 116, 165–166

Title visuals, 77, 80
Topic, 16
Translators, 39
Travel, 16–17
Twain, Mark, 6, 18, 98
Typing talks, 48

Unfriendly audience, 161–163, 177
Unruly audience, 163
USA Today, 100
U-shaped seating, 135–136

Verbal visuals, 78
Video recordings, 63, 120–121, 126,
    129, 144
Viewgraphs, 62, 81, 118, 136, 137
Visual aids
    advantages and disadvantages, 62–63
    benefits of using, 58
    dynamic, 71
    interaction with, 125
    making your own, 79, 185
    readability, 78
    types, 61

Washington, George, 18
Westinghouse, 116
Wharton School of Business, 57
Word charts, 61, 78
Workplace meetings, 17
Writing narration, 33